Contents

Introduction

100 Science Lessons is a series of year-specific teachers' resource books that provide a wealth of lesson plans and photocopiable resources for delivering a whole year of science teaching, including differentiation and assessment.

The series follows the *QCA Science Scheme of Work* in the sequencing of topics. However, instead of having six or seven units as in the QCA scheme, the book for each year contains eight units. These units are the familiar topics: 1. Ourselves, 2. Animals & plants, 3. The environment, 4. Materials, 5. Electricity, 6. Forces & motion, 7. Light & sound, 8. Earth & beyond. They appear in the same order in every book, but have sub-titles which describe the emphasis of the work in that year. For example, in this book Unit 1 is Ourselves: Teeth and food. By having eight units, this resource builds on the QCA scheme to accommodate the demands of the curricula for Wales, Scotland and Northern Ireland. It also creates opportunities to visit each topic in every year: after visiting a topic in synchrony with the QCA scheme, you can make a further visit the following year for extension or consolidation of the previous year's work. The Series topic map on page 208 shows how the topics are mapped out through the whole series.

Each unit is divided into a number of lessons, ending with an assessment lesson. The organisation chart at the start of each unit shows the objectives and outcomes of each lesson, and gives a quick overview of the lesson content (Main activity, Group activities, Plenary). The statements of the national curricula for England, Wales, Scotland and Northern Ireland (given in the grids on pages 196–207) provide the basis for the lesson objectives used throughout the book.

ORGANISATION (11 LESSONS)

	OBJECTIVES	MAIN ACTIVITY	GROUP ACTIVITIES	PLENARY	OUTCOMES
LESSON 1	● To ascertain the children's current knowledge of themselves, how they eat and the benefits of healthy eating from their work in Key Stage 1/Primary 1–3.	Assessment sheet focusing on knowledge and understanding of the body.	Brainstorm activity on one aspect of the body. Writing questions about themselves, food and teeth.	Discussion of issues raised, looking forward to the unit.	● Teacher can assess the level of understanding of the children in the class. ● Teacher can arrange the children in appropriate class groups.
LESSON 2	● To realise that food can be put into different groups. ● To understand one scientific grouping of foods.	Looking at a way of classifying food into three groups.	Sorting a bag of food shopping into food groups. Designing symbols for food groups.	Reinforcement of the concept of food groups.	● Can arrange food into groups for growth and for activity.

LESSON PLANS

Each lesson plan is divided into four parts: Introduction, Main activity, Group activities and Plenary session. In many of the lessons, the introduction is supported by background information and a vocabulary list that will help in delivering the lesson and support assessment of the work. The lesson introduction sets the context for the work. The Main activity features direct whole-class or group teaching, and may include instructions on how to perform a demonstration or an experiment in order to stimulate the children's interest and increase their motivation. There are then usually two Group activities to follow up this teaching. (In those lessons where a whole-class investigation takes place, there may be only a single Group activity related to this, and occasionally a 'circus' of group work is suggested.) Advice on differentiation and formative assessment linked to this work is provided. Finally, there are details of a Plenary session.

About 60% of the lesson plans in this book, including those for the assessment lessons, are presented in full detail. Many of these are followed by outlines for closely related lessons on the same topics or concepts, using the same background information. To avoid repetition and allow you to focus on the essentials of the lesson, these plans are presented as grids for you to develop. They contain the major features of the detailed lesson plans, allowing you to plan for progression and assessment.

100 SCIENCE LESSONS

N.Savage

YEAR 3

Scottish Primary 4

Published by Scholastic Ltd,
Villiers House,
Clarendon Avenue,
Leamington Spa,
Warwickshire CV32 5PR
Printed by Cromwell Press Ltd, Trowbridge

1234567890 1234567890

Series Consultant
Peter Riley

Author
Malcom Anderson

Editor
Janet Swarbrick

Assistant Editor
David Sandford

Series Designers
David Hurley
Joy Monkhouse

Designers
Rachel Warner
Paul Cheshire

Cover photography
Martyn Chillmaid

Illustrations
Kirsty Wilson

British Library Cataloguing-in-Publication Data
A catalogue record for this book is available from the British Library.

ISBN 0-439-01804-8

Teachers should consult their own school policies and guidelines concerning practical work and participation of children in scientific experiments. You should only select activities which you feel can be carried out safely and confidently in the classroom.

Acknowledgements
The National Curriculum for England 2000
© The Queens Printer and Controller of HMSO. Reproduced under the terms of HMSO Guidance Note 8.
The National Curriculum for Wales 2000
© The Queens Printer and Controller of HMSO. Reproduced under the terms of HMSO Guidance Note 10.

Detailed lesson plans

The lessons in this book have been designed to encourage and develop the children's investigative skills. Children at this stage are expected to plan and carry out a fair test with help and begin to explain why the test is fair. In this year, the children will be making predictions, planning (with help) a fair test, using appropriate equipment (although not always selecting it themselves), making observations and comparisons and presenting evidence in a variety of ways. They will also begin to use their scientific knowledge in explaining results and will begin to identify simple patterns in those results.

Objectives

The objectives of the lessons are derived from the statements in all the UK science curriculum documents. They are stated in a way that helps to focus each lesson plan and give a unique theme to each unit. At least one objective for each lesson is derived from the statements related to content knowledge. In addition, there may be one or more objectives relating to scientific enquiry; but you may choose to replace these with others to meet your needs and the skills you wish the children to develop. The relationship of the curriculum statements to the coverage of each unit's lessons is given in the grids on pages 196–207.

Wherever relevant, the focus and content of each unit coincides with that of the matching unit in the QCA *Science Scheme of Work*. However, we have not distinguished in the lesson objectives which content is specific to any one curriculum, and have left it to your professional judgement to identify those activities that are best-suited to the age and ability of your class and to the minimum requirements spelled out in your local curriculum guidance. If you wish to check whether a particular activity cross-references directly to your curriculum, please refer to the relevant grid on pages 196–207.

Resources and Preparation

The Resources section provides a list of everything you will need to deliver the lesson, including any of the photocopiables presented in this book.

Preparation describes anything that needs to be done in advance of the lesson, such as building flatbed catapults for forces work in Unit 6, Lesson 9 or sundials for work on the apparent movement of the Sun in Unit 8, Lesson 8. As part of the preparation for all practical work, you should consult your school's policies concerning the use of plants and animals in the classroom, so that you can select activities for which you are confident to take responsibility. The book *Be Safe!*, published by the Association for Science Education, is a useful addition to the staffroom bookshelf.

Background

The Background section provides relevant facts and explanations of concepts to support the lesson. In many cases, the information provided goes beyond what the children need to learn at Year 3/Primary 4; but you may need this further knowledge in order to avoid reinforcing any misconceptions the children may have.

Vocabulary

Each fully detailed lesson plan has an associated vocabulary list containing words that should be used by the children in discussing and presenting their work, and in their writing. The words relate both to scientific enquiry and to knowledge and understanding. You may wish to use these lists as the basis for a word bank that is displayed on the classroom wall and added to as new words are introduced.

It is important that children develop their scientific vocabulary in order to describe their findings and observations, and to explain their ideas. Whenever a specialist word is used, it should be accompanied by a definition, as some children in the class may take time to understand and differentiate the meanings of words. The use of specialist vocabulary, for example 'sub-soil' or 'bedrock', should be developed alongside the children's understanding of the concepts.

Introduction

The lesson introductions contain ideas to get each lesson started, to 'set the scene', and help the children relate it to previous lessons. You may also wish to make links with other lessons in your schemes of work, including curriculum areas other than science.

Main teaching activity

This section presents a direct, whole-class teaching session to follow the introduction. This will help you to deliver the content knowledge outlined in the lesson objectives to the children before they start their group work. It may include guidance on discussion, or on performing one or more demonstrations or class investigations to help the children understand the work ahead. These parts of the lesson are interactive, and suggestions are given for questions to engage and challenge the children's thinking.

The relative proportions of the lesson given to the Introduction, Main teaching activity and Group activities vary. If you are reminding the children of the previous work and getting them on to their own investigations, the group work may dominate the lesson time; if you are introducing a new topic or concept, you might wish to spend all or most of the lesson engaged in whole-class teaching.

Group activities

The Group activities are very flexible. Some may be best suited to individual work, while others may be suitable for work in pairs or larger groupings. In the detailed lesson plans, there are usually two Group activities provided for each lesson. You may wish to use one after the other, use both together to reduce demand on resources and your attention or, where one is a practical activity, use the other for children who complete their practical work successfully and quickly. Some of the Group activities are supported by a photocopiable sheet.

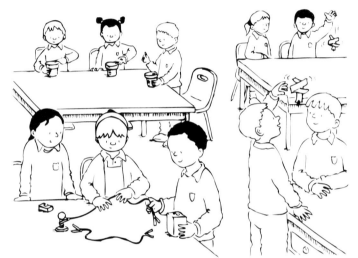

The Group activities may include some reading and writing. These activities are also aimed at strengthening the children's science literacy, and supporting their English literacy skills. They may involve writing 'Factfiles' and posters, developing scientific vocabulary, writing about or recording investigations, presenting data, explaining what they have observed, or using appropriate secondary sources. The children's mathematical skills are also developed through number and data-handling work in the context of science investigations.

Differentiation

For each of the lessons, where appropriate, there are suggestions for differentiated work to meet the different needs of children in the class. For example, strategies may be suggested to support recording for children who are lower attainers in writing. Differentiated Group activities are designed so that all the children who perform these tasks can make a contribution to the Plenary session. The activities are suitable for all abilities, with children contributing at their own level.

Assessment

Each unit begins with some means of finding out children's existing ideas in order to inform the teaching of the rest of the unit. Each lesson includes advice on how to assess the children's success in the activities against the lesson objectives. This may include questions to ask or observations to make to help you build up a picture of the children's developing ideas and tailor the planning of future lessons to the particular needs of the class. A separate summative assessment lesson is provided at the end of each unit of work, but it is expected that the ongoing assessments will also inform the summative assessments made.

Plenary

This is a very important part of the lesson. It is important not to let it get squeezed out by mistiming other activities in the lesson. Suggestions are given for drawing the various strands of the lesson together in this session. If an investigation has been tried, the work of different groups can be compared and evaluated. The scene may be set for another lesson, or the lesson objectives and outcomes may be reviewed and key learning points highlighted.

Homework

On occasions, some of the small tasks can be completed by the children as homework. Tasks such as observing the position of the Sun as it rises or sets, or the shadows under streetlamps can more easily be done outside the school day. Other lessons may offer opportunities for follow-up work, for example using the provided photocopiables at home, or to research a broader knowledge of the topic under discussion.

Outcomes

These are statements related to the objectives; they describe what most children should have achieved through the lesson.

Links to other units or lessons

The lesson may be linked to other lessons in the same unit to provide an alternative progression to the work or reinforce the work done, or it may be linked to other units or lessons elsewhere in the book. You may like to consider these links in planning your scheme of work – for example linking the work on the different properties of materials in Unit 4, Lesson 3 with knowing that some materials are magnetic and others are not in Unit 6, Lesson 3.

Links to other curriculum areas

These are included where appropriate. They may include links to subjects closely related to science, such as technology or maths, or to content and skills in subjects such as history or geography, also with references to other QCA *Schemes of Work*, where appropriate.

Lesson plan grids

These short lesson plans, in the form of a grid, offer further activity ideas to broaden the topic coverage. As the example below shows, they have the same basic structure as the detailed lesson plans. They lack the Introduction, Background and Vocabulary sections, but these are supported by the previous and related detailed lesson plans. Notes suggesting a Main activity and ideas for Group activities are provided for you to develop. Generally there are no photocopiables linked to these lesson plans.

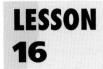

LESSON 16

Objectives	● To know that plants need leaves in order to grow well. ● To know that previous experimental results can help make predictions in new experiments.
Resources	Potted plants: one with leaves, one with leaves removed.

Main activity	Talk to the children about the work they have done previously about the parts of plants. Recall the parts they know about and talk briefly and in simple terms about the functions of those parts: roots take up water and nutrients and anchor the plant; stems carry water to the leaves and keep the plant upright; flowers produce seeds; leaves take in sunlight and make food.
	  Talk about what might happen if the plant was deprived of one of these parts, for example if all the leaves were removed.
	  Plan and carry out an investigation into the need plants have for leaves. Observe two plants (of the same species) – one that has leaves and one that has had its leaves removed. Keep them in the same conditions, observe what happens and measure growth over a period of time.

Differentiation	Differentiate by outcome.
Assessment	Discussion with children during their investigation and scrutiny of written work will indicate understanding. Look for evidence that the children know that without leaves the plant would not be able to grow. Higher-attaining children may be able to explain that without leaves the plant cannot produce food and therefore will not grow healthily.
Plenary	Discuss observations and draw conclusions about what happened to those plants without leaves that were not growing well. Reinforce the knowledge that leaves are important in order for plants to grow well.
Outcomes	● Can recognise that leaves are needed for healthy plant growth. ● Can describe an investigation of the relationship of plant leaves and plant growth. ● Can make observations and comparisons.

RESOURCES

Photocopiable sheets

These are an integral part of many of the lessons and are found at the end of the relevant unit, marked with the 'photocopiable' symbol 📄 . They may provide resources, instructions for practical work, more creative writing assignments, means of recording by writing or drawing and so on.

Classroom equipment and space

A wide range of resources is needed for the lessons in this book. However, every attempt has been made to restrict the list to resources that will be readily available to primary schools.

Each lesson plan includes a resources list. When you have planned which lessons you wish to use, you could make up your own resources list for the term's or year's work. Encourage your colleagues to do the same for other years, so that you can compare lists, identify times when there may be a high demand for particular resources and make adjustments as necessary. Educational resource companies such as TTS (Technological Teaching Systems, Unit 7, Monk Road, Alfreton, Derbyshire DE55 7RL; tel 01773 830255) can supply items such as switches for use in simple circuits (see Unit 5, Lesson 3) or bags of assorted springs (see Unit 6, Lesson 6).

ICT

Many of the lessons in this book can be enhanced by the use of ICT. As new products are entering the market all the time, few are specified in this book. However, you may like to plan your ICT work under these headings:

Information retrieval

Children should be encouraged to start to find information from secondary sources, including CD-ROMs and the Internet. Where this is the case, it is important that the children have a focus for their enquiries and that the materials offered are at an appropriate level, but that the task of information retrieval is sufficiently challenging. It is important to guard against children simply retrieving pages of information in answer to a question without understanding them. Prior to any information retrieval exercise, it is a good idea to examine the books, CD-ROMs or selected website(s) and set questions to guide the children so that they must interact with the material in some way as they prepare their answers. Interactive programs intended for Key Stage 1/ Primary 1–3 will be useful still to reinforce skills with many Year 3/Primary 4 children.

Databases

The use of databases can be developed in Year 3/Primary 4 to store information collected during scientific investigative work. Most children should be able to enter data into a predetermined database and use it to answer straightforward questions and produce bar charts, with higher attaining children turning questions into search criteria.

Presentations

Children should be introduced to a wide variety of methods to present their results and conclusions. This may include combining text and graphics.

A visual record of an investigation may be made by taking photographs (with a conventional or digital camera) or recording an activity with a video camera, and storing the information on the computer for use in a presentation. Visual records should be annotated to provide a complete record, not just a picture of the children's experiences. As well as displays and written records that may be produced, presentations may include video sequences that have been recorded during an investigation with a digital or video camera.

ASSESSMENT

The assessments in this book indicate the likely progress of children in Year 3/Primary 4. The statements relate specifically to work in this book, and are arranged in groups to reflect different levels. In this year's work, it is expected that most children will achieve National Curriculum (NC) Level 2/Scottish level B, and many will progress to Level 3/Scottish level C in at least some areas. Some children may not progress so well and achieve only Level 1/Scottish Level A, or be working towards Level 2/Scottish Level B.

It is important to determine what the children already know and understand before embarking on each unit. If appropriate, look at the previous book in the series, find the corresponding unit and check with your colleagues what work has been covered, particularly if children have just moved from Key Stage 1 to Key Stage 2 (in England or Wales) and/or have changed schools. Use the first lesson of each unit to talk to the children about what they know, and use the results to plan differentiated activities and provide materials as you teach the unit.

The last lesson in every unit focuses on summative assessment. This assessment samples the content of the unit, focusing on its key theme(s); its results should be used in conjunction with other assessments you have made during the teaching of the unit. The lesson comprises one or two activities which may take the form of a 'question and answer' session, photocopiable activity sheets or practical activities with suggested assessment questions for you to use while you are observing the children. These activities may include a mark scheme, but not related directly to curriculum levels of attainment. These tasks are intended to provide you with a guide to assessing how the children are progressing relative to an average expectation of Level 2/3 attainment or Level B/C in Scotland by the end of Year 3/ Primary 4.

A sample of the children's work from the lessons in this book, kept in a general portfolio, will be very useful in supporting your teacher assessment judgements.

SUPPORT FOR PLANNING

Developing your scheme of work

This book is planned to support the QCA *Science Scheme of Work* and the statements of the UK national curricula. In planning your school scheme of work, you may wish to look at the units in this book or throughout the series along with those of the QCA scheme. You may also wish to relate the objectives in your curriculum planning more directly to those of the curriculum documents. The grids on pages 196–207 show how the statements of the national curricula for science enquiry and knowledge and understanding for England, Wales, Scotland and Northern Ireland provide the basis for the lesson objectives used throughout the eight units in this book. In the grids, each statement is cross-referenced to one or more lessons to help with curriculum planning.

Planning progression

The Series topic map on page 208 shows the focus of each of the units in the books in this series, to help you work out your school plan of progression. By looking at the charts of curriculum coverage and the organisation chart for each unit, you can plan for progression through the year and from one year to the next, covering the whole of the work needed for Reception and Key Stages 1–2/Primary 1–7.

You may choose to use all or most of the lessons from the units in this book in their entirety, or make a selection to provide a 'backbone' for your own curriculum planning and supplement it with lessons you have already found successful from other sources. The pages in this book are perforated and hole-punched, so you can separate them and put them in a planning file with other favourite activities and worksheets.

TEACHING SCIENCE IN YEAR 3/PRIMARY 4

The units in this book introduce children to the work in the national curricula and build on the work done in Key Stage 1/Primary 1–3. It is expected that most children will attain at least NC Level 2/Scottish Level B as they work through this book, though some may still be working towards Level 2/Scottish Level B and many will attain Level 3/Level C in some areas.

An underlying theme of this book is the application of science knowledge to our everyday world. As the children move on from Key Stage 1/Primary 1–3 to Key Stage 2/Primary 4–7 and are beginning to mature and develop, this approach allows them to consider the ways in which science can alter our everyday life. This should help them see that it is important to know about science (to become scientifically literate) and to form opinions that, in future, can help in the sensible development of their world.

This book builds on earlier work and begins to develop children's knowledge, understanding and skill in planning and carrying out investigations, albeit with adult help and support. There is a particular focus on developing an understanding of what makes a fair test, how to plan a fair test and how to carry out a fair test.

A brief description of the unit contents follows, to show more specifically how the themes are developed.

● **Unit 1: Ourselves** focuses on 'Teeth and food'. It looks at food groups, healthy foods and at the importance of healthy eating. The unit also looks at types of teeth and the need for effective dental hygiene before moving on to consider the senses, starting from taste, and how our senses make us aware of our surroundings. Finally, the unit looks at human growth, including tooth replacement.

● **Unit 2: Animals & plants** focuses on 'The needs of plants and animals'. This unit looks at the life processes and needs of living things, including animal movement and growth and the importance of plants in our diet. This links on to optimal growing conditions for plants (in order to produce healthy crops, for example).

● **Unit 3: The environment** focuses on 'How the environment affects living things'. It considers the different environments of the world, climate and how climate affects where plants and animals live. The unit also looks at the environmental effects of litter and other waste and how some materials decay.

● **Unit 4: Materials** focuses on 'Natural & manufactured materials'. This unit looks at common materials and their uses, and how the properties of materials can be investigated to determine the best material for a particular purpose. It compares manufactured and natural materials, before looking in more detail at rocks and soil. Suggestions are provided, for example, for investigating the permeability of rocks and of soils and exploring how soil originates.

● **Unit 5: Electricity** focuses on 'Electricity and communication'. It stresses the importance of electrical safety, before looking at simple circuits which include switches and other devices. The children are introduced to using sound and light as a means of communicating, for example using Morse code.

● **Unit 6: Forces & motion** focuses on 'Magnets and springs'. This unit looks at push and pull forces in magnets, at materials that are magnetic and at the uses of magnets. It also looks at the forces exerted by springs and elastic bands and how that force can be varied. The unit concludes by considering and making links to relevant forms of energy and energy changes.

● **Unit 7: Light & sound** focuses on some 'Sources and effects' of light and sound. This unit develops the children's understanding of light and discusses how shadows are formed in relation to the sun. It also looks at colour and how colour is used in the natural and built environments for decoration and to give messages. The unit also looks at the variety of sound sources, the difference between soft and loud and high- and low-pitched sounds, and the uses (and misuses) of sounds.

● **Unit 8: Earth & beyond** focuses on 'The Sun and shadows'. This unit continues to develop ideas to do with shadows in Unit 7 by looking at how shadows cast by sunlight change during the day in shape, size and position. This leads on to looking at how the Sun appears to travel across the sky and how this can be safely investigated. The unit also looks at how we can tell the time using shadows through work on sundials and shadows.

Teeth and food

ORGANISATION (11 LESSONS)

	OBJECTIVES	MAIN ACTIVITY	GROUP ACTIVITIES	PLENARY	OUTCOMES
LESSON 1	● To ascertain the children's current knowledge of themselves, how they eat and the benefits of healthy eating from their work in Key Stage 1/Primary 1–3.	Assessment sheet focusing on knowledge and understanding of the body.	Brainstorm activity on one aspect of the body. Writing questions about themselves, food and teeth.	Discussion of issues raised, looking forward to the unit.	● Teacher can assess the level of understanding of the children in the class. ● Teacher can arrange the children in appropriate class groups.
LESSON 2	● To realise that food can be put into different groups. ● To understand one scientific grouping of foods.	Looking at a way of classifying food into three groups.	Sorting a bag of food shopping into food groups. Designing symbols for food groups.	Reinforcement of the concept of food groups.	● Can arrange food into groups for growth and for activity.
LESSON 3	● To know how to arrange a meal into food groups for growth and activity. ● To consider first-hand experience as a source of information in order to answer a question.	Looking at the contents of packed lunches.	Completing a worksheet to record contents of a packed lunch. Keeping a food diary.	Compiling a class food list from their packed lunches.	● Can arrange the food in their meals into groups for growth and activity.
LESSON 4	● To know about the quantities of different food groups that should be eaten. ● To know that a knowledge of food groups helps us to build healthy diets.	Assessing menus for their contents and forming a balanced diet.	Looking at shopping lists to assess them for balance and health. Letter writing about healthy foods.	Reinforcing the concept of healthy and unhealthy diets.	● Can assess how healthy their meal is. ● Can show how knowledge of food groups can help build a healthy diet.
LESSON 5	● To know that humans grow. ● To check observations and measurements by repeating them where appropriate. ● To use ICT to communicate data.	Looking at human growth and development.	Drawing personal time lines. Charting growth over periods of time.	Analysing of initial data.	● Can describe ways in which the body grows. ● Is aware that different people grow at different rates.
LESSON 6	● To know the different types of teeth and their functions.	Looking at and naming types of teeth.	Looking at our own teeth and recording on a worksheet. Using secondary sources to research information for a leaflet.	Taking part in a quiz about teeth to reinforce knowledge.	● Can recognise the different types of teeth. ● Can describe the function of different types of teeth.
LESSON 7	● To know that we have two sets of teeth.	Looking at losing teeth, at milk and permanent teeth and making models.		Discussion of the number of teeth the children have.	● Can recognise and describe the function of different sets of teeth.
LESSON 8	● To know that teeth and gums need care to stay healthy.	Using disclosure tablets. Looking at correct methods of brushing teeth. Designing a poster.	Survey of dental hygiene. Looking at dental health posters.	Discussion of the best advice regarding dental health.	● Can describe ways to care for teeth and gums. ● Can explain why tooth and gum care is needed.

ORGANISATION (11 LESSONS)

	OBJECTIVES	MAIN ACTIVITY	GROUP ACTIVITIES	PLENARY	OUTCOMES
LESSON 9	● To know that the senses make us aware of our surroundings.	Making a class concept map of 'The senses'.	Identifying senses, sense names and sensory organs. Crisp-tasting survey.	Taking part in a quiz on matching senses, names and organs.	● Can identify the senses and the sense organs.
LESSON 10	● To know that the senses, including taste, make us aware of our surroundings.	Taste tests for sweet, salty and bitter.		Explaining and describing taste experiences.	● Can perform activities on the senses.

	OBJECTIVES	ACTIVITY 1	ACTIVITY 2
ASSESSMENT 11	● To assess the children's knowledge and understanding of dental health, tooth types and functions. ● To assess the children's knowledge and understanding of the importance of eating a balanced diet.	Completing a 'Tooth facts' and 'Dental health' worksheet.	Completing a 'Food facts' and an 'Eating a healthy diet' worksheet.

LESSON 1

OBJECTIVE

● To ascertain the children's current knowledge of themselves, how they eat and the benefits of healthy eating from their work in Key Stage 1/Primary 1–3.

RESOURCES

Main teaching activity: A copy of photocopiable page 25 for each child, pencils.
Group activities: 1. Large sheets of paper, pens, pencils. **2.** Paper, pens, pencils.

BACKGROUND

In planning, developing and carrying out a unit of work with children it is important to give consideration to previous learning and current understanding. To ascertain the level of the children's understanding, carry out an initial assessment. This will give you a starting point from which you can move on and develop the children's understanding. It is important not to perceive that children are 'wrong' about a concept, but rather that they may need to develop their understanding of that concept to bring it nearer the generally accepted understanding. This lesson is intended to establish what is already known by the children about their bodies.

INTRODUCTION

Introduce the unit of work to the children by telling them they are going to begin a science topic called 'Ourselves'. Tell them the broad outline of the unit and that by the end of the unit they will understand more about how their bodies work and about themselves. Remind them that they will have already done some work about themselves and that you would like them to be able to tell you what they already know and understand. It is important therefore that, because this is all about them, they carry out this first task themselves and not working with their friends.

MAIN TEACHING ACTIVITY

Distribute the copies of photocopiable page 25. Ask the children to complete the worksheet first by making the illustration into a picture of themselves and then by writing as much as they can about themselves. Ask them to write words and phrases around their picture that reflect anything and everything that they know about their bodies, how they function, and so on. Ask them to think particularly about food and teeth: the benefits of food to their bodies and the things they may know about their teeth.

GROUP ACTIVITIES

1. Ask the children to work together in small groups, to choose one of the ideas or concepts they have written on their drawings and to brainstorm that idea. They should write down everything they know about, for example, sight, using words and pictures to explain their thoughts.
2. Ask the children to think of three questions that they would like to know the answers to about themselves, food and teeth.

DIFFERENTIATION

Lower-attaining children can be assisted with writing down their own ideas. Higher-attaining children can work unaided with a higher degree of understanding.

PLENARY

Discuss the pictures the children have drawn. Highlight some of the concepts they have written about and explain the areas they will be looking at over future lessons. Avoid suggesting that the children's concepts are wrong – the work they will be doing will develop their thinking from where they are now.

OUTCOMES

● Teacher can assess the level of the children in the class.
● Teacher can arrange the children in appropriate class groups.

LESSON 2

OBJECTIVES

● To realise that food can be put into different groups.
● To understand one scientific grouping of foods.

RESOURCES

Main teaching activity: Stand-up labels with the words 'Meat and eggs', 'Milk products', 'Cereals, fruit and vegetables' and 'Processed foods' written on them; a carrier bag of food including examples of energy-giving foods: carbohydrates and fats; body-building foods: proteins; and maintenance foods: vitamins and minerals (see table overleaf). If you don't get enough of each type of food, print out illustrations from your computer; most CD-ROM clip art collections have pictures of food.
Group activities: 1. Carrier bags; sets of stand-up labels with the words 'Meat and eggs', 'Milk products', 'Cereals, fruit and vegetables' and 'Processed foods' written on them; large sheets of paper, pens. **2.** Paper; drawing, painting and colouring materials.

PREPARATION

Prepare one carrier bag of shopping for you to use in your introduction which should contain examples from each of these groups: meat and eggs; milk products; cereals, fruit and vegetables; processed foods.

Prepare a carrier bag for each of the groups of children in your class containing a selection of the collected packets and food containers. Ensure there are examples from each of the food groups. Prepare stand-up labels for the Key Stage 1 food groups shown in the table overleaf.

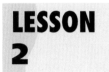

Vocabulary

body-building foods, energy-giving foods, growth, healthy, maintenance foods, activity

BACKGROUND

Food is needed to help our bodies to move, to grow and to repair themselves after being damaged. While there aren't any unhealthy foods, many people do eat unhealthy diets. The food and drink that we consume each day makes up our diet and it is important we eat a diet which contains a range of different foods, since these different foods serve different purposes. A balanced or healthy diet is one that consists of the appropriate types of food in the correct quantities. There are five main food groups.
● **Proteins:** essential for the growth and repair of the body. Muscles, skin, hair and nails are nearly 100% protein. Bone is part protein.
● **Fats and oils:** essential for the release and storage of energy and as an insulation.
● **Carbohydrates:** essential for the release of energy, for the storage of energy and as roughage for the movement of food through the gut. Fibre acts as roughage in the diet and prevents constipation.
● **Minerals:** essential for building bones and teeth, for the functioning of the nervous system and the production of haemoglobin in red blood cells.
● **Vitamins:** essential for the control of chemical reactions in the body and the control of deficiency diseases with symptoms such as poor vision, stomach ache, poor growth and weak bones.

However, these are often combined into three groups that can be thought of as energy-giving foods, body-building foods and maintenance foods.

Food group	Foods	Function
Energy-giving foods: carbohydrates and fats	bread, potatoes, pasta, rice, sugar, fatty and oily foods	Provide energy for activity, movement and warmth.
Body-building foods: proteins	meat, fish, eggs, dairy produce, seeds, nuts	Help with growth and repair of the body.
Maintenance foods: vitamins and minerals	red meats, milk, fresh fruit, vegetables	Maintain healthy bones and teeth. Prevent 'vitamin deficiency' diseases.

In addition to these foods we also need water and fibre. Whilst we could survive without food for several weeks, we could survive only for a few days without water. Most of the water we take in is through drinking, but most solid foods also contain water. Nevertheless, to maintain our bodily functions, we need to drink plenty of water every day.

INTRODUCTION

Ask the children to think about the different types of food they may see on a visit to a supermarket. *How are foods grouped together in the supermarket?* Use your carrier bag to show the children examples from the food groups: meat and eggs; milk products; cereals, fruit and vegetables; processed foods.

The children can help with this by coming to the front and having a 'lucky dip' into the bag. They then have to place the food by a card labelled with the appropriate category.

MAIN TEACHING ACTIVITY

Ask the children if they can think of any other ways of grouping the foods. Lead them into suggesting that we could group them by their functions and uses to our body. Introduce the idea that some foods give us energy, some foods help us to grow and some foods keep us healthy. Tell the children that each food belongs in one group and that together they are going to classify the foods in the bags you have prepared. Write three column headings on the board: 'Energy-giving foods', 'Body-building foods', and 'Maintenance foods'. Talk about each food group and tell the children about the types of food in each group and their function. (See Background.) Stress that energy-giving foods are good for activity; that body-building foods are good for growth, and maintenance foods keep us healthy.

GROUP ACTIVITIES

1. Distribute the bags of food, stand-up labels and sheets of paper. Ask the children to work in their groups to arrange their shopping into the three groups you have written on the board, using the stand-up labels as a guide to the sorting process. When sorted the children should record their work on a large sheet of paper using the column headings that are written on the board: 'Energy-giving foods', 'Body-building foods', and 'Maintenance foods'.
2. Ask the children to design symbols that could be used to accompany the food groups. You may like to compare them to computer icons. The designs should be based on the benefits to the body, for example energy-giving foods: an athlete; body-building foods: a weightlifter; maintenance foods: a toolkit.

DIFFERENTIATION

Make cloze procedure words available for lower-attaining children and support them in sorting foods. Ask higher-attaining children to write their own sentences about food types.

ASSESSMENT

Monitor the children's ability to sort the foods into groups by observation and by their completion of their work on writing sentences.

PLENARY

Gather the class together and discuss the Group activities. Ask children to bring foods out and make a simple display of foods in each group. Write the vocabulary list on the board, and use the words to reinforce the knowledge of food groups and what each gives to our bodies by completing these sentences together on the board:
Energy-giving foods like _____ are good for _____.
Body-building foods like _____ are good for _____.
Maintenance foods like _____ help to keep us _____.
Stress that energy-giving foods are good for activity, that body-building foods are good for growth, and maintenance foods help to keep us healthy, especially our teeth and bones.

OUTCOME
● Can arrange food into groups for growth and for activity.

LINKS
Unit 6, Lesson 11: different forms of energy.

LESSON 3

OBJECTIVES
● To know how to arrange a meal into food groups for growth and activity.
● To consider first-hand experience as a source of information in order to answer a question.

RESOURCES

Main teaching activity: Prepared word cards: 'Energy-giving foods', 'Body-building foods', 'Maintenance foods', 'apples', 'bread', 'butter', 'carrots', 'cheese', 'cream', 'fish', 'ice cream', 'meat', 'oil', 'oranges', 'pasta', 'potatoes', 'rice'; Blu-Tack; children's packed lunches.
Group activities: 1. Copies of photocopiable page 26; pens or pencils. **2.** Copies of photocopiable page 27; table of food groups (see Lesson 2 Background, page 14); flip chart or OHP; pens or pencils.

PREPARATION

Write to parents or guardians in advance of the lesson, explaining that the children are looking at food groups and asking them to ensure their child brings a packed lunch to school on one particular day. Try not to explain in too much detail to avoid parents putting in food types that perfectly match your groups, since this would not highlight the reality of packed lunch menus. Copy the table of food groups (see Lesson 2 Background, page 14) for whole-class use, for example on to a flip chart or OHP, for Group activity 2.

Vocabulary

balanced diet, bones, healthy diet, teeth

BACKGROUND

The main part of a balanced diet consists of carbohydrates, fats and proteins. Vitamins and minerals are needed but in much smaller quantities. However, if they are missing altogether, it could lead to ill-health, so the adoption of a balanced diet is important. Just as eating insufficient vitamins and minerals can lead to ill-health, so too can overeating. Eating more than is needed can lead to obesity and subsequent damage to the heart, bones and joints, together with high blood pressure and sometimes a general feeling of poor self-esteem. Fatty and sugary foods are generally the main culprits in overeating, so it is important to moderate the intake of these food types.

INTRODUCTION

Reinforce the food groups and how each of these groups carries out a particular function for us by asking the children to recall that energy-giving foods are good for activity, that body-building foods are good for growth and maintenance foods help to keep us healthy, especially our teeth and bones. Stick the prepared word cards: 'Energy-giving foods', 'Body-building foods', and 'Maintenance foods' on the board as column headings, then hold up a number of the word cards with food names written on them. Ask the children to put these in the correct food groups by sticking them in the right columns.

MAIN TEACHING ACTIVITY

Ask the children to think about how they could investigate the foods they eat. Ask them to open up their own packed lunch, to look at it and to try to sort the contents into the food groups. Remind the children of the importance of food hygiene. Ensure that they wash their hands prior to handling the packed lunch, and that they don't take the foods out of their wrappings if putting them out onto their desks.

GROUP ACTIVITIES

1. Ask the children to use the contents of their lunch pack to complete photocopiable page 26.
2. Ask the children to think about the meals they have eaten recently, for example breakfast or the previous day's evening meal. Ask them to complete photocopiable page 27 by writing down the foods they ate at each mealtime and then to put a tick in the appropriate column depending on whether the food's function is growth or activity. They can refer to the food group table on the flip chart or OHP. The children could then set up a database into which each child can input

their findings to give a class view of the foods eaten. Alternatively, this activity could be used as homework and photocopiable page 27 filled in as a diary over the following few days.

DIFFERENTIATION

Differentiation will be by the support given to individual children and the outcome of their work.

ASSESSMENT

Discuss with the children the foods they have eaten and their ability to sort their menus into food groups. Analysis of photocopiable pages 26 and 27 will support this assessment.

PLENARY

As the children complete Group activity 1, ask them to contribute to compiling a class chart showing the number of people with items in their lunch from each food group. When the data has been compiled help the children to interpret the data by asking questions such as: *Which food is the most popular? Is it healthy? Which food is the least popular? Is it healthy? Is our class a 'healthy-eating' class?*

Be careful not to make any child feel guilty about the contents of their packed lunch as this is something over which most young children have little or no control.

Discuss the menus of a few children (from photocopiable page 27) and compile a shared class list of foods from each food group.

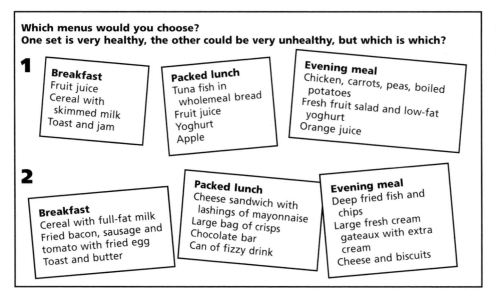

OUTCOME

● Can arrange the food in their meals into groups for growth and activity.

LINKS

Unit 6, Lesson 11.

LESSON 4

OBJECTIVES

● To know about the quantities of different food groups that should be eaten.
● To know that a knowledge of food groups helps us to build healthy diets.

RESOURCES

Main teaching activity: Sample menus (enlarged for class discussion) as shown below, one healthy and one unhealthy; OHP (optional).
Group activities: 1. Copy of photocopiable page 28 for each child, pens or pencils **2.** Paper, pens or pencils.

Which menus would you choose?
One set is very healthy, the other could be very unhealthy, but which is which?

1

Breakfast
Fruit juice
Cereal with
  skimmed milk
Toast and jam

Packed lunch
Tuna fish in
  wholemeal bread
Fruit juice
Yoghurt
Apple

Evening meal
Chicken, carrots, peas, boiled potatoes
Fresh fruit salad and low-fat yoghurt
Orange juice

2

Breakfast
Cereal with full-fat milk
Fried bacon, sausage and tomato with fried egg
Toast and butter

Packed lunch
Cheese sandwich with lashings of mayonnaise
Large bag of crisps
Chocolate bar
Can of fizzy drink

Evening meal
Deep fried fish and chips
Large fresh cream gateaux with extra cream
Cheese and biscuits

PREPARATION

Copy the menus shown opposite on to a flip chart or OHP for whole-class use.

Vocabulary

carbohydrates, fats, fibre, minerals, proteins, recommended daily allowance (RDA), vitamins, water

BACKGROUND

A balanced diet is one that helps the body to stay healthy and gives us a supply of carbohydrates, fats, proteins, vitamins, minerals, water and fibre. In order to get all this we need to eat a variety of foods. The quantities of food needed by each person will vary and be dependent on things like age, sex, height, weight, health and lifestyle. For example, those people who are involved in a great deal of physical work or exercise will need to eat more than those who lead a more relaxed and sedentary lifestyle. The balance of foods between food groups will also vary. People who have a tendency to very easily put on and retain weight may avoid fatty foods; similarly, those with certain medical histories may avoid certain foods. In general it is regarded as healthy to eat a balance of different foods, and not to eat from only one particular group. This is important since it is a balanced diet that provides us with all the nutrition that our bodies need.

Recommended Daily Allowances

Age group	Energy (kcal)	Protein (g)	Iron (mg)
Under 1	776	20	6
Age 5	1764	45	8
Boy 15–17	2964	75	15
Girl 15–17	2258	58	15
Man	2964	75	10
Woman	2164	55	12

INTRODUCTION

Begin the lesson by asking the children to share with the class their 'favourite meal': share yours too, it may be the same! Continue by asking the children to think about what life would be like if they were to always eat their favourite meal – how long would it be before they became bored with it?

MAIN TEACHING ACTIVITY

Ask the children if they can think of other, 'scientific' reasons why we don't always eat the same foods. Lead them to think about the importance of eating a variety of foods. Explain to the children that because different foods help our bodies to perform different functions it is important to eat a balanced diet.

Provide the sample menus and RDA figures, if appropriate, for the children to look at. Ask them to consider each menu and to decide if the menu seems to give a balanced diet. *What is 'good' about them? What is 'bad'? Is the 'very unhealthy' meal necessarily 'bad'?* (No, not if it is an occasional treat – no food is bad as such.)

GROUP ACTIVITIES

1. Distribute photocopiable page 28. Ask the children to consider the diets of the two people and to assess them for balance and health, then write a shopping list of their own.
2. Write a letter to a friend that explains the foods you should eat as part of a healthy diet.

DIFFERENTIATION

Work with lower-attaining children, helping them to read the lists. Higher-attaining children should be able to work unaided with differentiation by outcome.

ASSESSMENT

Using the photocopiable pages look for evidence of the children's understanding through their ability to explain the differences between the two lists. Look also for evidence among the higher attainers of their ability to write their own shopping list that has other healthy food ideas not already used.

PLENARY

Look again at the menus from the start of the lesson and ask the children to think about the unhealthy diet and to make suggestions for how it could be improved to make it healthy.

OUTCOMES

- Can assess how healthy their meal is.
- Can show how knowledge of food groups can help build a healthy diet.

LINKS

Unit 2, Lesson 3.
PSHE: developing a healthy, safer lifestyle.

LESSON 5

OBJECTIVES
- To know that humans grow.
- To check observations and measurements by repeating them where appropriate.
- To use ICT to communicate data.

RESOURCES

Main teaching activity: A collection of photographs from magazines to show the stages of human growth and development (birth to old age).
Group activities: 1. Photographs of the children at different ages (from birth to now), copies of a timeline, pens and pencils, glue. **2.** Computer and data-handling software.

PREPARATION

Write to the children's parents or guardians, asking them to encourage their child to bring a number of photographs of themselves to school. Ask them to ensure that their child's fingernails are cut the night before the lesson and then not again for at least one week and explain why! Prepare copies of the timeline, one per child.

Vocabulary

adolescence, baby, child, toddler

BACKGROUND

From birth, we begin to grow and develop until our bodies reach their optimum stage of development – usually late teens. After that, growth may be more related to diet than development. We grow at different rates depending on the stage we are at. As we grow, changes occur not only in our size but in our body proportions, diet, strength, power, senses and patterns of behaviour. As this occurs we pass through a number of distinct stages, as shown in the table on the right.

Stage of development	Approximate age range
Baby	0–1 years
Toddler	1–2.5 years
Child	2.5–11 years
Adolescent	11–18 years
Adulthood	18–65 years
Old age	65+ years

As well as physical and mental development, the range of rights and responsibilities also changes as we grow and develop.

INTRODUCTION

Remind the children that as they grow they gradually lose their milk teeth to be replaced by permanent teeth and that this is just one of the very many changes that will take place as they grow and develop.

MAIN TEACHING ACTIVITY

Ask the children to think about all the things that have happened to them over the past twelve months. Talk about how they have changed and that they will have grown a little bit in those twelve months. Show the children the photographs depicting the stages of human growth and, as a class, order them from birth to old age. Ask the children to think about how these people are different and what has happened to them over the years. Discuss how people have grown and when people tend to do most of their growing. Talk about how even when we have stopped growing there are parts of us that continue to grow (hair, nails, new skin).

GROUP ACTIVITIES

1. The children can draw personal timelines to show their own growth from birth to now, similar to the table shown below. They can use photographs they have brought in to help them illustrate the timeline. It should include pictures of themselves to show the stages of growth during each of the years shown and any significant events they can remember.
2. Ask the children to devise a simple chart on to which they record details of their growth over a period of time. Get them to measure the following:
- Height now and at weekly intervals for 3 months.
- Nail length now and over a period of one week.
- Hair length now and weekly over a period of 6 weeks.
A simple database program can be used to collate the information on an ongoing basis. Children can set up their page and enter initial information.

My timeline				
0	1 year	2 years	3 years	4 years
	5 years	6 years	7 years	8 years

DIFFERENTIATION

Lower-attaining children could use illustrations to show human growth on their timeline. Higher-attaining children use illustrations and text to show human growth on their timeline.

ASSESSMENT

Use the children's timelines to assess whether they have been able to show progression in and an understanding of human growth through their illustrations and writing.

PLENARY

Look at the initial data from the children's growth measurements, and compare children of the same age (to one month). Think about why some people are taller or shorter than others. As time passes and you have more data, reinforce the notion that people grow at different rates.

OUTCOMES

- Can describe the ways in which the body grows.
- Is aware that different people grow at different rates.

LINKS

PSHE: developing a healthy, safer lifestyle.

LESSON 6

OBJECTIVE

- To know the different types of teeth and their functions.

RESOURCES

Main teaching activity: Illustrations or models of teeth, hard fruits such as apples and pears.
Group activities: 1. Mirrors, copies of photocopiable page 29. **2.** Secondary sources of information about ourselves, food and teeth – books, videos, CD-ROMs, the Internet; paper, pens and pencils.

PREPARATION

Copy photocopiable page 29 for each child. Cut up fruit in to small portions.

BACKGROUND

Vocabulary

biting, canines, cutting, grinding, incisors, molars, premolars, tearing

The hardest part of the human body is the surface of the teeth. Made from enamel, this surface protects the teeth from being worn away and attacked by chemicals. Teeth play a vital role in the initial stages of food digestion in that, before it is swallowed, food is chewed. Most mammals have specialised teeth that are shaped in particular ways to carry out different tasks. Teeth are used to bite food, break it up and grind it into small pieces. Humans are omnivores (we eat both plants and animals as food), and our teeth are capable of eating both, unlike some other animals.

Carnivores (or meat-eaters) have teeth suited to killing other animals and tearing their flesh, whereas herbivores (plant-eaters) have teeth more suited to eating grass. As humans we have different types of teeth, each of which has a different function.

Tooth type	Shape	Function
Incisors	Sharp, chisel shape	Biting off food, cutting food
Canines	Sharp pointed shape	Biting off food, tearing food
Molars	Cube shape	Grinding, chewing and crushing food

Human babies are generally born without teeth and by the age of one their milk teeth have appeared. Between the ages of 6 and 12 these milk teeth are replaced by permanent teeth. The table below shows how many of each teeth we usually have.

We lose our milk teeth as we grow, but we can, and do, also lose our permanent teeth for a variety of reasons – through injury, gum disease or tooth decay. It is important, though, that we maintain healthy teeth for as long as possible so that we can chew properly and also be spared the pain of a decaying tooth. Most adults have 32 teeth in their second, or permanent, set. consisting of: 8 incisors, 4 canines, 8 premolars and 12 molars.

The part of the tooth you can see is the crown, which is about half of the full tooth. The crown is covered with enamel, below which is a layer of dentine. The centre of the tooth is filled with a soft pulp which contains the blood supply and nerve endings. Long roots anchor the tooth into the jaw.

Age	Tooth set	Tooth type	Number	Total
Birth	None			
1 year	Milk teeth	Incisors Canines Premolars	8 4 8	20
6–12 Adults	Permanent	Incisors Canines Premolars Molars	8 4 8 12	32

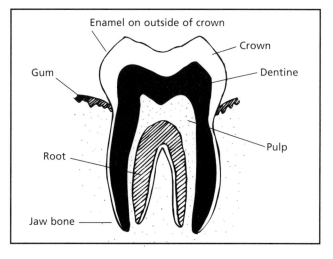

Labels: Enamel on outside of crown, Crown, Gum, Dentine, Root, Pulp, Jaw bone

INTRODUCTION

Ask the children to think about what they use when they are eating. Bring the discussion around to how they use their teeth.

MAIN TEACHING ACTIVITY

Look at your illustrations or models of teeth. Talk about how we use our teeth when eating, how we have different types of teeth, the names we give them and their functions. Think about the different types of teeth we have and the jobs they do. Hand out pieces of fruit so the children can watch each other eat and observe the functions of the teeth – incisors to bite; canines to hold and tear; molars and premolars to grind the food up. (The children will not have permanent molars yet.)

GROUP ACTIVITIES

1. Distribute a copy of photocopiable page 29 to each child. Tell the children to use mirrors to help them to see their own teeth. Tell them to complete the worksheet by drawing each tooth type and then writing about its function.
2. The children use secondary sources to find out how many teeth children and adults should have. Use this information to make an information leaflet about teeth.

DIFFERENTIATION

Differentiation will be by outcome. Lower attainers may need support in identifying the tooth types and could perhaps look only for two of the four tooth types. Higher attainers will be able to attempt all of the photocopiable page unaided.

ASSESSMENT

By observation and discussion with the children, assess their ability to recognise different types of teeth. The photocopiable page will provide documentary evidence.

PLENARY

Discuss the activity and have a quiz-style 'question and answer' session to reinforce knowledge of different types of teeth. Use the illustrations or model of the teeth as prompts.

OUTCOMES

- Can recognise the different types of teeth.
- Can describe the function of different types of teeth.

LESSON 7

Objective	To know that we have two sets of teeth.
Resources	Illustrations or models of teeth, mirrors, red paper, white paper, glue, scissors.
Main activity	Talk about losing teeth and the reasons why we lose teeth: replacement, disease and decay or damage. Develop the idea of the first teeth (milk teeth) being replaced by permanent teeth. Discuss how, as our teeth sets change and develop, so do the range and type of foods we eat. Use mirrors to enable the children to look at their teeth to assess permanent and milk teeth. Make models of gums and teeth using red paper for the gums and white paper for the teeth. The children can stick their teeth onto the gums to create a replica of their mouth.
Differentiation	Differentiate by outcome. Most children should be able to produce a model in this activity.
Assessment	Assess the ability to observe their teeth and draw a plan of their arrangement in the mouth.
Plenary	Gather the children together and discuss their findings. Talk about how many milk and permanent teeth the children have.
Outcome	Can recognise and describe the function of different sets of teeth.

LESSON 8

OBJECTIVE

● To know that teeth and gums need care to stay healthy.

RESOURCES

Main teaching activity: Disclosure tablets, children's own toothbrushes, toothpaste (these are often available in dental health packs that are frequently supplied to schools by toothpaste companies); cola soft drink; a small milk tooth (supplied by a child).
Group activities: 1. Paper, pens; computer and data-handling software. **2.** A collection of dental health leaflets available from dental surgeries, paper and art materials.

Vocabulary

acid, bacteria, gum disease, milk teeth, permanent teeth, plaque, tooth decay

BACKGROUND

As children lose their milk teeth they are replaced by permanent teeth. For various reasons these may not be so permanent. If we do not take care of both our teeth and gums we can lose even our permanent teeth. It is important, therefore, for the children to have some awareness of tooth decay and gum disease and how they can be prevented.

Tooth decay occurs when holes develop in what is the hardest substance in the body – tooth enamel. The holes are formed when acid is released from bacterial plaque that forms on the teeth. The presence of sugar in the mouth encourages the growth of the bacteria. The best way to prevent the build-up of plaque and tooth decay is to avoid consuming sweet and sugary foods and drinks. Regular brushing of the teeth and the drinking of fluoridated water also help to prevent the build-up of plaque and can strengthen the enamel.

Gum disease occurs when bacteria is able to get into the gaps between the gums and the surface of the teeth. This can lead to the fibres that hold the teeth in place becoming damaged, meaning the teeth can work loose and may be in danger of then falling out. Again, regular and correct brushing of the teeth can prevent this happening.

Prevention of tooth decay is helped by saliva, which is produced in the mouth while we are eating. Saliva is alkaline and this means it is able to help neutralise the acids produced by the bacteria in the mouth and can help to prevent tooth decay. However, the best ways of stopping tooth decay are to eat sensibly, without too much sugar, to clean teeth after each meal and visit a dentist for a check-up every six months.

INTRODUCTION

Ask the children to think back to the previous lessons and to recall why we sometimes lose teeth and, referring to the food the children eat, introduce the idea that sweet, sugary foods cause tooth decay. Explain how and why this happens (see Background). Demonstrate the effects that sweet, sugary foods have on teeth by leaving a small milk tooth in cola (the tooth enamel will break down and the tooth will decay).

MAIN TEACHING ACTIVITY

Ask the children to think of ways in which we could reduce the risk of tooth loss. If there is not a familiar toothpaste advert that you can refer to running on TV at the time you may need to introduce the idea of fluoridation and fluoride toothpaste. Discuss the importance of good dental health practice. Ask at least one child to use disclosure tablets to show where plaque builds up on the teeth. (Do this after break-time for 'best' results!) Then ask them to brush their teeth correctly: only correct brushing will remove all the disclosure colouring.

GROUP ACTIVITIES

1. Carry out a simple survey to find out how often the children brush their teeth. Use a simple database program to record the findings anonymously – there is no need to collect names, just the number of times per day that each child brushes their teeth. You may like to extend the survey to other classes in school. One group can visit each class to collect their data.
2. Ask the groups to work collaboratively to design posters that highlight and inform other children about the good and bad practices of dental hygiene. The children could use the dental health leaflets as a source of further information.

DIFFERENTIATION

Lower-attaining children's posters should be simpler and aim to contain just one clear message. Higher-attaining children's posters should be more complex and deliver a more coherent message. They could also be involved in interpreting survey data and presenting a graph of the results.

ASSESSMENT

Assess the posters to determine understanding and ability to describe ways to care for teeth. Ask the children to explain their posters.

PLENARY

Summarise the learning by asking the children what advice they would give you if you were concerned about your dental health.

OUTCOMES

- Can describe ways to care for teeth and gums.
- Can explain why tooth and gum care is needed.

LESSON 9

OBJECTIVE

- To know that the senses make us aware of our surroundings.

RESOURCES

Main teaching activity: Large sheets of paper, pens; A4-sized pictures (suitable images are available on many clip art packages for ICT use) to illustrate the sense organs; large print labels of the names of the organs, the senses and functions of the sense organs (also used in Plenary).
Group activities: 1. A copy of photocopiable page 30 for each child, **2.** Bags of flavoured crisps, pen and paper.

Vocabulary

eyes, ears, tongue, nose, skin, sight, sound, taste, hearing, smell, touch

BACKGROUND

In order to survive, all living things need to have a system that allows them to respond to changes and events that are occurring around them. Humans have a sensory system which keeps us in touch with our surroundings by processing information received from our surroundings and sent to our brain. In common with other mammals, we have a number of sensory organs that help us to monitor and make sense of our environment. Although our sensory system can respond to many things, we tend to regard ourselves as having just five senses with associated sensory organs (see table above).

Sensory organ	Sense	Information received by sense organ
Eyes	Sight	Colour, shape, movement
Ears	Hearing	Sound, position (therefore balance)
Tongue	Taste	Sweet, sour, bitter, salty
Nose	Smell	Smells
Skin	Touch	Feel of things, temperature, sensation

The information received by the senses is sent around the nervous system of the body as a series of nerve impulses. The central nervous system (the brain and the spinal cord) responds in an appropriate way. For example, if you touch an object the receptors in your skin detect a great deal of information about that object, including whether it is hot or cold. If it is hot your central nervous system will instantly send a message back saying 'that object is too hot to hold, let go!' There are many other examples that you could use to illustrate the role of our senses in making us aware of our surroundings. These changes in our surroundings that our bodies detect are called stimuli; our reactions to them are called responses.

- **Sight:** our eyes help us to detect light and to form images. The iris controls the amount of light entering the eye; the lens and cornea focus that light onto the retina at the back of the eye. Here, light-sensitive cells send a message to the brain which interprets the image.
- **Sound:** our ears detect sound because of the movement of the air (vibration). When, for example, someone bangs a drum, the skin vibrates. This causes the air in contact with it to also vibrate and these vibrations, like ripples on a pond, spread out. As that vibrating air enters your ear then a series of vibrations occur in the ear drum and the ear bones. This causes the fluid-filled 'cochlea' to vibrate. Nerve cells detect this movement and send a message to the brain.
- **Smell:** we detect smells using groups of sensory cells, called receptors, in the nasal passages.
- **Taste:** we detect tastes using groups of sensory cells, called receptors, located on the tongue.
- **Touch:** we are able to detect the many sensations associated with touch because of the receptors in the skin which are sensitive to touch, pain and temperature.

INTRODUCTION

Begin by asking the children to think about their favourite foods. Invite some children to share with everyone a description of the foods they really enjoy. Ask the children to say why they enjoy the food, and they should begin to talk about liking the taste.

MAIN TEACHING ACTIVITY

Continue by asking the children to tell you more about their favourite foods, asking them to talk about other ways of identifying and enjoying foods apart from taste. Move the discussion on to learning about their surroundings: the classroom, the weather, various atmospheric smells or sounds, and so on. Ask the children to think about how we know about all these things. Encourage the children to think about the senses as a means of making us aware of our surroundings. Use A4-sized pictures of the sense organs to illustrate the discussion.

As a class, draw a concept map of the senses in which you include all the senses, the sensory organs and any other relevant information. Use this to help support the Group activities. Start with 'The senses' in the centre and write all the children's ideas and contributions around this. Then ask the children to try to link up words which are connected in some way and to say what that link is. For example, for eyes—sight, the link would be 'We use our eyes to see things'. This could be used as the basis for a 'senses' display.

GROUP ACTIVITIES

1. Distribute copies of photocopiable page 30. Tell the children to fold the page in half on the central line (the 'valley' fold) and back on the line to the left of centre (the 'mountain' fold). The sheet can then be completed with detailed information on the senses, sensory organs and functions of the senses according to the children's knowledge (as an assessment, perhaps) or by research.
2. Carry out a 'Tasty crisp survey', but ask: *Can you identify flavours of crisps blindfolded?* Ask the children to hold their noses to see if it makes a difference to their ability to choose. Encourage the children to decide on a suitable way of recording and presenting the findings.

DIFFERENTIATION

Lower-attaining children use secondary sources to help. Higher attainers work unaided with understanding.

ASSESSMENT

Does the children's work on the photocopiable page indicate that they can identify the senses and show that they understand how senses tell us about our surroundings?

PLENARY

Have a quiz where the children have to match your A4 pictures of the sense organs with their names, senses and functions. Highlight how much our senses work together, such as the relationship of smell to taste.

OUTCOME

● Can identify the senses and the sense organs.

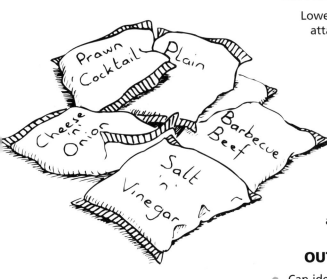

LESSON 10	Objective	● To know that the senses, including taste, make us aware of our surroundings.			
	Resources	A variety of foods (sweet, salty and sour); paper and pens.			
	Main activity	Use a variety of foods to get the children to distinguish and classify foods into one of these tastes: sweet (sugar cakes), salty (salted crisps), bitter (lemons). Get the children to record their results in a table, like the one shown on the right.	Sweet	Salty	Bitter
	Differentiation	Most children should be able to work on this task since the different tastes are quite distinctive.			
	Assessment	Through discussion with the children, identify if they demonstrate understanding of what the senses tell us.			
	Plenary	Ask the children to explain their findings and to describe what effect the different tastes had on them.			
	Outcome	● Can perform activities on the senses.			

UNIT 1 OURSELVES

LESSON 11

OBJECTIVES
● To assess the children's knowledge and understanding of dental health, tooth types and functions.
● To assess the children's knowledge and understanding of the importance of eating a balanced diet.

RESOURCES

Assessment activities: 1. Copies of photocopiable page 31; pens or pencils. **2.** Copies of photocopiable page 32; pens or pencils.

INTRODUCTION

Begin the Assessment activities by giving the children a vocabulary test. This could be oral or written. Remember the activity is an assessment of scientific knowledge and understanding. Either give a word and ask for a definition or give a definition and ask for a word.

ASSESSMENT ACTIVITY 1

Distribute copies of photocopiable page 31 to the children and allow them time to complete it individually. You may wish to tell the children that you wish to find out what they have understood and that it is important to complete the sheet individually. You will need to collect these in to mark them effectively.

Answers
For Assessment activity 1 the children should answer that it is important to look after our teeth because they help us to tear, break, cut up and eat our food. To keep our teeth healthy we should eat sensible food with not too much sugar, clean our teeth regularly (at least twice a day), and visit the dentist every six months.

Looking for levels
For Assessment activity 1, all the children should be able to describe orally and in words a number of relevant tooth facts. Most children will be able to answer the questions correctly. More able children should be able to give a more reasoned answer with greater use of appropriate vocabulary.

ASSESSMENT ACTIVITY 2

Distribute copies of photocopiable page 32 to the children and allow them time to complete it individually. You may wish to tell the children that you wish to find out what they have understood and that it is important to complete the sheet individually. You will need to collect these in to mark them effectively.

Answers
For Assessment activity 2 the children should answer that it is important to eat a healthy balanced diet because our bodies need different types of nutrients that different foods can give us. Too much of one food type would therefore be unhealthy. They should know that their diet was unhealthy if it consists of all the same types of food, for example too much fat or sugar.

Looking for levels
For Assessment activity 2, all the children should be able to plan a healthy meal. Most children will be able to answer the questions correctly. More able children should be able to give a more reasoned answer with greater use of appropriate vocabulary.

PLENARY

You may wish to give some feedback to the children, celebrate their achievements and correct any areas of recurrent misunderstanding.

Name

Myself

Make this picture into a picture of you.
Write labels in the spaces around the picture for all the things that you
know about your body and how it works. One label has already been
put on for you.
Think particularly about how you eat and how food benefits you.

Eyes are used
for seeing

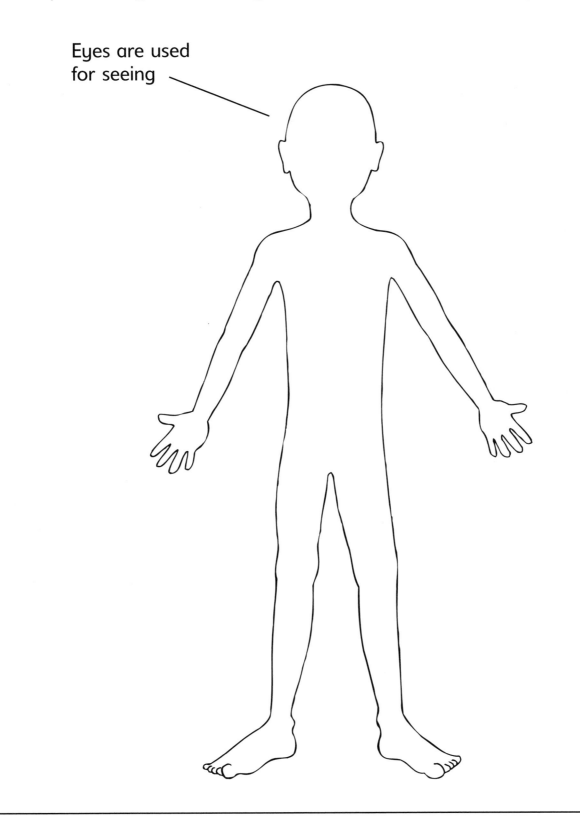

My lunch

Look at the food in your packed lunch. It looks lovely, but what is in it?
Lay out your packed lunch in front of you.
Draw pictures of all the food.

Now write down the name of each item in your packed lunch under these headings.

Energy-giving foods	Body-building foods	Maintenance foods

Which foods in your packed lunch are you looking forward to eating the most and why?

_____

_____

Name

Food groups

Write in the table the foods you have eaten in the past 24 hours for breakfast, lunch, evening meal, supper and any other snacks.

✓Tick the correct food group.

Foods eaten at mealtimes	Food groups	
	Body-building (for growth)	Energy-giving (for activity)
Breakfast		
Lunch		
Evening meal		
Supper		
Snacks		

Going shopping

Different people eat different kinds of foods.
Here are the food shopping lists for two people. Look at them carefully.
Think about the balance of the foods on each list.

LIST A Super Supermarkets LTD

BANANAS
CARROTS
APPLES
CHICKEN
YOGHURT
SKIMMED MILK
LOW FAT SPREAD
RICE
PASTA
WHOLEMEAL BREAD
FISH

LIST B Super Supermarkets LTD

CHIPS
CREAM
SAUSAGE
FULL FAT MILK
CHOCOLATE BISCUITS
BUTTER
FIZZY DRINKS
CHEESE
CHOCOLATE BARS

1. Write your thoughts about the balance of food on each list.

List A _____

_____

List B _____

_____

2. a) Which diet is healthy and balanced? _____

   b) Which diet is unhealthy and unbalanced? _____

Now write your own shopping list. Include a range of items to give you a healthy, balanced and tasty diet. A few 'treats' are allowed!

My shopping list

Name

My teeth

Look at the diagram of some teeth below. Colour the teeth to show the position of each type.

Incisors – red   Canines – blue   Molars – green

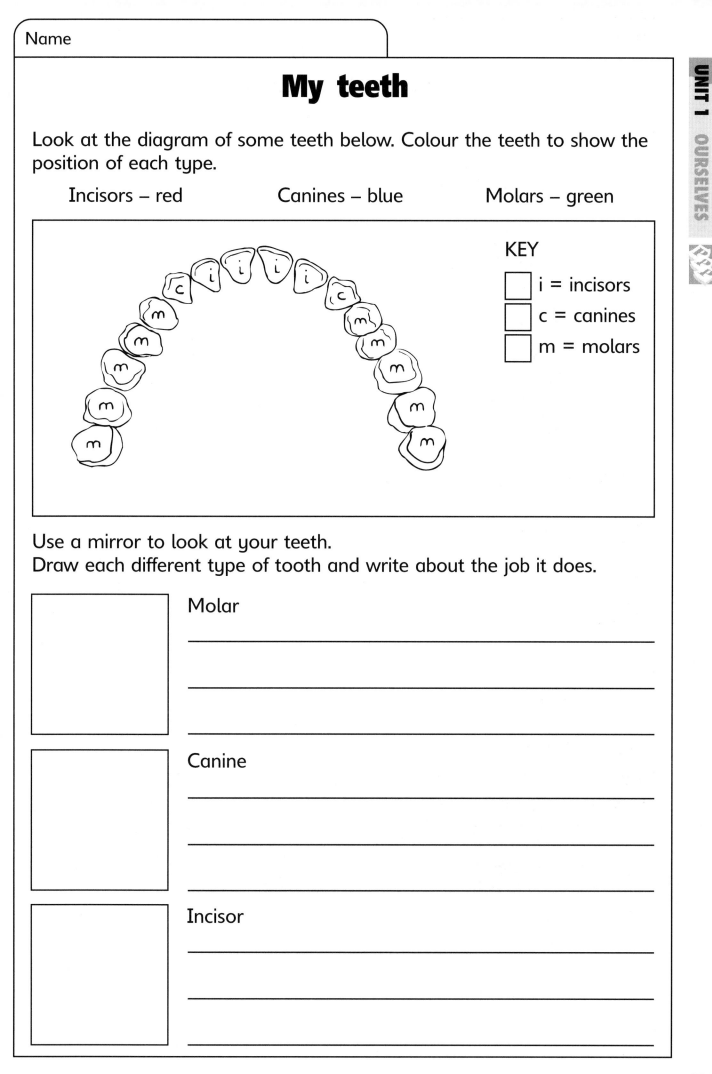

KEY

☐ i = incisors

☐ c = canines

☐ m = molars

Use a mirror to look at your teeth.
Draw each different type of tooth and write about the job it does.

Molar

_____

_____

_____

Canine

_____

_____

_____

Incisor

_____

_____

_____

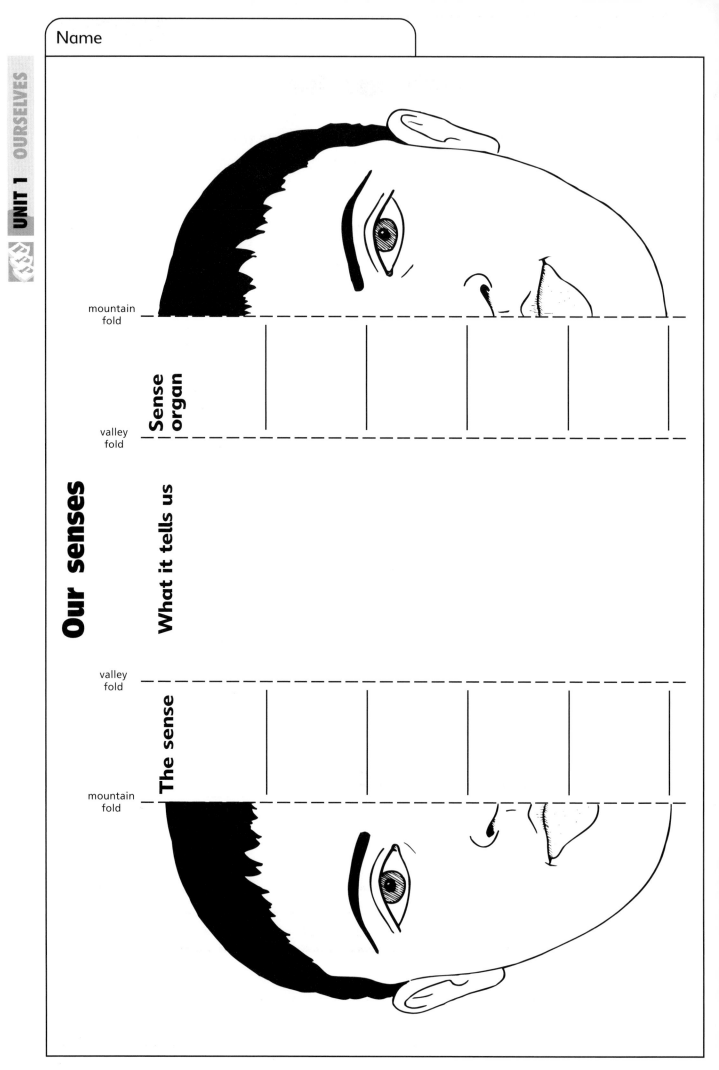

Name

Our senses

mountain fold

Sense organ

valley fold

What it tells us

valley fold

The sense

mountain fold

Name

Teeth and food

What have you learned about teeth? Write in the tooth all you know about teeth. Write about their growth, why they are important and how to look after them.

Teeth facts

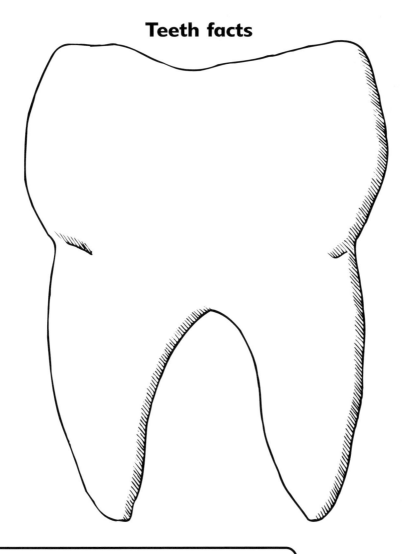

Why is it important to look after your teeth?

_____

_____

What should you do to make sure your teeth are healthy?

_____

_____

Teeth and food

Think about all the things you have learned about food. Draw and write what you would include in a healthy balanced meal on these plates.

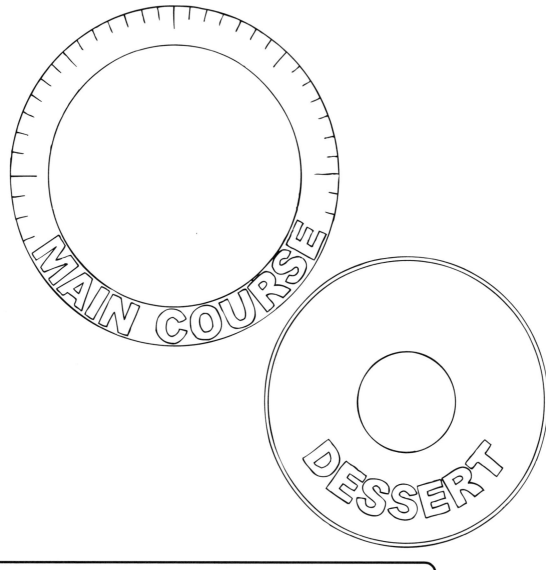

MAIN COURSE

DESSERT

Why is it important to eat a healthy balanced diet?

_____

_____

How would you know if your diet was healthy or not?

_____

_____

The needs of plants and animals

ORGANISATION (19 LESSONS)

	OBJECTIVES	MAIN ACTIVITY	GROUP ACTIVITIES	PLENARY	OUTCOMES
LESSON 1	● To ascertain children's current knowledge of the needs of plants and animals from their work in Key Stage 1/ Primary 1–3.	Concept mapping.	Completing a worksheet on plants and one on animals.	Discussion of the outcomes of the assessment.	● Teacher can assess the level of the children in the class. ● Teacher can arrange children in appropriate class groups.
LESSON 2	● To know that there are certain processes which can be used to identify a living thing.	Identifying differences between living and non-living things.	Looking at evidence of life processes. Identifying living and non-living things.	Reinforce seven life processes: (MR FERGS).	● Can recognise movement, growth, nutrition and reproduction as processes which occur in living things.
LESSON 3	● To know that different animals move in different ways. ● To make observations in obtaining evidence.	Minibeast safari.	Observational drawings. Compiling animal movement factfile.	Reinforcement of how animals move.	● Can describe how different animals move on land. ● Can make observations to obtain evidence.
LESSON 4	● To know that animals have senses that make them aware of their surroundings. ● Make predictions about what will happen.	Identifying animal senses. Carrying out investigation into animal senses.	Planning an investigation. Recording observations.	Discussion of findings from investigation.	● Can recognise the sense organs of some animals. ● Can describe how some animals use their senses. ● Can make predictions about what will happen.
LESSON 5	● To know that animals grow and reproduce. ● To suggest questions, ideas and how to test them. ● To present results and draw conclusions.	Discussing animal growth and change.	Measuring growth in animals. Researching animal growth.	Children explain investigative work.	● Can plan an experiment to measure the growth of animals. ● Can suggest questions, ideas and how to test them. ● Can present results and draw conclusions.
LESSON 6	● To know that animals grow and reproduce.	Using secondary sources to research animal growth, reproduction and development.		Share findings to compare how different animals reproduce.	● Can describe how an animal changes as it grows. ● Can compare how different animals reproduce.
LESSON 7	● To know that animals have different diets.	Comparing foods eaten by humans and other animals.	Looking at food eaten by humans and animals. Researching simple food chains.	Share findings of animal diets.	● Can identify the different sorts of food eaten by animals.
LESSON 8	● To know that animals have different diets. ● To use ICT to communicate data.	Survey of pet owners to determine foods eaten by pets.		Present findings and draw conclusions.	● Can identify the different sorts of food eaten by animals. ● Can use ICT to communicate data.
LESSON 9	● To know that most of our diet comes from plants.	Identifying foods that come from plants and animals. Supermarket visit.	Looking at food chains. Tracing foods back to plants.	Discussion from visit to supermarket.	● Can recognise that most of our diet comes directly from plants.
LESSON 10	● To know that plants are carefully tended so that they produce large crops.	Preparation of a 'Guide to caring for plants' booklet.		'Question and answer' session with guest gardener.	● Can recognise that plants need care in order for them to supply us with food.

ORGANISATION (19 LESSONS)

	OBJECTIVES	MAIN ACTIVITY	GROUP ACTIVITIES	PLENARY	OUTCOMES
LESSON 11	● To know that the roots take up water and anchor the plant to the ground. ● To use systematic observation and measurement.	Looking at plant specimens.	Drawing a labelled diagram of a plant. Investigating the function of roots as water carriers.	Review the investigation and draw conclusions.	● Can describe two functions of roots. ● Can use systematic observation and measurement.
LESSON 12	● To know that water travels in tiny 'pipes' through plants. ● To know that information from previous experiments can be used in planning new experiments.	Observing the effects of a stick of celery standing in coloured water as a way to show the pipes in the stem of a plant.		Reinforce the concept through discussion of the effects on the celery.	● Can recognise the importance of previous information in planning experiments. ● Can recognise where water moves up inside a plant. ● Can recognise the importance of leaves in drawing water up the plant.
LESSON 13	● To know that plants need water, but not an unlimited amount, for healthy growth.	Investigations with water as a variable factor in plant growth.		Groups to report back and together draw conclusions.	● Can recognise that too little or too much water prevents healthy plant growth.
LESSON 14	● To know that different plants prefer different places in which to grow.	Plan a wild plant survey.	Carry out the survey. Present results of observations.	'Wild plant' quiz.	● Know that different plants prefer different places in which to grow.
LESSON 15	● To know that plants need light for healthy growth.	Investigations with light as a variable factor in plant growth.		Groups to report back and together draw conclusions.	● Can recognise that light is needed for healthy plant growth.
LESSON 16	● To know that plants need leaves in order to grow well. ● To know that previous experimental results can help make predictions in new experiments.	Investigations involving plants with and without leaves to determine importance of leaves.		Groups to report back and together draw conclusions.	● Can recognise that leaves are needed for healthy plant growth. ● Can describe an investigation on the relationship of plant leaves and plant growth. ● Can make observations and comparisons.
LESSON 17	● To know that temperature affects plant growth.	Investigations with heat as a variable factor in plant growth.		Groups to report back and together draw conclusions.	● Can recognise that temperature affects plant growth.
LESSON 18	● To know that experimental work can be related to the growing of food plants. ● To make predictions about what will happen. ● To consider what makes a fair test. ● To make observations. ● To present results in drawings and tables. ● To draw conclusions and make generalisations.	Planning an investigation into plant growth using different variables to determine ideal conditions.	Carry out the investigation. Record findings as a diary.	Groups to report back and together draw conclusions.	● Can describe the conditions plants need for healthy growth. ● Can explain why plants need roots and leaves. ● Can make predictions about what will happen. ● Can consider what makes a fair test. ● Can make observations. ● Can present results in drawings and tables. ● Can draw conclusions and make generalisations.

	OBJECTIVES	ACTIVITY 1	ACTIVITY 2
ASSESSMENT 19	● To assess the children's level of understanding of animal growth, movement and diet. ● To assess the children's level of understanding of the needs of plants, their functions and uses.	Completing a worksheet to assess level of understanding of plants.	Completing a worksheet to assess level of understanding of animals.

LESSON 1

OBJECTIVE

● Teacher to ascertain children's current knowledge of the needs of plants and animals from their work in Key Stage 1/Primary 1–3.

RESOURCES

Main teaching activity: Flip chart or board, pens.
Group activities: 1. Copies of photocopiable page 55, pens, pencils. **2.** Copies of photocopiable page 56, pens, pencils.

BACKGROUND

This first lesson in Unit 2 is designed to assess the children's current knowledge and understanding of plants and animals based on work they will have carried out in Key Stage 1/Primary 1–3. The tasks in the lesson can be used individually or together. The children should already be familiar with the differences between plants and animals and be able to sort a group of common living things into plants and animals. They should have an understanding that plants can be sorted into further sub-groups and that flowering plants produce seeds from which seedlings grow. They will also be familiar with the need for water and light for seedlings to grow. They will have developed their understanding that animals can also be separated into groups and that animals change and can reproduce as they grow older.

INTRODUCTION

Tell the children that they are going to be thinking about some things that are all around us – plants and animals – and that by the end of this work they will understand more about how important plants and animals are and what it is that is important to them.

MAIN TEACHING ACTIVITY

Remind the children that they will have already done some work about plants and animals and that you would like them to tell you what they already know and understand. Begin by asking the children to give some words and phrases that they can remember. Write these down on your board or flip chart. Build these up until you can ask the children to begin to link the words into a concept map. These links should be made where they can give a suitable explanation.

GROUP ACTIVITIES

1. Distribute copies of photocopiable page 55 and ask the children to work individually on them. It would be useful to read through the sheet first with all the children and to explain what they need to do. Take care not to explain the answers. It may be appropriate to read the questions to some children while they are carrying out the assessment. The children should draw and label a diagram of a plant and then draw four stages of plant growth to show how the plant begins as a tiny seedling and grows into a healthy plant.
2. Distribute copies of photocopiable page 56 and ask the children to work individually on them. From work carried out in Year 2, the children are asked to draw examples of animals from groupings such as mammals, birds, reptiles, fish, insects and so on. The second part of the activity asks the children to explain in words and pictures the life cycle of an animal.

DIFFERENTIATION

Differentiate by outcome.

ASSESSMENT

Through observation of the concept map contributions and the photocopiable pages you should be able to assess children's level of understanding. They should all be able to give you some ideas about plants and animals and be able to distinguish between the two. Most should be able to identify the parts of a plant and members of the animal groups. Some should be able to explain the life cycle of an animal in detail.

PLENARY

Discuss the tasks, highlighting some of the concepts the children have written about, the similarities and differences of plants and animals and their key characteristics. Explain the areas they will be looking at over future lessons. Avoid suggesting the children's concepts are wrong, but say that the work they will be doing will develop their thinking from where they are now.

OUTCOMES
● Teacher can assess the level of the children in the class.
● Teacher can arrange children in appropriate class groups.

LINKS
Art: observational drawing.

LESSON 2

OBJECTIVE
● To know that there are certain processes which can be used to identify a living thing.

RESOURCES
Main teaching activity: A small pet such as a hamster, a large stone.
Group activities: 1. Two sheets of paper, writing and drawing materials available for each child. **2.** Copies of photocopiable page 57 for each child, pencils, four objects per group (see Preparation).

PREPARATION
Give each group undertaking Group activity 2 four objects to describe as 'living' or 'not living', for example: a plant, a book, a ball, a fish (for example, a goldfish in a bowl). The items you select can be varied depending on the ability of the group. For example, some children may be able to deal with less obvious examples such as seeds, fruit or cut flowers, which it can be argued are still living things since they still exhibit the characteristics of living things or have the potential to do so. Perhaps think about 'never lived' and 'were once alive' as groupings to help the sorting.

BACKGROUND

This lesson introduces the concepts of alive/not alive and identifies the characteristic life processes, which are then explored individually and in more detail through the subsequent lessons in the unit. You may prefer to use this lesson later on in this unit or your scheme of work as a summative, rather than an introductory, lesson.

It is possible to sort the things we see around us into one of three groups: living – those that are alive (plants and animals, for example); once living – those that were once living, but are now dead (wooden furniture, for example); never lived – those things that have never been alive (water or air, for example). It is not always an easy process to decide which group things belong to, as we can sometimes see the characteristics of living things in things that have never lived. Water, for example, moves and makes a noise, but it is not a living thing. Fire is even more confusing! So it is important for children to think carefully about the life processes in order to determine whether or not something is a living thing.

Nearly all living things can be classified as either 'plants' or 'animals', and all have a number of characteristics that they share:

Vocabulary
breathing, characteristics, dead, excretion, feeding, growth, life processes, living/alive, moving/movement, never lived, non-living, reproduction, respiration, sensing/sensitivity

Life process	Animals	Plants
Movement	Animals move all or parts of their body and can move from place to place.	Plants do not move from one place to another, but may be able to move in response to a stimulus, for example flower position relative to a light source.
Reproduction	Animals produce young.	New plants grow from seeds or small parts of the parent plant.
Feeding	Animals eat other animals or plants to give them energy.	Plants make their own food using carbon dioxide and energy from the Sun.
Excretion	Waste substances such as food remains, some gases and other chemicals need to be removed from animals' bodies.	Plants need to get rid of waste gases and water.
Respiration	Animals use oxygen to turn food into usable energy.	Plants use oxygen to turn food into usable energy.
Growth	Animals usually stop growing when they reach adulthood. Parts of the body like hair and nail continue to grow, and parts can self-repair.	Plants continue to grow for as long as they live.
Sensitivity	Animals notice and respond to stimuli in their surroundings.	Plants grow towards the light, respond to day length and to chemicals in the plant and the environment.

NB: 'Respiration' is not 'breathing', but what happens in cells (partly as a result of breathing in animals) to release energy – breathing is really an excretion process, but at this level it is acceptable to think of them as parts of the same process.

INTRODUCTION

Ask the children if they are 'alive' (many will have experienced the loss of relatives or pets). Ask: *How do you know?* Highlight the life processes from their suggestions. At this stage, the children should easily identify movement, feeding and growth from their work in Y2/P3, and maybe reproduction if they have younger siblings. They should be reminded of their senses (from work in KS1/P1–3). Excretion is easily introduced by reminding them of the need to use the toilet, but you will need to explain that we also need to remove waste gases, water and other chemicals, some of which we breathe out after we've breathed in the air that is vital for us to live. So there's breathing too.

Keep it simple and describe these processes with examples and in terms with which the children should be familiar. They will revisit these criteria throughout their science lessons into Key Stage 3/Secondary 1–2 and beyond, with the examples becoming more problematic and the language and definitions more sophisticated.

MAIN TEACHING ACTIVITY

Ask the children to look at the pet and the stone you have brought in and to compare them. Remind them to be quiet and gentle with the pet. Compile a list of characteristics of the pet and the stone. Ask the children to think about anything that is similar and those things that are different. Try to identify which of these characteristics determine that the pet is a living thing.

GROUP ACTIVITIES

1. Ask the children to sort and record on two separate sheets of paper their observations of the living and non-living things: the pet and the stone that you have brought in. They should write its name and then list the characteristics of each. For the pet, the list should include references to all seven life processes. The rock will not exhibit any of these characteristics. (Alternatively, this could be a teacher-led, whole-class or large group activity to make a list on the flip chart.)
2. Give each child a copy of photocopiable page 57 and each group four objects to discuss and describe: some living and some non-living. Again they should be judged against the list of life processes to identify whether the object is living or non-living.

DIFFERENTIATION

Support lower-attaining children with a word list of life processes, perhaps introducing the mnemonic MR FERGS (movement, respiration, feeding, excretion, reproduction, growth, sensing). Higher-attaining children can work unaided, and may display deeper understanding through their writing. Use less obvious objects in Group activity 2 for more able children (see Preparation).

ASSESSMENT

Through scrutiny of their work, observation and discussion, assess the children's understanding. All the children should be able to discriminate between living and non-living things and begin to understand the characteristics of living things. Most of the children will know about the life processes and some will be able to explain them in greater detail.

PLENARY

Gather the children together and discuss the work they have done. Together, complete on the board the sentence: 'I can identify if something is a living because it can...' Introduce higher-attaining children to the mnemonic MR FERGS (or MRS GREN where F becomes N for nutrition).

OUTCOME

● Can recognise movement, growth, nutrition and reproduction as processes which occur in living things.

LINKS

Unit 1, Lessons 3-5: human feeding.
Unit 1, Lessons 7–10: human senses.

LESSON 3

OBJECTIVES

- To know that different animals move in different ways.
- To make observations in obtaining evidence.

RESOURCES

Main teaching activity: Equipment necessary for a 'minibeast safari' (see Preparation); fish in a tank (optional), flip chart or board.
Group activities: 1. Art materials. **2.** A copy of photocopiable page 58 for each child, pencils, additional reference materials on animal movement (optional).

PREPARATION

Choose an area for your 'safari' and check the availability of minibeasts there and their specific locations. Consult with your school policy on outdoor study and arrange any necessary additional adult support. Gather together pooters, sweep nets, containers with lids, trays etc, if you intend to collect animals while outside.

Vocabulary
crawling, flying, hopping, running, sliding, swimming, walking

BACKGROUND

There are two types of movement among animals, including humans: voluntary and involuntary. Even when animals are still, there is always some involuntary movement going on in the body: the heart is beating, blood is moving around the body and the animal is breathing. We do not choose to make these movements, our bodies make them for us. Voluntary movements occur when animals choose to move, either a part of their body, or their entire body from one place to another.

Animals move voluntarily in a variety of ways and for a variety of reasons. These may include: catching prey to eat for food; escaping danger; to move from one place to another seasonally; to move for breeding. Some animals are able to move in more than one way, others in just one.

Movement	Examples of animals
Walking upright	humans
Walking on four legs	dogs, horses
Swimming	fish, marine mammals such as whales
Crawling	lizards, toads
Sliding	snakes
Hopping	kangaroos, some birds
Running	cheetahs, antelope
Flying	birds, bats

Movement occurs in different ways and depends on the animal's shape, size and surroundings. The types of movement can be grouped together as: moving on land with legs; moving on land without legs; flying; and swimming.

- **Moving on land with legs:** animals that have legs and have to use them in a co-ordinated way to move efficiently. We move our legs alternately; when some birds use their legs they do the same, while others hop along both feet together.

Some animals use different ways of co-ordinating their legs depending on the speed they are travelling. The cheetah, for example, moves diagonally opposite pairs of legs together when walking, but front legs together, then back legs together when running.

- **Moving on land without legs:** animals like snakes, slugs, snails and worms move by sliding along. Whilst slugs and snails move on a large muscle (the foot) as it contracts in waves, snakes can move in any one of four sliding movements. They can move in curves which push against the ground, sliding the snake forwards, or they can anchor their tail against something before stretching forward and bringing the tail along after. Snakes can also slide by raising and lowering their belly scales or simply by throwing themselves forward.

- **Flying:** an animal flies through the air by pushing backwards, creating a force called a 'reaction' in the opposite direction, allowing the animal to travel forwards. This force has two parts. As a bird flaps its wings the air flowing over it creates 'lift' which helps the bird to stay in the air. The other is 'drag' which is caused as the bird pushes against the air, slowing the bird down.

- **Swimming:** although through a different medium, the principle of swimming is similar to that of flying in that the animal has to create a backward force to give forward movement. A fish swims by pushing against the water with its fins or its whole body.

INTRODUCTION

Talk about how animals get their food. Apart from pets, most animals have to move in some way to get to their food – to graze or to catch their prey. Even spiders who may catch food in their webs need to move to the food. Discuss how, by moving, animals can also avoid becoming food for other animals.

MAIN TEACHING ACTIVITY

Ask the children to think about the ways in which animals can move about. Make a list on the flip chart. Consider how, in comparison, we move about. *Is it similar or different? Can we move in the same ways as animals? Can we move in different ways? Can animals move as easily and in as many different ways as us?*

Go on a 'minibeast safari' to observe some small animals on the move. If possible, carefully collect some specimens using pooters, sweep nets and containers for the children to observe in the classroom. It is essential that these creatures are returned as soon as possible after the lesson.

GROUP ACTIVITIES

1. Encourage the children to make careful observational drawings of the creatures you bring back to the classroom and make notes regarding where the creature was found and how it moves. Emphasise the need to care for these creatures. You might like to 'import' some fish too, so the children can observe swimming.
2. The children complete page 58 that asks them to think about the ways in which animals move. They are asked to think of six different animals (here meaning any living thing that is not a plant) that move in different ways. The children should think about the way each animal moves before drawing them in motion.

DIFFERENTIATION

Make available a number of suggestions of animals that move in different ways for lower-attaining children. Higher-attaining children can work unaided with more complex and detailed illustrations.

ASSESSMENT

Use the children's completed photocopiable pages to decide if they have been able to identify a range of animal movements. During the Group activities ask questions such as: *How does the worm move? Can you show me something that crawls?*

PLENARY

Use the findings of the minibeast safari to illustrate and reinforce the point of different animal movements. Ask some children to show the rest of the class examples of how different animals move.

OUTCOMES

● Can describe how different animals move on land.
● Can make observations to obtain evidence.

LINKS

Unit 2, Lesson 7: the variety of animal diets.

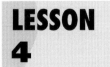

LESSON 4

OBJECTIVES
● To know that animals have senses that make them aware of their surroundings.
● Make predictions about what will happen.

RESOURCES

Main teaching activity: A pet, a flip chart or board, pens.
Group activities: 1 and 2. Copies of photocopiable pages 59 and 60, pens, pencils.

PREPARATION

Arrange for a child to bring to school for this lesson a small, friendly pet that can be observed and studied, such as a hamster. Contact the child's parents or guardian regarding the pet, and arrange suitable accommodation and food for the animal.

Vocabulary

hearing, sight, taste, touch, smell

BACKGROUND

Senses keep us in touch with our surroundings. Our sense organs send messages to our brains and we respond accordingly. Different animals rely on different senses depending on their way of life. To survive in the wild animals need to be able to respond to the environmental conditions in which they find themselves. For some animals these responses are long-term, for example some animals respond to the lowering of temperatures as winter approaches by building nests and hibernating. Other animals will respond to short-term situations, such as the presence of a predator who may threaten their lives. Like humans, other animals have a number of sensory organs that enable them to respond to the many and varied environmental conditions. Some animals have developed one or two particularly keen senses whilst other senses may be less efficient. Birds of prey, for example, have particularly good eyesight to enable them to spot their prey; cats have a keen sense of hearing and good eyesight, and dogs have a well-developed sense of smell.

INTRODUCTION

Ask the children to think about work they have done about themselves (from Unit 1 in this book, for example) and how they are able to find things out about their environment: *How are animals able to do the same?* Discuss the sense organs of animals.

MAIN TEACHING ACTIVITY – PART 1

Look at the pet that you have brought into the classroom. Ask the children to indicate the various sensory organs that the pet has. Write these on the board. Introduce the idea to the children that, just like us, animals use their senses to make them aware of their environment. Ask the children to suggest ways that we could prove this.

GROUP ACTIVITIES

1. Give each child a copy of photocopiable pages 59 and 60. Ask them to work in groups to plan an investigation to show how the pet uses its senses.

MAIN TEACHING ACTIVITY – PART 2

Gather the groups back together and discuss their ideas and plans for carrying out an investigation. Ask them to remain in their groups and to observe and record what happens when you: place food in with the animal; make a sound (be careful not to scare the animal); change the intensity of light; touch the animal.

GROUP ACTIVITIES

2. The observations the children have made and a record of what you have all done together can be made on copies of pages 59 and 60. Ensure the children make predictions about what they think will happen when, for example, the pet is presented with food (apart from eating it), and that they have observed which senses it uses to identify the object.

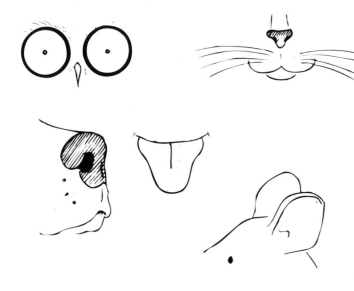

DIFFERENTIATION

Lower-attaining children may need assistance in planning the investigation and identifying what they will do. Higher-attaining children will plan to carry out the investigation unaided with some clear, well-thought-out conclusions and observations being made.

ASSESSMENT

Can the children identify the senses of the animal? Do they have an awareness of how the animal uses them?

PLENARY

Bring the class together to discuss their findings. Discuss their predictions and what actually happened. Ask the children to share with the others their observations and to identify the senses and sensory organs used by the animal.

OUTCOMES
● Can recognise the sense organs of some animals.
● Can describe how some animals use their senses.
● Can make predictions about what will happen.

LESSON 5

OBJECTIVES
● To know that animals grow and reproduce.
● To suggest questions, ideas and how to test them.
● To present results and draw conclusions.

RESOURCES
Main teaching activity: Pictures of humans and other animals at various stages of development (birth, childhood, teenager, adult, old age).
Group activities: 1. Copies of photocopiable pages 59 and 60, young stick insects (which are used in this lesson as an example), suitable containers. **2.** A variety of secondary sources such as books, CD-ROMs and videos; a copy of photocopiable page 61 for each child.

PREPARATION
Ideally, you will need young creatures ready for observation, such as young stick insects. These can be obtained from many pet shops or direct from companies such as: Small-Life Supplies, Station Buildings, Station Road, Bottesford, Notts, NG13 0EB (tel 01949 842446; www.small-life.co.uk). Stick insects are quite easy to care for.
● **Feeding:** most eat bramble (blackberry) leaves. The Indian stick insect (the most common variety) also eats privet and ivy leaves. In all cases the leaves should be sprayed daily with water.
● **Housing:** the cage needs to be tall, around 46cm (18in), with mesh sides.
● **Handling:** many stick insects are easy to handle. Lift adults by the middle of their bodies and medium-sized insects by their tails. It's best not to touch baby stick insects as they are delicate.
● **Temperature:** stick insects do not need heated cages – they can live very well in a room that is comfortably warm in the day and cooler at night. It is best to avoid putting the cage on a window sill as the insects may overheat in the summer and get too cold in the winter.

Vocabulary
adults, babies, growth, reproduction

BACKGROUND
Reproduction and growth are two of the seven processes shared by all living things. Living things cannot live forever so it is important that, for the continuation of the species, they are able to reproduce. The following detailed information is provided to support your understanding.

Reproduction
Among living things reproduction occurs in two quite different ways: sexual and asexual. (Human sexual maturity is discussed in *100 Science Lessons: Year 5/Primary 6* and the stages in reproduction in *Year 6/Primary 7.*)
● **Sexual reproduction:** almost all animals and some plants reproduce sexually. Sexual reproduction involves the mating of a male and a female and the fertilisation of the female egg cells with the male's sperm (in animals) or pollen (in plants). As both parents contribute part of themselves to the fertilised egg, then the offspring will have similarities to each. It will not, however, be identical to its parents. Some organisms, like worms, have both male and female parts and are called 'hermaphrodites'. This means they do not need other individuals for sexual reproduction to take place, but avoid self-fertilisation where possible. Sexual reproduction is more complicated than asexual reproduction, but has one important advantage. Because it involves mixing the characteristics of two parents, the offspring are unique and have their own genetic characteristics.
● **Asexual reproduction:** this requires only one parent and is the method of reproduction of most plants and some animals. Asexual reproduction occurs when cells divide, producing new cells. Each new cell is a copy of an old one. Therefore, in asexual reproduction, all the offspring from the parent are identical to each other and to the parent. Asexual reproduction is much more efficient than sexual reproduction in that it only requires one parent and uses/wastes less of the energy and resources of that individual. On the other hand, because it effectively produces clones sharing the same genetic material, any defect or disease affecting the parent can also affect the offspring.

Growth
Most offspring get bigger as they get older and develop. Growth takes place in plants and animals not by the individual cells getting bigger, but by those cells dividing. Plants carry on growing by this division of cells all their lives. In most animals, cell division slows down once the adult body shape has been achieved. A plant grows when cells at the tips of the roots and

branches divide so that the roots and branches get longer. At the same time, cells in the stem divide to make it thicker. The cells in an animal, like a human, do not all grow at the same rate. In the human body cells in, for example, the arms and legs grow quicker than those in the head, thus as animals grow, their shape changes, rather than just being a much larger version of the young offspring.

INTRODUCTION

Ask the children if any of them have baby brothers or sisters. Ask them to tell everyone a little about them: *How big are they? What foods do they eat? What do they do all day? Who do they look like?* Tell the children that one of the most important parts of living is being able to reproduce – to have young.

MAIN TEACHING ACTIVITY

It is not necessarily appropriate to go into much detail about the biology of reproduction – the 'how'. Rather, ensure that the children fully understand that all plants and animals need to reproduce – the 'why'. Ask these questions: *Why do plants and animals reproduce?* (To maintain their numbers.) *What happens to the young plants and animals?* (They begin to grow.) Talk a little about growth and how both plants and animals grow. Discuss how animals tend to change shape as they grow and reach a stage when they stop growing (adulthood). Illustrate this with a number of pictures of adults at various stages of development.

GROUP ACTIVITIES

1. Using stick insects as a basis for this activity, ask the children to plan and carry out an investigation to observe the growth, over a period of time, of these creatures. Remind them that they must try to ensure that their investigation is a fair test and that they should: make a prediction about the growth; make observations and comparisons; present their results in drawings and writing; draw conclusions from their results. The investigation writing frames on pages 59 and 60 can be used as a guide for the children.
2. Tell the children that they are going to think about young and old animals and how they change. The children should complete photocopiable page 61 that compares young and old animals. The children should use secondary sources (if needed) to complete the missing illustrations and information for each animal. The correct adult and diminutive names should be: frog: tadpole; pig: piglet; penguin: (penguin) chick; bear: (bear) cub; cat: kitten; hen: chicken.

DIFFERENTIATION

Lower-attaining children may plan an investigation in less detail. Higher-attaining children could plan a more complex investigation observing a number of animals as a comparison and drawing conclusions. If appropriate insects are available the investigation from Group activity 1 can be carried out, otherwise just use it as a planning exercise.

ASSESSMENT

In planning and carrying out the investigation, look for evidence that the children can: make a prediction about the growth; make observations and comparisons; present their results in drawings and writing; draw conclusions from their results.

The second Group activity should indicate that the children have an understanding of the life cycle of an animal. Talk with the children, asking them to explain the life cycle to you.

PLENARY

The group can explain the plans for their investigations, what they predict and how they will observe and measure the growth.

OUTCOMES

● Can plan an experiment to measure the growth of animals.
● Can suggest questions, ideas and how to test them.
● Can present results and draw conclusions.

LINKS

Unit 1, Lesson 5: human growth.

LESSON 6

Objective	● To know that animals grow and reproduce.
Resources	Completed photocopiable page 61 from the previous lesson; secondary sources of information such as books, CD-ROMs, Internet access; writing and drawing materials.
Main activity	Use photocopiable page 61 with secondary sources to find out about the growth, development and reproduction of the animals on the sheet. Tell the children that some of the animals were born live from their mothers, while others hatched from eggs. Ask them to complete a table like the one below. (For the purposes of this activity assume that frogspawn is a type of egg.) Some examples may be: eggs – tadpole, penguin, chicken; live – piglet, bear, cat. Then tell the children to choose one of the animals and find out as much as they can about their young. They should try to find out how they reproduce, for how long the young are inside their mother and how many babies are usually born at the same time, for example. The children can present their findings as a poster. Factors to consider may include: how animals change as they get older (in terms of size, shape, colour); how the animals reproduce (eggs or live young); number of young produced; how long they live for. | Eggs	Live
Differentiation	Lower-attaining children could concentrate on fewer aspects of the animal. Higher-attaining children can give more detailed explanations presented with a deeper understanding.
Assessment	Discuss the children's findings with them. Ask the children to explain how their chosen animal grows and reproduces and ask questions that will indicate a level of understanding, such as: *Tell me how your animal reproduces and grows. What do the young look like? In what ways are they similar or different to the adults? Do they hatch from eggs or are they born as live animals?*
Plenary	Share findings with each other and consider how different animals reproduce.
Outcomes	● Can describe how an animal changes as it grows. ● Can compare how different animals reproduce.

LESSON 7

OBJECTIVE

● To know that animals have different diets.

RESOURCES

Main teaching activity: Board or flip chart and felt-tipped pen.
Group activities: 1 and 2. Photocopiable page 62; long strips of paper (for food chains); reference sources about animals such as books, videos, CD-ROMs, Internet access.

PREPARATION

Ensure suitable secondary source material is available.

Vocabulary
carnivore, food chain, food web, food, herbivore, omnivore, processed

BACKGROUND

In years past, people got their food by gathering seeds and fruit and by hunting. Today, most of our food is produced for us, by farmers and food processing companies, and instead of gathering the food ourselves we visit shops and supermarkets to buy our food. In the wild, things are very different. Animals in the wild eat very different foods and spend much of their time finding and eating food. Animals that eat plants do not usually need to move very far to feed since plants tend to be rooted in one place and do not move about unless blown by the wind. On the other hand, carnivores (meat-eaters) usually have to catch their food.

The 'diet' of an animal is its complete food intake. Some animals have very varied diets, others tend to eat only a limited range of foods. The plants and animals living in a community are closely linked through their feeding habits as they may feed on other members of the same community. For example, a rabbit eats plants, and in turn is eaten by a fox. So we get a food chain: plants are food for rabbits which are food for foxes.

Since some animals eat a varied diet it is possible to see that these food chains can very quickly build to form a food web with great interdependence between the plants and animals in the web. For example, should there be a lack of food for smaller creatures at the lower end of a food chain this has a 'knock-on' effect as you travel higher up the chain. Hence, if for some reason there was a problem with the growth of suitable plant life, the number of rabbits may be reduced which in turn could affect the number of foxes.

INTRODUCTION

Begin by talking to the children about the foods that their pets may eat, ask them a few silly questions such as: *Does your pet rabbit each jam sandwiches? Did your goldfish have a boiled egg for breakfast? Does your hamster enjoy a tasty trifle?*

MAIN TEACHING ACTIVITY

Ask the children to think about the different types of food that they eat. If they have already looked at Unit 1 you could refer back to their work. Compile a simple list on a board or flip chart. Now ask the children to think about the food that is eaten by an animal. Again, make a list. Compare the lists: while some foods may be similar, in general the foods eaten by animals will be different. Encourage the children to think about the ways in which an animal's food is different – human food is often cooked or processed whereas food for wild animals is raw and unprocessed, for example. Talk about food chains and the way in which animals and plants are food for other animals. Give an example of a food chain.

GROUP ACTIVITIES

1. Give out copies of page 62 for the children to complete. While some of the basic foods may be the same, encourage the children to think about how our food is eaten raw, cooked or processed. The children should use a range of secondary sources to find out about the range of foods eaten by one particular animal. Encourage them to relate what is eaten to where the animal lives. They should use the 'Animal diet factfile' sheets to record their findings.
2. Working together in small groups, the children should go on to use their research skills and findings to build up a simple food chain based on the diet factfile. These can be drawn on strips of paper for illustration and display.

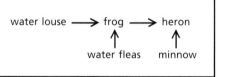

DIFFERENTIATION

Lower-attaining children draw simple 'chains' of only one or two relationships. For higher attainers introduce the concept of a simple food web by linking sets of food chains together as shown in the example opposite. (Food chains and webs are explored in more detail in *100 Science Lessons: Year 4/Primary 5*.)

ASSESSMENT

Look at the children's work for evidence of an understanding of the different diets eaten by humans and animals and also between different animals.

PLENARY

Share the findings of the children's research into animal diets as a means of reinforcing the knowledge and understanding of differing animal diets.

OUTCOME

● Can identify the different sorts of food eaten by animals.

LINKS

Unit 1, Lessons 3–5: human feeding.

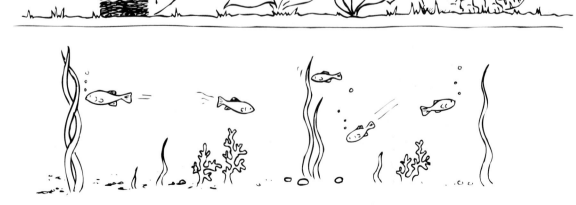

LESSON 8

Objectives	● To know that animals have different diets. ● To use ICT to communicate data.
Resources	Computer and data-handling software.
Main activity	Design and carry out a survey of the pet owners amongst the children to determine the foods eaten by particular pets, favourite foods and any unusual diets or food items. Use data-handling software to record, interpret and present findings.
Differentiation	Support lower-attaining children with data collection. Higher-attaining children can begin to ask questions about the data they have collected such as 'What is the most popular food eaten by rabbits?'
Assessment	Assess ability to explain findings and to carry out the data research.
Plenary	Present findings, discuss and try to draw some conclusions about foods eaten by different pets.
Outcomes	● Can identify the different sorts of food eaten by animals. ● Can use ICT to communicate data.

LESSON 9

OBJECTIVE

● To know that most of our diet comes from plants.

RESOURCES

Main teaching activity: 1. Flip chart, paper, pens, pencils. **2.** Computer and online shopping disk (optional); extra adult supervision (if visiting a shop or supermarket).
Group activities: 1 and 2. Paper, pens, pencils.

PREPARATION

If arranging to visit a local shop or supermarket, contact the manager first to arrange permission, and arrange extra adult supervision for each group. If this is not a practical option, you could obtain online shopping software and install it on the class computer.

Vocabulary

animals, food chains, plants

BACKGROUND

A characteristic of all living things is the necessity to feed. Almost all plants and animals depend directly or indirectly on the Sun for that food. Unlike animals, plants are able to make their own food. They do this through the process of photosynthesis where plants use carbon dioxide, water and the energy from the Sun to make a type of sugar that is the plant's source of energy. The plant then becomes food for animals, which in turn may be food for other animals, including humans. Thus most of the food we eat in our diet can be traced back along a food chain to plants and ultimately the Sun. These links in the food chain are often difficult to trace when faced with some of the processed foods we eat today and the many additives and preservatives they contain. None the less, the bulk of foods that children will come across will be just one link in a food chain where we as humans are at the very end.

INTRODUCTION

Ask the children to tell you some of the foods they have eaten recently. Write them down on the board. Ask the children to consider where the food came from originally, before it arrived in the shops. Ask them to see if they can put the food into groups, not according to the type of food or its benefits to us, but in some other way. Guide their thinking towards the idea of food from plants and food from animals.

MAIN TEACHING ACTIVITY – PART 1

As a whole-class activity, the children should now rewrite their earlier food suggestions, this time in two lists on the flip chart, one headed 'Plants', the other headed 'Animals'. Before recording their ideas, encourage the children to predict which they think will give the longest list, then discuss the table. After filling in the table ask the children to think about the food that is eaten by those who are in the 'Animals' list, and what those animals that provided the food were fed on themselves.

GROUP ACTIVITIES

1. The children should then trace back some of the food they have eaten to its source in a food chain. Draw these as a series of linked illustrations. Challenge the children to see if they can find a food that does not start with a green plant.

2. Ask the children to work in groups to share and explain to each other their food chain drawings. At this stage the children should then be able to come to an understanding that, either directly or through a food chain, most of our diet comes from plants.

MAIN TEACHING ACTIVITY – PART 2

Arrange a visit to a local shop or supermarket or, if that is not possible, obtain an online shopping disk from one of the major supermarkets. These are often organised into aisles, just like the real thing. Either using the computer or in the real supermarket, allocate groups of children an aisle. Their task is to record and consider the foods in that aisle and determine if they come directly from plants or animals. The results will reinforce the principle that most of our diet comes from plants.

DIFFERENTIATION

Lower-attaining children could use magazines to find photographs to cut and paste into a food chain. Higher attainers could try to find the longest food chain they can. They could begin to think about joining food chains into food webs.

ASSESSMENT

Marking the children's work will give an indication whether or not they have understood the concept. All the children should have been able to sort the foods into groups, so will have understood that foods come from one of these two sources. Most should have been able to understand that most of our food can be traced directly or indirectly back to plants.

PLENARY

Discuss the findings from the supermarket visit, reinforcing the concept of plants being the major source of food and highlighting one or two foods that make food chains where plants are at the bottom of the chain, such as milk and some meats.

OUTCOME

● Can recognise that most of our diet comes directly from plants.

LINKS

Unit 1, Lessons 3–5: human feeding.

LESSON 10

Objective	● To know that plants are carefully tended so that they produce large crops.
Resources	Find a parent or grandparent who is a keen gardener to visit the school to talk about looking after plants.
Main activity	Ask your gardening expert to talk to the children about growing plants and looking after them so that they produce a good crop. The children can then prepare a 'Guide to Caring for Plants' booklet.
Differentiation	Lower-attaining children's guides could be illustrations with the addition of key words. Higher-attaining children could give more thorough written descriptions to show understanding of the need for plant care.
Assessment	Through observation and discussion, identify those children who understand how to care for plants.
Plenary	Have a 'question and answer' session, with the children as the 'experts' answering questions from your guest.
Outcome	● Can recognise that plants need care in order for them to supply us with food.

LESSON 11

OBJECTIVES

● To know that the roots take up water and anchor the plant to the ground.
● To use systematic observation and measurement.

RESOURCES

Main teaching activity: Washed weeds with roots in shallow trays, a copy of photocopiable page 63 for each child.
Group activities: 1. Copies of photocopiable page 63. **2.** Copies of photocopiable page 64, beakers, washed weeds (complete with roots), water, cling film.

PREPARATION

Dig up and clean sufficient weeds to provide one for each group.

Vocabulary

anchor, roots, water

BACKGROUND

Roots are vital to the well-being of a plant. Gardeners go to great lengths to develop a healthy and substantial root system on their plants. It is this system that performs two very important functions in the plant and without such a system the plant would become unhealthy and die.

The first function is that of supplying water to the plant. If a plant becomes short of water it will eventually wilt and die: the plant needs water in order to survive. The roots of the plant draw up water and trace minerals from the ground. These are transported from the roots to the leaves where photosynthesis takes place. The plant also loses some of this water as it evaporates into the air from the leaves and flowers. This water loss is called transpiration. The water in the roots and stems moves due to a combination of pushing and pulling. The roots often push the water a little way up the stem while the evaporation from the leaves draws up more water to replace that lost.

As well as taking up water for the plant, the roots also perform another very important function: the root system acts as an anchor to hold the plant firmly in place. Without a well-established root system to keep the plant in place it would rock about and become loose; very soon it would fall over, become unhealthy and die. The root system of a plant is very often quite extensive and can spread out as far and wide as the branches above ground. The roots of some larger plants and trees are also very strong and can cause serious structural damage if allowed to develop near buildings.

INTRODUCTION

Ask the children to think about what they feel like on a lovely, hot and sunny day, particularly when they are inside or if they have just been for a long walk or finished playing games. Encourage them to think about being hot and in need of some refreshment. Ask them to think about what being thirsty does to you.

Show them a wilting plant and ask them to think about what this plant may need and why it is wilting. They should suggest that the plant needs a 'drink' of water. Draw again on the analogy of themselves needing water and the plant needing water. Ask the children to think about how we drink to take in water and how the plant might take in water through its roots.

MAIN TEACHING ACTIVITY

Distribute the weeds that you have prepared and copies of photocopiable page 63. Ask the children to take great care as they will be using the plants later in an investigation. Ask them to look carefully at the plant, its roots, stem and leaves. Talk about how water moves up the roots and stem to the leaves and about the functions of the roots, stem and leaves.

GROUP ACTIVITIES

1. Ask the children to draw a labelled diagram of their plant on a copy of photocopiable page 63. They should then pair up the names of the parts with the description of their function.
2. Suggest to the children that, while we think water is taken up through the roots of the plant, we need to be sure and so they are going to carry out an investigation to show that water does travel through the roots of the plant. The children will need copies of page 64, the weeds, plastic beakers, water and cling film. During the investigation, which could last a week, the children will need to observe the water levels every day and record their observations on page 64. At the end of the investigation there are two questions to answer that will help the children to draw some conclusions.

DIFFERENTIATION

Support lower-attaining children during the setting up of the investigation and use a simplified scale on the beaker (or write on the beaker with a waterproof pen to mark the falling water level). Higher-attaining children will give reasoned answers to questions and may have a beaker marked in smaller units, such as millilitres, that can be read off and recorded.

ASSESSMENT

Mark the children's work to show understanding of the functions of the roots. Have they been able to identify the two functions? During the investigation, assess the children's ability to take simple measurements.

PLENARY

Bring the children together, with their plants, and ask each group to describe what has happened to theirs. (The water levels will have dropped.) You may need to reinforce the idea that because the beaker was sealed the water could not have 'escaped' directly into the air, so it must have been taken up by the plant's roots and travelled through and out of the plant.

OUTCOMES

- Can describe two functions of roots.
- Can use systematic observation and measurement.

LESSON 12

Objectives	● To know that water travels in tiny 'pipes' through plants. ● To know that information from previous experiments can be used in planning new experiments.
Resources	Celery, containers, food colouring.
Main activity	As an introduction to the lesson, take a bunch of cut flowers and put them in a vase of water. Talk to the children, asking them to tell you why we put cut flowers into water. Talk about the tiny pipes through which a plant carries the water. Look at the ends of the cut flowers. The children will find it difficult to see any pipes clearly. Continue by suggesting that if they place a stick of celery in a container of coloured water the children will be able to see the pipes. Leave it for a few days. Cut the stalk and examine the end of the celery. The children can write and draw about their observations of how water travels in tiny pipes through plants.
Differentiation	Lower-attaining children present their findings simply using annotated drawings. Higher-attaining children present their findings in written narrative using illustrations with clear explanations and evidence of understanding.
Assessment	Examine the children's work. Consider if their explanations are sufficiently accurate to demonstrate that they understand the concept of water travelling through pipes.
Plenary	Discuss the investigation and the colour of the celery. Reinforce the concept of water travelling up the stem of the celery.
Outcomes	● Can recognise the importance of previous information in planning experiments. ● Can recognise where water moves up inside a plant. ● Can recognise the importance of leaves in drawing water up the plant.

LESSON 13

Objective	● To know that plants need water, but not an unlimited amount, for healthy growth.
Resources	Seeds, compost, water.
Main activity	In the context of previous work related to plants, grow a packet of seeds. When they have germinated and grown into small seedlings set up an investigation in which you have a number of samples each receiving varying amounts of water: some are under-watered, some over-watered, some not watered at all. Observe and measure the growth and general health of the plants over a period of time.
Differentiation	Differentiate by outcome.
Assessment	Discussion with children during the investigation and scrutiny of written work will indicate understanding. Ask the children to explain their investigation and what the results mean. Ask questions such as: *Why did this plant die? Do you think plants like to stand in water? What happens if you over-water a plant?*
Plenary	Discuss the results of the investigation, draw conclusions related to the amount of water plants need. The children should find that too little or too much water is not going to benefit a plant. Too little and the plant will dry out and die, too much and the roots may rot, also causing the plant to die.
Outcome	● Can recognise that too little and too much water prevents healthy plant growth.

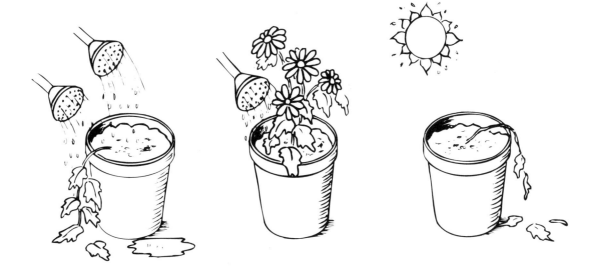

LESSON 14

OBJECTIVE
● To know that different plants prefer different places in which to grow.

RESOURCES
Main teaching activity: Secondary sources of information, a map of your locality, paper, pens, pencils.
Group activities: 1. Paper, pens, pencils, clipboards. **2.** Secondary sources of information, paper, pens, pencils, art materials.

PREPARATION
Ensure that a variety of common wild plants are growing in your chosen locations.

BACKGROUND
As most gardeners will tell you, certain plants like to grow in particular types of soil and thrive or otherwise in certain conditions. Many garden centres will set out their stocks of plants according to whether those plants prefer, for example, clay soil or sandy soil; whether they should be planted in a shady site or a sunny site and so on. As we look around our environment we are able to see a real variety of wild plants that also prefer certain conditions. Some, such as the dandelion, grow well in dry open sunny sites whilst others, such as mosses, prefer the shady dampness offered by a sheltered north-facing position.

Vocabulary
wild plant, survey, hedges, waste ground, field

INTRODUCTION

Begin the lesson by telling the children that they are going to be explorers and that they are going to explore local plant life. Ask the children if they can name any wild plants that they know of and that they think they may be able to see and possibly identify locally. Most of the children should be able to identify some common wild plants such as the dandelion, daisy and buttercup. It may be worth discussing here the difference between a wild plant and a weed. (Weeds are plants that are not wanted in the location where they are growing.)

MAIN TEACHING ACTIVITY

Together, plan a wild plant survey. Ask the children to suggest areas in the locality in which they could look to survey the wild plants growing there. Try to get a range of different places, such as the school field, under a hedge, in a wild area or on waste ground. (These will depend on the location of your school.) Have available a range of secondary sources of information that the children can use to familiarise themselves with some of the possible wild plants they may see. Discuss with the children exactly what it is they are going to be observing, for example the characteristics of the location (damp, dry, dark, light and so on) or the plants growing there.

GROUP ACTIVITIES

1. Let the children carry out their survey. They should record their observations in an appropriate way. They could devise a record sheet that includes detail such as: place, date and season, the conditions and plants growing there. A sketch of the location and the individual plants could also be made.
2. On return to the classroom, the children should try to identify the wild plants they have seen using secondary sources as an aid. The children could present their findings in the form of a location sketch, painting or collage, which may also give extra detail on the plants seen.

DIFFERENTIATION

Lower-attaining children could present their observations in a simple picture form. Higher-attaining children could present their observations with additional research and background information.

ASSESSMENT

All of the children should be able to identify a few of the more common wild plants. Most should be able to identify more common wild plants and understand that they grow in different places. Some may be able to explain more about each of the common wild plants they have seen and begin to explain where they generally grow.

PLENARY

Bring the children together and discuss their observations from their surveys. Have a simple quiz where the children have to try to identify a wild plant from the description you give of the plant and where it typically grows. For example: *This plant has a yellow flower and grows in fields and meadows.* (A buttercup.)

OUTCOME

● Know that different plants prefer different places in which to grow.

LINKS

Unit 3, Lessons 2–4.

LESSON 15

Objective	● To know that plants need light for healthy growth.
Resources	Seeds, compost, pots.
Main activity	Set up a number of investigations with plants where light is a variable factor. These could include: growing seeds with and without light; leaving some seedlings in the dark and bringing others out; keeping existing plants in light and dark conditions; studying covered and uncovered patches of grass.
Differentiation	Differentiate by outcome.
Assessment	Discussion with children during their investigation and scrutiny of written work will indicate understanding. Ask the children to explain what they have done in their investigation and what they have found out. Do the children understand that for healthy growth plants need light?
Plenary	Ask each group to report back their findings. Bring results together and encourage the children to draw conclusions. Highlight that the plants deprived of light have not grown as well or as healthily as those with the benefit of light.
Outcome	● Can recognise that light is needed for healthy plant growth.

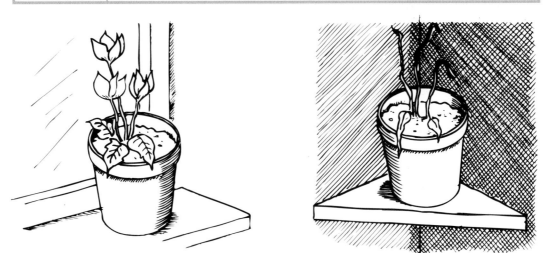

LESSON 16

Objectives	● To know that plants need leaves in order to grow well. ● To know that previous experimental results can help make predictions in new experiments.
Resources	Potted plants: one with leaves, one with leaves removed.

Main activity	Talk to the children about the work they have done previously about the parts of plants. Recall the parts they know about and talk briefly and in simple terms about the functions of those parts: roots take up water and nutrients and anchor the plant; stems carry water to the leaves and keep the plant upright; flowers produce seeds; leaves take in sunlight and make food.
	   Talk about what might happen if the plant was deprived of one of these parts, for example if all the leaves were removed.
	   Plan and carry out an investigation into the need plants have for leaves. Observe two plants (of the same species) – one that has leaves and one that has had its leaves removed. Keep them in the same conditions, observe what happens and measure growth over a period of time.

Differentiation	Differentiate by outcome.
Assessment	Discussion with children during their investigation and scrutiny of written work will indicate understanding. Look for evidence that the children know that without leaves the plant would not be able to grow. Higher-attaining children may be able to explain that without leaves the plant cannot produce food and therefore will not grow healthily.
Plenary	Discuss observations and draw conclusions about what happened to those plants without leaves that were not growing well. Reinforce the knowledge that leaves are important in order for plants to grow well.
Outcomes	● Can recognise that leaves are needed for healthy plant growth. ● Can describe an investigation of the relationship of plant leaves and plant growth. ● Can make observations and comparisons.

LESSON 17

Objective	• To know that temperature affects plant growth.
Resources	Seedlings, warm and cold places.
Main activity	Grow a number of seedlings where the only variable is temperature. Heated and unheated propagators would give the ideal variables. Try to ensure that light and other conditions remain the same for all the samples.
Differentiation	Differentiate by outcome.
Assessment	Discussion with children during the investigation and scrutiny of their written work will indicate understanding. Ask the children to explain to you the conditions in which their plants were kept and what happened to each. They should be able to explain to you that plants with insufficient heat will not grow as well as those with sufficient heat. Similarly, some plants may not like too much heat and would again not remain healthy.
Plenary	Discuss the results of the investigation, draw conclusions related to the effect variables in temperature have on plants. The children should discover that too much or too little heat are not ideal conditions for healthy growth.
Outcome	• Can recognise that temperature affects plant growth.

LESSON 18

OBJECTIVES

- To know that experimental work can be related to the growing of food plants.
- To make predictions about what will happen.
- To consider what makes a fair test.
- To make observations.
- To present results in drawings and tables.
- To draw conclusions and make generalisations.

RESOURCES

Main teaching activity: Paper, pens, pencils.
Group activities: 1. Cress (or other fast-germinating seeds), compost; eight small containers per group, sticky labels, photocopiable page 65, pens, pencils. **2.** Paper, pens, pencils.

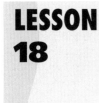

Vocabulary

conclusion, fair test, observation, prediction, results

BACKGROUND

There are about 380 000 known species of plant in the world, the most abundant and successful being those which reproduce by making seeds. There are two main groups of seed-bearing plants:

- flowering plants, which produce seeds that are enclosed in a fruit
- non-flowering plants, which produce seeds that are not enclosed in a fruit (such as ferns).

The abundance and success of plants is of benefit to man since we harvest and eat a large range of fruits, vegetables, cereals and grain as food. Many food crops are grown throughout the world and are a major part of the diets of large parts of the world population. It is man's general success in growing crops that has helped to sustain life throughout the world, despite problems in some countries.

It is the plant's unique ability to make its own food that has been the source of food for mankind. Without plants, animals (including humans) would die. Plants need water, light, moderate temperatures and carbon dioxide in order to survive. Plants will suffer and die if they do not get the correct amount and balance of these things. Too much or not enough water, insufficient light, too high or low a temperature will all affect the growth of plants. This lesson brings together the work from previous lessons into one investigation. It is designed to encourage the children to consider factors that affect the growth of plants in combination with each other.

INTRODUCTION

Remind the children of the recent lessons they have had and the investigations they have carried out looking at plants, particularly plants and light, plants and water, plants and temperature. Reinforce the previous learning, asking questions such as: *What things do plants need to grow? Can anybody tell me what effect light has on plants? If I kept a plant in very cold temperatures what would happen to it? Tell me why water is important to plants.* Address any misunderstandings that may become apparent as a result of such questions and ask other children to share and discuss solutions.

MAIN TEACHING ACTIVITY

Tell the children that they are going to carry out an investigation to try to find out the ideal conditions for growing plants, particularly those that we can use for food. Together discuss how this could be done. Ask the children to plan a fair test that would investigate the growth of plants with combinations of these variables – light, heat and water. Ask the children to work out how many different combinations there are and therefore how many samples they will need to grow. They will also need to consider: how much water they will give the plants and how often (perhaps daily, every three days, weekly); where to keep the plants needing light and those needing dark (perhaps in a store room, on a window sill); where to keep those that need heat or not (perhaps in a cold store room, outside, in a fridge).

Plant	Water?	Light?	Heat?
1	Yes	Yes	Yes
2	Yes	Yes	No
3	Yes	No	No
4	No	Yes	Yes
5	No	No	Yes
6	Yes	No	Yes
7	No	No	Yes
8	No	No	No

This gives eight samples with one given all the variables, one given none of the variables and six with combinations of one or two of the variables.

GROUP ACTIVITIES

1. Make the resources the children need available, and distribute and talk through photocopiable page 65. The children can then work in groups of three or four to set up their part of the investigation. Remind them to put sticky labels on the pots that include the group's names, the plant number, the conditions (whether given water, light or warmth).

2. Ask the children to write the first part of the record of their investigation. This can be in diary format, but needs to include details of: what they are investigating, how they are carrying out the investigation, what they think will happen, and what they have done so far.

DIFFERENTIATION

Prepare a writing frame to support lower-attaining children in recording their observations under the following headings: 'What we are investigating', 'How we are carrying out the investigation', 'What we think will happen', and 'What we have done so far'. Higher-attaining children record observations in a way they decide.

ASSESSMENT

During the investigation, try to find time to talk to each child about the investigation. Try to elicit their level of understanding of what they are doing and why. Marking of the children's completed work should also be indicative of understanding. The children should have been able to keep accurate records of their work, presenting their results and drawing some conclusions that would indicate they understand that seeds that have water, light and heat grow better, and maybe suggest why.

PLENARY

At the end of the first investigation lesson, ask some children to talk about how they have set up the investigation. Remind the children of the aims and also to continue to observe their seeds on a daily basis. At some point each day, set aside a few minutes for groups to report on any progress. Remind the groups to record everything they observe during the experiment.

OUTCOMES

● Can describe the conditions plants need for healthy growth.
● Can explain why plants need roots and leaves.
● Can make predictions about what will happen.
● Can consider what makes a fair test.
● Can make observations.
● Can present results in drawings and tables.
● Can draw conclusions and make generalisations.

LINKS

QCA Scheme of Work for Science, Unit 3B: helping plants grow well.

LESSON 19

OBJECTIVES
● To assess the children's level of understanding of animal growth, movement and diet.
● To assess the children's level of understanding of the needs of plants, their functions and uses.

RESOURCES

Assessment activities: 1. Copies of photocopiable page 66; pens or pencils. **2.** Copies of photocopiable page 67; pens or pencils.

INTRODUCTION

Begin the assessment by having a vocabulary quiz. Either give a word and ask for the definition or give a definition and ask for the word. Here are some words to use: carnivore, herbivore, food chain, swimming, crawling, flying, sight, hearing, touch, smell, taste, reproduction, growth, plants, animals.

ASSESSMENT ACTIVITY 1

Distribute copies of photocopiable page 66 to test the children's understanding and let them complete it individually. The test would be best marked yourself, however you may wish the children to mark each other's. You may need to scribe for some of the children.

Answers
1. Roots collect water from the ground and anchor the plant into the ground; stems hold the plant upright and carry water from the roots to the leaves; leaves produce food for the plant; flowers produce seeds. 2. The drawing should show a wilting plant and the words should suggest that the plant may be wilting due to a lack of water. 3. There should be appropriate examples of plant- and animal-originated foods. 4. Most of our food comes from plants.

Looking for levels
All the children should be able to answer questions 1 and 2 on photocopiable page 66 correctly. Most should be able to answer question 4 and some will be able to answer question 3.

ASSESSMENT ACTIVITY 2

Distribute copies of the photocopiable page 67 to test the children's understanding and let them complete it individually. The activity is designed to assess the children's understanding of animal growth, movement and diet.

Answers
1. The correct order of numbers under the pictures from left to right is 3, 1, 2.
2. Examples could be as shown in the table opposite.
3. A rabbit eats grass, a lion eats antelope, a kestrel eats mice, a seal eats fish and a blackbird eats snails.

Movement	Animal
Walks	human, dog, horse
Swims	fish, whale
Crawls	lizard
Slides	snake
Flies	bird, bat
Hops	kangaroo

Looking for levels
All of the children should be able to answer the first question on photocopiable page 67, with most also being able to correctly answer the second two questions.

PLENARY

You may wish to review the unit with the children and work through any misconceptions that the children still have.

Name

What can you remember about plants?

Draw a picture of a flowering plant and label these parts of the plant:

leaf
flower
stem
root

Imagine you planted a seed.
Draw what you think you would see each week over four weeks.

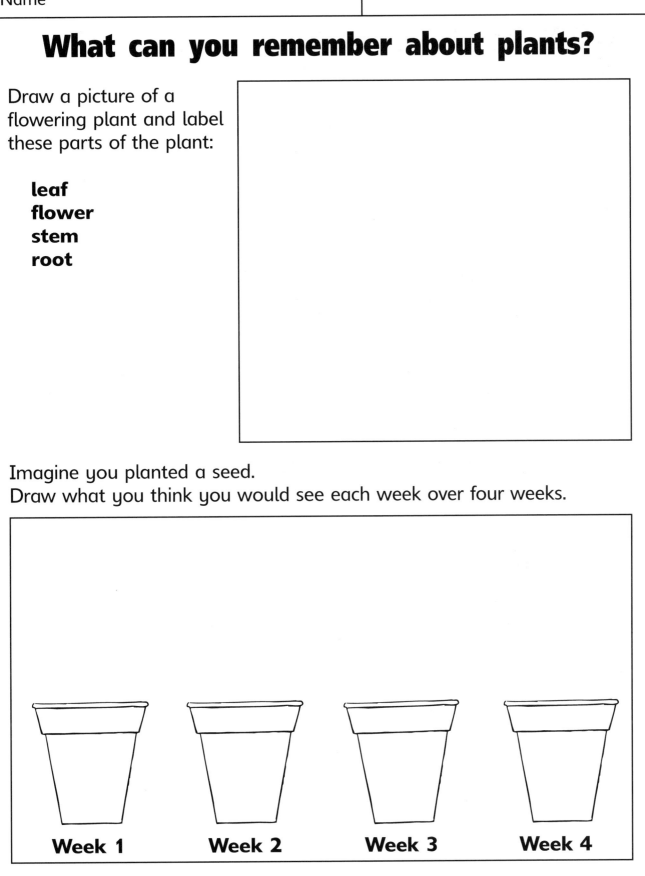

Week 1   **Week 2**   **Week 3**   **Week 4**

What must you do to make sure your seeds grow?

_____

_____

Different kinds of animals

Draw pictures of four different animals. Try to show animals from four different groups such as a mammal, a bird, a fish and an insect.

Use words and pictures to describe how an animal changes from when it is born to when it grows up.

Name

Is it living?

Look at the objects in front of you. Draw a picture and name each one.
Put a tick in the boxes for each object to say if it has each life process.

Name and picture of object			
Does the object possess these life processes?			
Can move on its own			
Makes young			
Needs food			
Has to get rid of food remains or harmful chemicals			
Respires/breathes			
Grows			
Can sense its world			

Is it, or has it been, a living thing?
Write the name of each of your objects under one of these headings:

Living	Once lived	Never lived

Animal movements

Think of six different animals that move in different ways.
Draw and write about each animal on the move.

Animal Movement Factfile

The _____

moves by _____.

The _____

moves by _____.

The _____

moves by _____.

The _____

moves by _____.

The _____

moves by _____.

The _____

moves by _____.

Name

Our scientific investigation

Name _____ Date _____

Our question:

What we will do to find the answer:

What we will need:

What we think will happen:

Our scientific investigation (continued)

This is what we did:

This is what we found out:

This is what we now know:

Name

Young and adult

Look at these pictures of young and adult animals.
Complete the pairs and fill in their names.
Some of the young animals have special names. See if you can find the correct names.

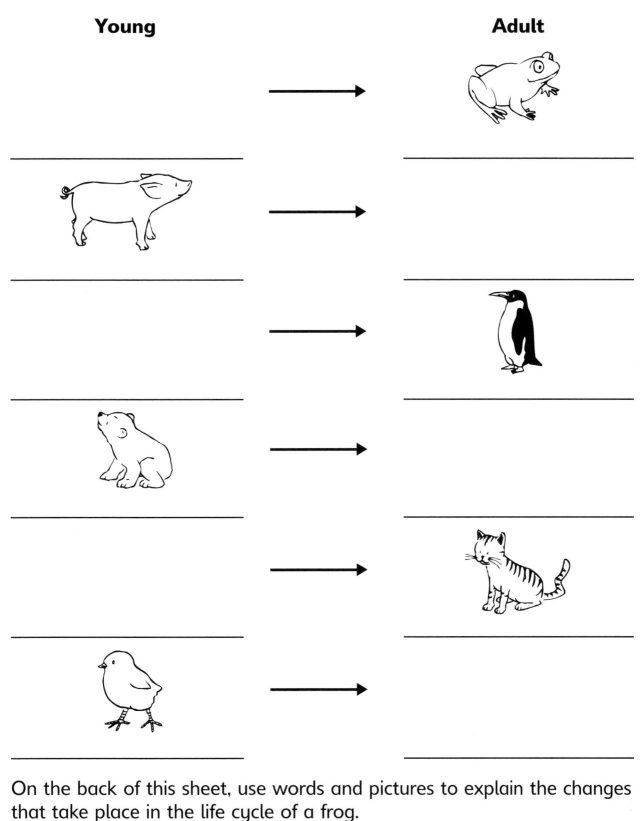

Young   **Adult**

On the back of this sheet, use words and pictures to explain the changes that take place in the life cycle of a frog.

Food

Write down the foods you and your family like to eat in the 'Foods eaten by humans' column.

Then think about the foods that animals eat. Write these down in the 'Foods eaten by animals' column.

Foods eaten by humans	Foods eaten by animals

Now choose one animal and find out as much as you can about where it lives and what it likes to eat.

Animal Diet Factfile

Name of animal:

Habitat (where it lives):

Main foods eaten:

Name

Plant parts

Look carefully at the plant in front of you. Draw it in the box below.
Label these parts of the plant:

roots

stem

leaves

Each part of the plant has a special job to do.
Match the part of the plant with its job.

(**leaves**)

(**roots**)

(**stem**)

These take water into the plant from the soil.

These are where the plant makes its food.

This keeps the plant upright.

One of these parts of a plant has another job. Which one is it and what does it do?

_____

_____

Name

Roots

You are going to carry out an investigation to show that water is carried up the roots of a plant. Use your weed, beaker, cling film and water to set up your investigation as shown in this diagram.

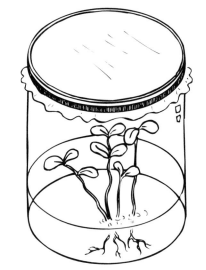

Why is it important to put a seal around the top of your beaker?

_____

_____

_____

Now put your plant in a safe place and record the water level every day, starting with today.

Date	Days after start	Water level
Difference between first and last water levels		

What has happened to the water level during your investigation?

_____

_____

Why do you think this has happened?

_____

_____

Name

Growing seeds

Use this table to record the conditions that your plant will be kept in

Plant Number	Water?		Light?		Heat?	
	Yes	No	Yes	No	Yes	No
1						
2						
3						
4						

Use the table below to keep a record of how well your plant is growing. You may want to draw or write your observations down. You may be able to measure the growth of your plant.

	Day 1	Day 2	Day 3	Day 4	Day 5
1					
2					
3					
4					
	Day 6	Day 7	Day 8	Day 9	Day 10
1					
2					
3					
4					

As you observe your plant what do you begin to notice?
Remember to write down everything that is happening in your diary.
At the end of two weeks what has happened?
Write down which of your plants has grown the best. What do you think this tells us about the conditions that your plant was kept in?

The needs of plants and animals

1. What job does each of these plant parts do?

roots _____

stem _____

leaves _____

flower _____

2. Draw an unhealthy plant.

Write why you think it may be like this.

_____

_____

_____

_____

3. What have you eaten in the past two days? Fill in the table to show whether it was food from an animal or from a plant.

Food from animals	Food from plants

4. Complete this sentence:

Most of our food comes from _____.

The needs of plants and animals

1. Number these pictures to show the life cycle of a frog.

 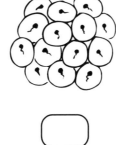 

2. From this list write down how each of these animals moves.

walks   swims   flies   crawls   slides   hops

_____	_____	_____
_____	_____	_____

3. Draw a line from each animal to the food it eats.

Animal	**Food**
Rabbit	Fish
Lion	Grass
Kestrel	Snails
Seal	Mice
Blackbird	Antelope

UNIT 3

How the environment affects living things

ORGANISATION (10 LESSONS)

	OBJECTIVES	MAIN ACTIVITY	GROUP ACTIVITIES	PLENARY	OUTCOMES
LESSON 1	● To ascertain the children's level of knowledge and understanding about the environment from their work in KS1/P1–3.	Completing a worksheet to assess understanding of animal habitats, seasonal changes and the environment.	Writing a list of seasonal characteristics. Using secondary sources to research human effects on the environment.	Discussion of outcomes and looking forward to the unit.	● Teacher can assess the level of the children in the class. ● Teacher can arrange children in appropriate class groups.
LESSON 2	● To understand how the climates of world environments differ.	Researching people who live in different climates.		Sharing research findings.	● Can understand how the climates of world environments differ.
LESSON 3	● To develop an understanding of the characteristics of different climates.	Describing individual climates.		Role-play a TV holiday programme.	● Has developed an understanding of the characteristics of different climates.
LESSON 4	● To know that the world environment can be divided into parts. ● To think about how to collect sufficient evidence. ● To use simple measuring equipment safely. ● To present results in tables.	Completing a class weather study.	Week-long individual weather study. Looking at different environments and writing a postcard.	Children share postcards with the class.	● Can recognise the major environments on the planet. ● Can describe how the atmosphere brings changes in the weather.
LESSON 5	● To know that the climate affects where plants and animals live.	Identifying different climates by criteria: heat, moisture, temperature.	Using secondary sources to research details of animals living in a chosen environment. Making 'estate agent' descriptions of environments.	Creating an environmental 'estate agency'.	● Can recognise places with different climates. ● Can describe some of the living things that live in rainforests, deserts and at the poles.
LESSON 6	● To know that living things in a habitat are affected by light and shade, dryness and moisture, heat and cold. ● To make predictions.	Walking around the school grounds to look at two contrasting environments.	Looking at characteristics of contrasting environments. Using secondary sources to research living things seen on the walk.	Discussion of findings in the environment.	● Can recognise how environmental factors vary in a habitat. ● Can recognise a relationship between environmental factors and the distribution of plants and animals.
LESSON 7	● To know that litter is an environmental problem.	Looking at litter. Carrying out a litter survey and planning an anti-litter campaign.		Children share plans for an anti-litter campaign.	● Can explain why litter in the environment is harmful to living things including humans.
LESSON 8	● To know that some materials decay and some do not and how we can use this in waste disposal.	Studying different materials as they decay.		Discussion of investigation and materials that did or did not decay.	● Can recognise that some materials decay and some do not.
LESSON 9	● To know that there are many waste products that can affect the environment.	Studying waste produced in the locality.	Mapping the locations of waste products seen. Creating posters to show the effects of waste on the environment.	Displaying maps and posters.	● Can recognise a range of wastes that can affect the environment.

ORGANISATION (10 LESSONS)

OBJECTIVES	ACTIVITY 1	ACTIVITY 2
● To assess the children's level of understanding of animal habitats and environments of the world. ● To assess the children's level of understanding of the environmental effects of waste products.	Completing a worksheet to identify different habitats and creatures living there.	Designing an environmental awareness poster.

ASSESSMENT 10

LESSON 1

OBJECTIVE

● To ascertain the children's level of knowledge and understanding about the environment from their work in Key Stage 1/Primary 1–3

RESOURCES

Main teaching activity: A copy of photocopiable page 79 for each child.
Group activities: 1. Paper, pens, pencils. **2.** Books, CD-ROMs, Internet access.

BACKGROUND

This unit builds on the children's previous understanding of the environment through the work they have carried out on habitats, the animal and plant life within a habitat and the seasonal changes in plants and animals. It takes the children on to learn about world environments, the effects of climate on plants and animals, environmental factors in differing habitats and waste in the environment.

INTRODUCTION

Begin by asking the children a number of questions like: *Do moles live in trees? Do fish live on dry land? Do polar bears live in the desert? Do camels walk across the ice?* While these questions may be silly, they will capture the imagination of the children and you will begin to gain an understanding of what knowledge the children have. Ask the children if they can think of any similar questions.

MAIN TEACHING ACTIVITY

Continue by asking the children if they know what the word 'habitat' means. Say that you would like them to show you what they already know and understand about habitats and how the seasons can affect habitats. It is important, therefore, that they carry out this first task themselves and not working with their friends. Distribute copies of photocopiable page 79 and ask the children to work individually on them.

GROUP ACTIVITIES

1. Ask the children to write a list of the characteristics of each season, for example in the UK summer usually has longer daylight hours, warm weather, flowers in bloom and in winter many trees have lost their leaves and the weather is cold. The children should record their work in an imaginative way that reflects the season, for example written inside the outline of a snowman for winter.
2. Use secondary sources such as books, CD-ROMs or websites to find out about the effects we are having on our environment. Think about what has changed recently in the local environment and about places in the world where man has not had a dramatic effect. You could visit the websites for organisations such as the Royal Society for the Protection of Birds (www.rspb.org) or the World Society for the Protection of Animals (www.wspa.org.uk). These and many other environmental organisations have sections for young people and provide environmental information.

DIFFERENTIATION

Lower-attaining children may complete the task with the help of a word bank. Encourage higher attainers to add reasons for their choices.

PLENARY

Discuss the task the children have completed, highlighting some of the concepts the children have covered and explaining the areas they will be looking at in future lessons. Avoid suggesting that the children's concepts are wrong – the work they will be doing will develop their thinking from where they are now.

OUTCOMES

- Teacher can assess the level of the children in the class.
- Teacher can arrange children in appropriate class groups.

LESSON 2

Objective	• To understand how the climates of world environments differ.
Resources	Pictures of people from different climatic regions of the world, secondary sources of information, paper, pens, pencils.
Main activity	Use pictures of people dressed appropriately for the different climates of the world as a basis for discussion about how these climates differ. For example you could use pictures of people dressed in warm clothing suited to very cold conditions (polar climate), people dressed in minimal clothing who live in very warm conditions (tropical climate) and those dressed for a temperate climate. Ask the children to draw their own pictures of people who live in these three different climates and describe the characteristics of the climates using secondary sources of information.
Differentiation	Lower attainers concentrate on one of the three climatic regions. Higher attainers consider all three regions and research each.
Assessment	Through scrutiny of their work, questioning and observation, assess the children's understanding of how climates of the world differ. Can they identify three distinct climates?
Plenary	Bring the children together to share their findings. Reinforce the idea of different climates in the world and use the work of the children to begin to find simple differences and similarities between the regions.
Outcome	• Can understand how the climates of world environments differ.

LESSON 3

Objective	• To develop an understanding of the characteristics of different climates.
Resources	Secondary sources of information, atlases, paper, pens, pencils.
Main activity	Ask the children to imagine they are one of the people they drew in Lesson 2 and to write about the sort of place in which they live. The children could use secondary sources of information to identify a particular country that has, for example, a tropical climate to write and draw about in a holiday brochure style, with an emphasis on the climate. These could then be compiled into a large class holiday booklet.
Differentiation	Lower attainers could write about a country with which they are familiar. Higher attainers could research an unfamiliar country and write a clear detailed description.
Assessment	Through scrutiny of their work, questioning and observation, assess the children's understanding of and ability to describe one particular climate.
Plenary	Bring the children together and role-play a television holiday programme. The children should pretend they are presenters reporting on a particular country, again with an emphasis on climate.
Outcome	• Has developed an understanding of the characteristics of different climates.

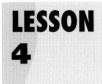

LESSON 4

OBJECTIVES
● To know that the world environment can be divided into parts.
● To think about how to collect sufficient evidence.
● To use simple measuring equipment safely.
● To present results in tables.

RESOURCES

Main teaching activity: Class weather chart, weather measuring and observation equipment such as thermometers, an anemometer; flip chart or board, OHP (optional).
Group activities: 1. Copies of photocopiable page 80. **2.** Pens, pencils, colouring materials, postcard-sized cards for each child.

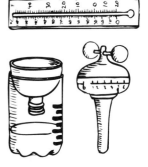

PREPARATION

Prepare a class weather chart based on photocopiable page 80. You will need to mark on a temperature range depending on the season. Prepare a piece of card the size of a postcard for each child.

Vocabulary

cities, deserts, forests, freshwater, grasslands, lakes, land, mountains, oceans, polar, rivers, seashore, sea water, towns, tundra, wetlands, woodland

BACKGROUND

Living things are found everywhere in the world: on land, in the air, in water and underground. Different living things live in different places, these are called habitats. While children will be familiar with habitats in their local environment, there are millions of other habitats in the world offering a variety of conditions, some hot, some cold, some dry, some wet. It is the surroundings, not the actual location, that makes an environment. The place where something lives is generally called a 'habitat', whereas 'environment' is the term used to describe the surroundings of a habitat. These surroundings affect the things that exist there. The factors that contribute to creating a particular environment may include such physical things as temperature and rainfall, or biological things such as the creatures living there. For example, when ecologists study the environment of an animal such as a rabbit, they study everything – living and non-living – that is connected with it. This includes animals that hunt it, its food, other rabbits, the weather, air and soil. So we can see that there is a very diverse range of environments into which our world can be divided. The environments give character to a number of 'ecosystems'. An ecosystem is a community of living things, for example a lake or a forest. These ecosystems can be broadly grouped into land, sea (salt water) and freshwater.

One of the main factors that characterises an environment is climate. There are different climates ranging from extremely cold and dry at the poles to hot and wet at the Equator. Living things like plants and animals have often changed so that they can be more suited to the local conditions in which they live.

INTRODUCTION

Tell the children that for this science topic they are going to be thinking about the environment and how we can affect it. Tell them the outline of the unit and that by the end of the unit they will understand more about how important the environment is and why it is important to them.

Begin by asking the children to think about where they live: the town, city, village or rural location. *What is it that makes that place what it is?* Ask questions about the characteristics of their local environment, such as: *Is it built up? Are there any parks or fields? Is it near the coast? Are there rivers or lakes nearby?*

Now compare the local environment to somewhere further afield – even abroad if you have Internet links with a school a long way away. Introduce the idea that there are a number of different types of 'environments' in the world. Ask the children if anyone can guess what we mean by an environment. Explain that it is everything that is around us – our surroundings – that makes a place what it is.

Land	Sea (salt water)	Freshwater
Seashore	Seashore	Rivers and lakes
Polar and tundra	Beaches	Wetlands
Towns and cities	Seas and oceans	
Mountains		
Grasslands		
Forests and woodland		
Wetlands		
Deserts		

MAIN TEACHING ACTIVITY

Ask the children to think about different types of environments there are in the world. Copy the headings 'Land', 'Sea (salt water)' and 'Freshwater' from the table above onto the board or OHP and ask the children to help you fill in the table. Explain any words such as 'polar' or 'tundra' they may be unfamiliar with.

Introduce the idea that one of the factors that influences the environment is the weather. Talk about the types of weather we generally have, how our weather changes from day to day, and seasonal variations. Explain that each day they are going to study and record the weather. Children can take it in turns to complete a class weather chart for each day. They will need to record: temperature, measured using a simple thermometer; wind speed, measured using an anemometer; cloud cover in terms of 'no cloud', 'some clouds', 'very cloudy'; general comments like 'It is wet and windy today'.

Ask the children to draw illustrations to show typical weather in each of the four seasons.

GROUP ACTIVITIES

1. Give each child a copy of photocopiable page 80 to help them make individual weather records which they can keep for themselves each day for a week.
2. Give each child a postcard-sized piece of card and ask them to think about the range of environments in the world. Tell them to imagine that they are on holiday in an environment very different from home. Ask them to write a postcard from that place describing its characteristics and climate.

DIFFERENTIATION

Support lower-attaining children in identifying types of environments. The descriptions on the postcards from higher-attaining children should be clear and explicit.

ASSESSMENT

Are the children able to identify environments and their characteristics? Most children will be able to identify some environments, but some may identify less familiar ones such as polar, tundra and wetlands.

PLENARY

Discuss the environments the children have identified. Ask some children to read out their postcards. Reinforce the concept of the world being made up of a number of different environments. Remind the children about their weather study and the observations they are going to carry out.

OUTCOMES

- Can recognise the major environments on the planet.
- Can describe how the atmosphere brings changes in the weather.

LINKS

Geography: weather around the world (QCA *Geography Scheme of Work,* Year 3, Unit 7).

LESSON 5

OBJECTIVE

- To know that the climate affects where plants and animals live.

RESOURCES

Main teaching activity: A copy of photocopiable page 81 for each child.
Group activities: 1. Secondary sources of information related to climate; pens, white and coloured paper, art materials. **2.** Paper, pens, pencils.

PREPARATION

Copy photocopiable page 81. Ensure secondary resources, various types of paper, pens and art materials are available.

Vocabulary
climate, cold, environment, hot, temperature, temperate

BACKGROUND

The climate of an area or region depends on its position on the Earth's surface. For example, land near the Equator has a hot climate because it gets sunshine from almost directly overhead. As you travel further away from the Equator, the climate gets cooler until you reach the North and South Poles where the Sun is always low on the horizon and the temperatures are constantly low. There are, however, other factors that affect climate: the oceans carry warmth around the world and affect the land climate, as do winds and the height of land above sea-level. Climates

Climate	Characteristics
Polar	Very cold and dry strong winds
Tundra	Cold with low rainfall and short summers
Mountain	Climates depend on latitude and altitude
Cool temperate	Not very hot summers or very cold winters
Warm temperate	Mild wet winters, hot dry summers
Desert	Very hot days and very cold nights, very little rain
Monsoon	Sudden changes from dry to wet weather
Tropical	Very hot with heavy rainfall

are classified into eight main groups, within which there are also variations.

The climate of a region affects the plants and animals that live there. Different plants and animals are able to thrive in different climates. For example, bears are well-suited to living in polar regions because of their diet of fish and their thick fur. On the other hand, an elephant would not survive in such conditions due to its diet of vegetation, the slow speed at which it moves and its unprotected skin. A number of climatic factors affect living things and their environment. These include temperature, light intensity, rainfall and wind speed. The most profound of these climatic factors is without doubt temperature. Generally, living things prefer to live in an environment with warm temperatures and a supply of water and food. This is why as you travel from temperate climates to ones that are more extreme, like the poles or deserts, there is a marked reduction in the number of species of living things to be found.

INTRODUCTION

Remind the children of their work from the last lesson and how they were identifying different environments. Ask them to recall some of those. Also remind them that they have been studying the weather. Discuss the weather findings briefly and ask the children to sum up the weather over the past week. Has it been warm and dry, sunny, wet and windy, cold and frosty? Ask the children to think about how our weather changes and what happens to plants and animals when it does. Some children will be able to tell you about hibernation or migration, although they may not recall the correct terms.

MAIN TEACHING ACTIVITY

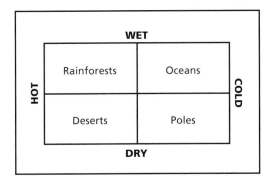

Talk about why some animals, particularly birds, tend to move around to different environments. Introduce the idea that the climates within environments are not always suitable for plants and animals at all times of the year and that some plants and animals prefer different climatic conditions. Give examples of climatic conditions with different combinations of heat and moisture: hot and dry; hot and wet; cold and dry; cold and wet. Photocopiable page 81 provides a simple Carroll diagram on which the children can see the different combinations of temperature and moisture to help them identify four examples of environments with these climates.

GROUP ACTIVITIES

1. In pairs, the children can use secondary sources of information to find out about some of the living things that live in a chosen climate. Research could be presented in a novel way, for example information about rainforests on paper the shape of a large tree, the poles on paper the shape of an iceberg and deserts the shape of a sand dune.

2. Ask the children to write an estate agent-style description of three or four habitats of living things, for example 'Accommodation under deceptively spacious damp and dark stone. Would ideally suit someone who does not like the Sun…'

DIFFERENTIATION

Lower-attaining children use secondary sources to help with ideas. Higher-attaining children will make greater use of estate agent jargon in descriptive writing.

ASSESSMENT

Most children should be able to complete photocopiable page 81. Discuss with the children their ideas to gain an idea of their level of understanding.

PLENARY

Create an 'Environmental estate agents' window to display the children's descriptions and ask the children to read them to the class.

OUTCOMES
● Can recognise places with different climates.
● Can describe some of the living things that live in rainforests, deserts and at the poles.

LINKS

Unit 8, Lesson 5: the relationship of the Earth in space to the seasons we experience.
Geography: weather and climate.
Literacy: using jargon.

LESSON 6

OBJECTIVES
● To know that living things in a habitat are affected by light and shade, dryness and moisture, heat and cold.
● To make predictions.

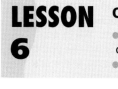

RESOURCES
Main teaching activity: A copy of photocopiable page 82 for each child; a simple plan of the area to be visited; a clipboard and pencil for each child.
Group activities: 1. Paper, pens and pencils. **2.** Secondary sources of information, paper and art materials.

PREPARATION

Plan to visit an area where the children can study two contrasting environmental conditions, such as two areas of your school field or local park. Ensure that you have adequate adult supervision. Ask some parents to help you and, if they are going to lead a group, ensure your adult helpers are well briefed and know what they are looking for. Organise your visit to allow plenty of time for both fieldwork and follow-up. Draw and copy a simple plan of the area you are going to visit for each child.

Vocabulary
cool, dark, dry, habitat, light, warm, wet

BACKGROUND

Living things, plants and animals interact with their environments in order to create habitats. A habitat is simply the place where a plant or animal lives. Habitats vary greatly in size, from large forests to small puddles, but all have to satisfy the needs of the animals and plants that live there. Not only do they vary in size: habitats also vary greatly in character. Some are hot, some cold, some light, some dark, some dry, some wet. Whatever their differences they all have the same function – the support of living things. It is these differences in habitats that means different habitats are capable of supporting varying types of plants and animals.

INTRODUCTION

Children always enjoy going outside and hunting around. In this lesson, the children will get the opportunity to do just that. Ask the children to think about where they would choose to live if they had unlimited money: in what sort of house, in which location and why. After a short discussion ask them to imagine they are a tiny woodlouse and to think about where they would choose to live and why. Encourage the children to think about the conditions that would be most suitable. Some creatures like hot and dry conditions, others prefer dark and damp conditions. Explain that they are going to look in some different habitats to find out what type of creatures are living there and why they think that may be so.

MAIN TEACHING ACTIVITY

Distribute the plans and copies of photocopiable page 82. Encourage the children to choose two contrasting areas around the school grounds, for example from the playground, a playing field, under a hedge, a garden, a pond, a wildlife area. Before visiting the sites, ask children to predict the animals they expect to find in each area.

Take a walk around the school grounds, visit a local park or wild area with a variety of habitats. Ask the children to use photocopiable page 82 to help them record the living things they see in the two contrasting habitats, for example under stones or in damp walls and in bushes or hedges. They should complete the photocopiable page with details of each habitat and what they saw. Some children will also be able to mark these locations on their plan. Observe birds feeding in the playground (after break is a good time, especially if the children have been eating snacks). As you walk around, talk with the children about what animals they have found and where they were found.

GROUP ACTIVITIES

1. Back in the classroom, ask the children to use drawings and writing to describe the differences between the two areas they studied. Ask them to think about why the two areas are different and whether they found the animals they expected.

2. Ask the children to use secondary sources to find out more about any of the living things they saw. They should present their findings in an imaginative way, perhaps in the shape of the creature they are writing about.

DIFFERENTIATION

Lower-attainers record their observations simply and easily on the photocopiable page. Higher-attainers also record observations and locations on the plan. They could indicate minibeasts found at each location using a colour code to show the distribution.

ASSESSMENT

Assess the ability of the children to carry out the observations and record their findings.

PLENARY

Discuss with the children the creatures they have found in a number of locations. Draw conclusions about the creature's habitat preferences.

OUTCOMES

● Can recognise how environmental factors vary in a habitat
● Can recognise a relationship between environmental factors and the distribution of plants and animals.
● Can make predictions.

LESSON 7

Objective	● To know that litter is an environmental problem.
Resources	Paper and art materials.

Main activity	Identify a local area to visit to look at the litter there. Carry out a litter survey. Be very conscious of health and safety issues: the spread of diseases, the dangers of cuts from glass and of discarded syringes. The children must not touch any of the litter, particularly outside school. Also be vigilant for risks from dog faeces, for example in public parks. Consider: *Where is most of the litter? Why is it there? Are there any litter bins and are they in the best places?* (Mark positions on a map and relate to paths, dog-walking routes and so on.)
	   Discuss why litter is a problem. (Because it's a danger to animals, it helps spread diseases, it smells and so on.)
	   Design and run an anti-litter campaign in school with posters, leaflets and an assembly presentation. If you contact a local shopping centre, they may be willing to provide a more public forum for the children's work.

Differentiation	Differentiate by outcome.
Assessment	Discuss the children's campaign proposals, looking for an understanding that litter is a problem.
Plenary	Discuss their findings and plans for an anti-litter campaign.
Outcome	● Can explain why litter in the environment is harmful to living things including humans.

LESSON 8

Objective	● To know that some materials decay and some do not and how we can use this in waste disposal.
Resources	Trays, soil, leaves, cardboard, aluminium foil, orange peel, an apple core, a crisp bag.
Main activity	Bury the same six items deep in several pots full of soil, or in the school garden. Vary the conditions, try: warm and dry, warm and wet, cold and dry, cold and wet. Check at weekly intervals to monitor and note the rates of decay. Take photographs, perhaps, with a camera as evidence. At the end of three or four weeks, draw some conclusions by asking: *Which has decayed the most? Which has not decayed at all? Which materials would be suitable for disposal in a landfill site? Which materials should be disposed of in some other way?*
Differentiation	Differentiate by outcome.
Assessment	Through observation and questioning identify the children's level of understanding of decaying materials.
Plenary	Gather together to discuss observations at regular intervals.
Outcome	● Can recognise that some materials decay and some do not.

LESSON 9

OBJECTIVE

● To know that there are many waste products that can affect the environment.

RESOURCES

Introduction: A bag of classroom waste, gloves, a bag to put the waste into,
Main teaching activity: Photocopiable page 83, paper, pens.
Group activities: 1. Paper and pencils. **2.** Pictures and samples of waste packets, large sheets of paper, glue, art materials.

PREPARATION

Arrange to make a visit around your locality to identify the types of waste being produced and to carry out a study of waste products from the home, transport and industry. Visit the location for your walk and ensure there are appropriate examples for the children to see and that the route you will take is safe. Ensure you have adequate adult supervision for the visit. Ask some parents to help and brief them as to the purpose of the visit.

Vocabulary

exhaust, fumes, landfill, litter, recycling, refuse, waste

BACKGROUND

By its very nature, the industrial society of which we are a part produces, whether we like it or not, a huge amount of waste. What is more, it is not just manufacturers and producers of goods that are to blame. As consumers, we too are responsible for many of the waste products that can affect the environment, not just in our demand for things to look attractive and to be well packaged, but more so in the way we dispose of the waste we produce. In recent years, our society has become increasingly concerned about the industrial and domestic waste we all produce, its management, disposal and the effects on the environment.

   Some of these effects are local to us all (for example litter). The effects of nuclear waste, and damage caused to the ozone layer are global issues. This lesson will concentrate not on the global issues, but on the effects that waste like rubbish and fumes have on the environment. Recent legislation has been introduced in an attempt to regulate the production of waste and its disposal, since it is not always the waste itself that causes environmental concern, rather the way its disposal is managed. The children will be familiar with very many waste products, and many will be aware of the environmental concerns they raise. On the right are examples of some waste products, where they are found and their environmental effects.

   As part of this work it may be possible to arrange for a local industrialist and/or a local authority waste officer to come and talk about the problems of waste and how they are dealing with it.

Location	Waste products	Type of waste	Environmental effects
Home	Litter, packaging, food waste	Rubbish	Danger to wildlife, danger of disease
In the street	Vehicle exhausts	Fumes	Air pollution
	Litter	Rubbish	Danger to animals and humans, attraction of vermin
Factories	Fires	Fumes	Air pollution
	Production waste and scrap	Rubbish	Disposal of potentially dangerous waste
	Smoke and smells	Fumes	Air pollution

INTRODUCTION

Ask the children to guess what is in your bag. Wearing gloves, transfer items from the rubbish bag into the second bag. (Later dispose of both carefully.) The children will fairly quickly work out it is rubbish. Show them the quantity of waste they have produced in just one day in the classroom. Ask the children if they know what will happen to this waste and all the waste from school. They may be able to tell you that it will be taken away by the refuse collectors (for dumping or incineration, usually). In some areas, there are recycling schemes that require the waste to be sorted before collection. Pose a few questions and seek responses: *But where is the rubbish taken to? What happens to it? What about all the other waste we produce? What effect does waste have on our environment? What kinds of waste are there?* Tell the children that together they are going to find the answers to some of these questions.

MAIN TEACHING ACTIVITY

Prior to the visit, discuss with the children what types of waste they think they will observe and where it will be. Try to move them beyond litter, to think about fumes from cars, for example.

As they walk around, they should use photocopiable page 83 to record their observations.

On return to the classroom, discuss what the children saw and recorded, and consider the effects that the waste may be having and what could be done about the problem.

GROUP ACTIVITIES

1. Following the visit, the children should draw a map of the area they have surveyed and use a key to record where certain waste products were found. This will give some indication of particular problem areas. For example, at a bus stop there may be litter and traffic fumes.
2. Collect pictures or samples of waste products (be sure they are clean and safe) to produce posters explaining the effects that waste has on the environment. For example, display plastic bags and bottles to highlight them as a danger to wildlife; use pictures of cars to highlight car exhaust fumes and their effect on people's health.

ASSESSMENT

Assess the children's ability to understand and appreciate the range of waste produced. Their work should reflect their understanding, having identified a range of waste products during the visit.

DIFFERENTIATION

Lower-attaining children concentrate on identifying one or two types of waste. Higher-attainers look for a wider range of waste products and draw more specific conclusions.

PLENARY

Bring the class together to look at the maps of waste and the posters. Ask the children to explain their findings, and involve the children in a discussion reinforcing the types of waste and their effects on the environment.

OUTCOME

● Can recognise a range of wastes that can affect the environment.

LINKS

PSHE: care for the environment; personal responsibility; health and safety issues.
Geography: investigating the local area (QCA *Geography Scheme of Work*, Year 3, Unit 6).

LESSON 10

OBJECTIVES

● To assess the children's level of understanding of animal habitats and environments of the world.
● To assess the children's level of understanding of the environmental effects of waste products.

RESOURCES

Assessment activities: 1. A copy of photocopiable page 84 for each child, pens, pencils, colouring materials. **2.** Large sheets of paper, art materials.

INTRODUCTION

Begin the Assessment activities by giving the children a vocabulary test, which could be oral or written. Remember the activity is an assessment of scientific knowledge and understanding. Either give either a word and ask for a definition or give a definition and ask for a word.

ASSESSMENT ACTIVITY 1

Distribute copies of photocopiable page 84 to the children and allow them time to complete it individually. You may wish to tell the children that you wish to find out what they have understood and that it is important to complete the sheets individually. You will need to collect these in order to mark them effectively.

Answers
I am a hot place with lots of tall trees – rainforest
It is very cold here all year long – polar region
I am hot during the day but cold at night – desert
I am a very wet place and I can be calm or rough – ocean
I begin my journey in the hills and travel towards the sea – river.

Looking for levels
Assess the children's work for evidence of understanding. Most children should be able to match the habitat descriptions with their names. While most should be able to name creatures living in each habitat, the list will vary in complexity. Lower-attaining children may be able to name only one or two creatures, whereas higher-attaining children ought to be naming a varied selection.

ASSESSMENT ACTIVITY 2

Ask the children to design an environmental awareness poster that explains the dangers to the environment of litter and encourages people to be litter conscious. It should make people aware of the quantities and types of waste that we all produce and how we can prevent damage to the environment.

Looking for levels
Most children will be able to create a poster for Assessment activity 2. Lower-attainers will be able to create a poster with a single simple message, whereas higher-attainers will produce one that is more complex and puts forward clear points and arguments.

PLENARY

Discuss the Assessment activities and address any misconceptions still held by the children. For example, young children may commonly believe that animals grow thick fur so they can live where it is cold. (Animals don't decide to equip their bodies to live in a particular environment.) Young children may also believe that all of the effects we have on the environment are negative. (We do many things to create and improve environments.)

Name

In the garden

These animals live in this garden, but they have different habitats.
Draw an arrow to where in the garden you think each animal might live.
Say why you think it lives there.

A fox lives here because _____ _____	A squirrel lives here because _____ _____	A blackbird lives here because _____ _____
A slug lives here because _____ _____	A snail lives here because _____ _____	A hedgehog lives here because _____ _____

Add to the picture to show that it is autumn in the garden.
Do you know anything that might harm the plants and animals?
Tell your teacher or write about it on the back of this sheet.

Name

My weather chart

Use this sheet to record your weather observations over one week.

	Monday	Tuesday	Wednesday	Thursday	Friday
Morning temperature in degrees Celcius					
Afternoon temperature in degrees Celcius					
Wind					
Cloud					
General comments					

Name

Looking at climates

Draw a picture in each box to show the different climates in the world. For example in the box where the climate is both wet and hot you could draw a place such as a rainforest.

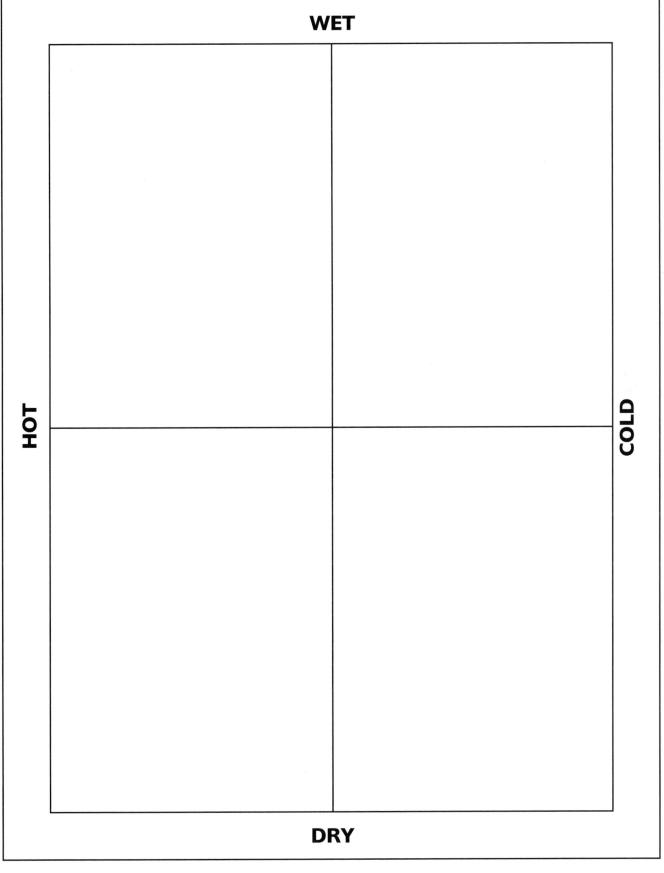

Name

Habitats

Look carefully at two different habitats in which an animal lives. Use this sheet to record what you observe.

Habitat name or description	Light or dark?	Hot or cold?	Creatures found Name or drawing	How many? Estimate

Name

What a waste!

Go on a walk around your locality. As you walk, look out for examples of waste products. Make a note of where you are, what you saw and from where the waste was being produced.

Location	Waste seen	Producer		
		Home	Transport	Industry

Look at the results of your survey. Which types of waste did you see most examples of?

_____

_____

What effects do you think each type of waste has on the environment?

Type of waste	Effects on the environment

How the environment affects living things

Draw a line to match the description with the name of the habitat.

Description

Habitat

I am a hot place with lots of tall trees.

ocean

It is very cold here all year long.

desert

I am hot during the day but cold at night.

river

I am a very wet place and I can be calm or rough.

rainforest

I begin my journey in the hills and travel towards the sea.

polar region

Different creatures like to live in different conditions. Write the names of as many creatures as you can think of that live in each of these places. On the back of this page draw an example from each habitat.

Under a hedge	
Around houses	
Under a stone	
In a wood	
In a garden	

UNIT 3   THE ENVIRONMENT

UNIT 4

Natural & manufactured materials

ORGANISATION (15 LESSONS)

	OBJECTIVES	MAIN ACTIVITY	GROUP ACTIVITIES	PLENARY	OUTCOMES
LESSON 1	● To ascertain the levels of the children in their understanding of materials from their work in Key Stage 1/ Primary 1–3, particularly in relation to simple properties and how they can be changed by heating and cooling.	Concept mapping.	Sorting materials. Changing materials worksheet.	Review concept maps, reinforce learning about changing materials by heating and cooling.	● Teacher can assess the level of the children in the class. ● Teacher can arrange children in appropriate class groups.
LESSON 2	● To know a range of common materials and that a material may have different uses.	Using senses to identify materials.	Materials survey worksheet. Identifying materials used.	Feedback from Group activities.	● Can recognise common materials. ● Can describe how some materials have several uses.
LESSON 3	● To know that different materials have different properties. ● To know that any material may have more than one property.	Describing the properties of materials.	Identifying the properties of given materials. Tabulating properties by criteria.	'Guess the material' quiz.	● Can state one or two characteristics of a range of common materials. ● Can compare the properties of different materials.
LESSON 4	● To know that materials are selected for making objects due to their properties. ● To understand that the use and wear an object will need to withstand governs the materials from which it can be made.	Identifying why objects are made from particular materials.		Agreeing why certain materials are used.	● Can recognise how materials are selected for their properties when an object is being made.
LESSON 5	● To know that the properties of materials can be compared by investigation. ● To plan and carry out a fair test, make predictions, and observations and draw conclusions.	Identifying which properties can be investigated and how. Ensuring fair tests.	Planning an investigation. Carrying out and recording the investigation. Making and testing carrier bags.	Sharing group investigations and findings.	● Know that the properties of materials can be compared by investigation. ● Can plan and carry out a fair test, make predictions, and observations and draw conclusions.
LESSON 6	● To use materials for a specific purpose and to test their suitability for that purpose. ● To identify what scientific questions need to be asked.	Using appropriate materials to suit a function.		Drawing conclusions about the best materials.	● Can use materials for a specific purpose ● Can test their questions about the material's suitability for that purpose.
LESSON 7	● To know that some materials occur naturally and others do not.	Sorting materials into 'natural' and 'man-made'.	Looking for materials that derive from plants, animals and under the ground. Survey of objects made from man-made and natural materials.	Quiz, identifying the mystery material.	● Can recognise that some materials occur naturally and others do not.

100 SCIENCE LESSONS ● YEAR 3 / UNIT 4

85

ORGANISATION (15 LESSONS)

	OBJECTIVES	MAIN ACTIVITY	GROUP ACTIVITIES	PLENARY	OUTCOMES
LESSON 8	● To be able to compare finished objects with raw materials.	Sorting raw materials, processed materials and finished objects into groups.		Sharing ideas and reinforcement of lesson objectives.	● Can compare finished objects with raw materials.
LESSON 9	● To be able to recognise and describe a range of different rocks.	Observing, examining and naming rock samples.	Grouping rocks by characteristics. Using secondary sources.	Using descriptions of rocks to help others identify rock samples.	● Can recognise and describe a range of different rocks. ● Can put rocks into groups.
LESSON 10	● To know that rocks can be tested for their wear.	Compare rock samples for wear by rubbing.		Ranking rocks for wear.	● Can compare and rank rocks according to their ease of wearing.
LESSON 11	● To know that rocks can be tested for their permeability.	Compare rock samples for permeability by dripping water.		Concluding which rock samples are least permeable.	● Can compare and rank rocks according to their permeability.
LESSON 12	● To know there are different kinds of soil. ● To know that there is rock beneath soil.	Learning how soil is formed.	Describing soil samples. Using secondary sources.	Looking at coloured layers in soil.	● Can describe how soil lies on top of rock. ● Can recognise that there are different kinds of soil.
LESSON 13	● To know that different soils have different-sized particles and different colours.	Mixing soil with water and observing settlement.		Discussion of the different layers from different soil samples.	● Can compare soils in terms of particles and colour.
LESSON 14	● To know how to compare the permeability of soils. ● To plan and carry out a fair test.	Demonstration of testing soil permeability.	Devising and carrying out a fair test into different soil samples. Growing cress in different soils.	Reinforcing the concept of permeability and why some land does not drain well.	● Can compare the permeability of soils. ● Can plan and carry out a fair test.

	OBJECTIVES		ACTIVITY 1	ACTIVITY 2
ASSESSMENT 15	● To assess the children's knowledge and understanding of materials and their uses. ● To assess the children's knowledge and understanding of rocks and soils.		Completing a worksheet, identifying materials used in houses and why they are used.	Completing a worksheet on uses of rock and how soil is formed.

LESSON 1

OBJECTIVE

● To ascertain the levels of the children in their understanding of materials from their work in Key Stage 1/Primary 1–3, particularly in relation to simple properties and how they can be changed by heating or cooling.

RESOURCES

Main teaching activity: Flip chart or board; large sheets of paper, pens, a small number of common objects from the classroom.
Group activities: 1. A selection of everyday materials such as paper, plastic, metal, wood, water, wool, cotton and so on; large (A2) sheets of art paper, marker pens or thick crayons for recording. **2.** Copies of photocopiable page 103, pens, pencils, drawing materials.

Vocabulary

cooling, heating, ice, materials, steam, water

BACKGROUND

This first lesson reintroduces the children to materials. They should already have done some work about the properties of materials and how materials can be changed. They should have some understanding of a range of everyday materials and know that some materials are natural while others are manufactured (man-made). They should also have some understanding that materials can be changed physically or by heating and cooling, for example through experience of baking or clay modelling.

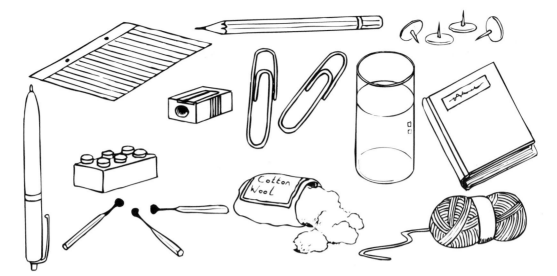

INTRODUCTION

Begin the lesson by showing the children the objects that you have collected. Try not to talk about the identity of the objects so much as the materials from which they are made. Encourage the children to look carefully and to say what each object is largely made from. Remind the children that they have already done some work on materials and that in this lesson you are going to see what they can remember from that work.

MAIN TEACHING ACTIVITY

Review the children's work on materials by working with them to draw a concept map. Use a flip chart or board to record key words and facts from the children as they brainstorm the ideas they have learned in Key Stage 1/Primary 1–3. When you have these words and phrases scattered around the board, attempt to link the phrases and also justify those links. For example, the children should be able to name a range of everyday materials and might identify that some are natural while others are manufactured.

GROUP ACTIVITIES

1. Give the children a collection of materials or pictures of materials and ask them to sort them according to their own criteria, and to explain what the criteria are. These could be hard/soft, heavy/light, magnetic/non-magnetic, shiny/dull and so on. This could be a collaborative task recorded on large sheets of art paper. Ask higher-attaining children to present their findings in a table.
2. Distribute photocopiable page 103 and ask the children to recall their work on how materials change when subjected to temperature changes.

DIFFERENTIATION

Differentiation will be by outcome due to the nature and focus of the lesson.

ASSESSMENT

Note the children's individual contributions to the concept mapping exercise as an indication of their general understanding. Most children should be able to name some materials and say a little about how they are used. Most should be able to describe what happens to water when it is heated and cooled. The lower-attaining children may not have reached this level of conceptual understanding.

PLENARY

Review the children's work. Return to the concept map and ask the children if they would like to add or change anything. Reinforce the key points raised in the concept mapping. Ask each group to explain their sorting work in Group activity 1. Check each child's work on photocopiable page 103. With the class, revise how these materials change when they are heated or cooled.

OUTCOMES

● Teacher can assess the level of the children in the class.
● Teacher can arrange children in appropriate class groups.

LESSON 2

OBJECTIVE

● To know a range of common materials and that a material may have different uses.

RESOURCES

Main teaching activity: A selection of everyday materials such as paper, plastic, metal, wood, water, wool, cotton and so on.
Group activities: 1. Copies of photocopiable page 104, clipboards, pens, pencils.
2. Paper, pens, pencils.

PREPARATION

Decide and agree where around school your class will be surveying materials.

BACKGROUND

Vocabulary

brick, glass, metal, paper, plastic, sight, stone, touch, wood

No matter how we choose to classify different materials, it is important to remember that all materials ultimately come from the natural resources of the Earth; either in a form that makes them useful immediately, like wood, or as a raw material in the production of other materials, such as oil for plastics.

Our ability to manipulate the materials around us has played a major part in our development from the ages of stone and iron for tools and weapons, to the modern age of synthetic and 'man-made' materials. This unit considers in more depth the sources of our materials and how their uses and properties must be matched up.

The designs of many everyday items today may have changed little since their invention, but the materials they are made from have often been replaced by newer alternatives.

Many materials can serve the same purpose, and some materials can serve many different purposes, as shown in the table below.

Object	Old material	New material
Kettle	Steel	Plastic
Window frames	Wood	uPVC
Carrier bag	Paper	Polythene
Bottles	Glass	Plastic

Clearly this range can be expanded very significantly. However, what is key is that to make good use of the range of available materials it is necessary to know about and understand their properties in order to choose the best material for the job. Children often have the idea that when we talk about 'materials' we mean 'fabrics'. However, the word 'material' is used to describe the full range of substances that things are made from such as wood, metal, plastic,

Material	Range of uses
Glass	Windows, bottles, beakers, ornaments, lenses, mirrors
Wood	Window frames, furniture, buildings, pencils, paper, fences
Plastic	Bottles, furniture, pens, boxes, packaging, containers

paper, pottery, glass and so on. In the scientific world, the word 'material' is used to describe an even wider spectrum of substances. When scientists refer to 'materials' they think and talk about the whole physical substance of the Universe.

INTRODUCTION

Bring into the classroom an unusual or old object that the children will not especially recognise, or something that has changed over recent years: perhaps a 78rpm record, a flat iron or a chamber pot! Ask the children to look at the object and then tell you what they think the item may be used for. Discuss how they identified the object – which senses did they use? Relate the activity to their earlier work on the senses and how they use their senses to inform them about the world around them.

MAIN TEACHING ACTIVITY

Present the children with a selection of samples of materials. Ask them to tell you how they would identify each material. Talk about how they find out about anything to do with the world around them (if appropriate, relate the discussion to the work carried out in Unit 1 about the senses). Encourage the children to recall the senses they would use in identifying an unknown material – sight and touch mainly.

GROUP ACTIVITIES

1. Distribute copies of photocopiable page 104 and tell the children that they are going to use their senses to identify a range of materials around the school that have been used to make particular objects. Go out and survey the chosen area to complete the photocopiable sheet.

Object and material	How we identified it
Wooden chair	By the look (and smell?) of the wood
Plastic spoon	By the feel of the plastic

2. When they have completed their investigation, ask the children to think about how they knew, or what helped them to decide, what an object was made from. They should find a way to record their thoughts.

DIFFERENTIATION

When carrying out the survey allow lower-attaining children to initially look for just one item in each group. Encourage higher-attaining children to look for more complex objects that are made from several materials.

ASSESSMENT

All the children should know that they use their senses to help them identify materials, and which senses are most often used. Most should be able to complete Group activity 1 and be able to identify the uses of these materials.

PLENARY

Ask the children to feed back their findings, giving examples of objects made from particular materials and the materials used in various objects.

OUTCOMES

● Can recognise common materials.
● Can describe how some materials have several uses.

LINKS

Unit 1, Lessons 9–10: using our senses.

LESSON 3

OBJECTIVES

● To know that different materials have different properties.
● To know that any material may have more than one property.

RESOURCES

Main teaching activity: A selection of materials, flip chart or board, pens.
Group activities: 1. Copies of photocopiable page 105; materials, including glass (in a window), paper, steel, plastic, wood, clay. **2.** Paper, pens, pencils.

Vocabulary

clay, glass, hard, opaque, paper, plastic, properties, rough, smooth, soft, steel, translucent, transparent, wood

BACKGROUND

To make the best use of materials it is important to know the properties they possess so we can select the correct material for the job we are doing. For example, we construct buildings using concrete, bricks, steel and so on because we know that they are strong, durable and available relatively cheaply. Similarly, we use plastic for bottles because it is cheap, lightweight, can be coloured, moulded and recycled. Of course, whole objects can be made from a number of different materials, as well as their individual components. Likewise, one material can be made into very many different objects. In deciding which material to use for a particular purpose, the manufacturer needs to consider the range of different properties that the material possesses and may sometimes have to compromise on some aspects of the properties of some materials.

The material may be: hard or soft; heavy or light; opaque, transparent or translucent; smooth or rough; reflective or non-reflective; rigid or flexible; easily cut, moulded or otherwise changed; cheap or expensive; smelly; easily available; magnetic or non-magnetic; able to conduct electricity or be an insulator; a good insulator of heat; recyclable. Some of these properties are explored in this unit, and others are touched on in other units (such as magnetism in Unit 6), or in future years of the *100 Science Lessons* series.

INTRODUCTION

Recap on how the children identified the various materials in the previous lesson. Then ask: *How would you tell the difference between two different people?* Begin to introduce the children to the idea that just like humans have certain things about them that make them who they are, so too can materials have certain 'properties'.

MAIN TEACHING ACTIVITY

How would you tell the difference between two different materials? We use our senses to help us identify materials, but how do we sort one material from another? How do we know that what we are touching is glass?

Have a selection of materials for the children to look at and handle. Talk about the properties of those materials, asking the children to describe those properties such as: hard or soft; opaque, transparent or translucent; smooth or rough. You may like to keep the range and number of properties limited at this stage (depending on the ability of your class), as too many could lead to some confusion. Compile a list of properties that the children could use in describing materials (see Background). This should be revision, so try to extend the properties identified to take in the children's more recent experiences.

PROPERTIES			
Hard	**Soft**	**Smooth**	**Rough**
metal	plastic	glass	stone

GROUP ACTIVITIES

1. Distribute copies of photocopiable page 105. Ask the children to compile lists of properties of these common materials. For example: glass – rigid, transparent, smooth, reflective and so on. (You may prefer to amend the sheet to match the materials you have available.)

2. Ask the children to use the information from Group activity 1 to draw up a table similar to that above to show which materials have particular properties such as hard, soft, smooth, rough.

DIFFERENTIATION

For lower-attaining children, limit the number of properties used to describe each material. Ask higher-attainers to look at the table prepared in Group activity 2 and try to group the materials according to specific criteria, for example all the materials that are reflective or are soft. Encourage using Carroll diagrams (one criterion only).

ASSESSMENT

All the children should be able to identify a number of properties such as hard, soft, smooth, rough and so on. Most should be able to look at examples of materials and list some properties that each has. Some will be able to use that information to group materials by these properties in increasingly sophisticated ways.

PLENARY

Ask the children to think of a material and to begin to describe it by referring only to its properties; the other children must try to guess the identity of the material.

OUTCOMES

● Can state one or two characteristics of a range of common materials.
● Can compare the properties of different materials.

LINKS

Unit 6, Lessons 3–5: exploring the functions and uses of magnets.
Unit 6, Lessons 8–10: exploring elasticity.
Unit 7, Lessons 5–7: the occurrence and uses of lights, reflective materials and colour in the environment.
Unit 8, Lessons 2–3: exploring which materials make the best shadows, reinforcing transparent, translucent and opaque.
Maths: organising data in tables and charts, for example into a Carroll diagram.

LESSON 4

Objective	● To know that materials are selected for making objects according to their properties. ● To understand that the use and wear an object will need to withstand governs the materials from which it can be made.
Resources	A variety of classroom objects, a video of glassmaking or similar material changing.
Main activity	Look at a variety of objects and suggest reasons why a particular material was used in its making. Ask the children to give sensible reasons why each object is made from the material it is. Ask them to suggest alternative materials that could be used and to say why. Suggest materials that would be unsuitable, again ask the children to say why they are unsuitable. Refer back to the survey of materials around the school in Lesson 2 – does the place where the object is used affect the choice of materials it is made from: *Why are our chairs made from metal or plastic and not finely carved wood?*
Differentiation	Differentiate by outcome. Most children should be able to explain why certain materials are or are not suitable, for example an extreme suggestion such as 'A teapot made of chocolate would melt'. Higher attainers will give a fuller, more reasoned explanation for less absurd examples and more 'everyday' objects.
Assessment	Through scrutiny of the children's work and discussion with them, assess their understanding of the suitability of materials for particular uses.
Plenary	Discuss the findings and come to some agreement about the use of certain materials due to their properties, for example wood is used for furniture because of its looks and strength. Show the children a video where materials are being used to make things, for example wooden furniture or glass bottles. Focus on the appropriacy of these materials. This is followed up practically in Lesson 5, Group activity 3, but you may like to discuss and plan for that activity as part of this lesson.
Outcome	● Can recognise how materials are selected according to their properties when an object is being made.

LESSON 5

OBJECTIVES

● To know that the properties of materials can be compared by investigation.
● To plan and carry out a fair test, make predictions and observations and draw conclusions.

RESOURCES

Main teaching activity: Copies of photocopiable page 106 for each child or pair (or an enlarged copy displayed for whole-class use), appropriate pens or pencils.
Group activities: 1. Paper, pens, pencils, **2.** A selection of man-made and natural materials, such as stone, brick, paper, cloth, clay, plastic, steel, wood; carrier bags made of paper, fabric, rafia, leather and different types of plastic; copies of photocopiable pages 59 and 60 (see Unit 2).
3. Different materials, including paper, fabric, rafia, leather and different types of plastic; copies of photocopiable page 107; adhesives and or sticky tape; needles and a variety of threads (optional); scissors; weights (for example, large potatoes); thin card (see Preparation).

PREPARATION

The template on photocopiable page 107 is for half a bag and needs enlarging to A3 size, copying onto thin card and perhaps assembling before the children can use it to draw and cut out bag shapes. You may prefer to make the bag template from card for the children first (see instructions on photocopiable page 107).

BACKGROUND

Vocabulary

absorbency, elasticity, hardness, magnetic, reflective, strength

In order to make the best use of materials, it is essential to know and understand their properties and to know how they will perform under certain conditions. Often this knowledge can be gained from simple observation, at other times we need to carry out an investigation into the properties of a range of possible materials and compare the results of those investigations to make the best choice. Investigations into materials involve doing things to the material such as exerting a force and trying to break it and measuring the effects. This lesson offers a 'pure' science investigation through which to explore this, but also offers a design and technology task, relating the appropriacy of a material to its purpose when made into an object. You may prefer to use only one of these tasks, use both in a circus, or use them sequentially.

In carrying out the activities in this lesson you will need to support the children as they continue to develop their investigative skills. While many of them may have done similar tests before (for example in Key Stage 1/Primary 1–3 it is common to explore suitable waterproof materials for a teddy's umbrella), they may not have carried out an investigation so systematically or with consideration of controlling any of the variables.

INTRODUCTION

Begin by talking about why we need to know about the properties that certain materials possess. Discuss the outcomes of the previous lesson in the context of establishing a suitable material from which to make a carrier bag.

Property	Description of material	What could you test?	How could you test it?
Strength	strong/weak	How much force is needed to break it?	Hang weights on.
Elasticity	elastic/inelastic	Does it spring back after being stretched or compressed?	Apply push and pull forces.
Hardness	hard/soft	How easily can you change its shape by squeezing it?	Try to squash it into a different shape.
Reflective	reflective/ non-reflective	Can you see a reflection in it?	Shine a light at it, look for your reflected face.
Magnetic	magnetic/ non-magnetic	Is it attracted by a magnet?	Use a magnet to try to attract the material.
Absorbency –probably a new word!	absorbent/ waterproof	Does it absorb or repel water?	Drip water on to the material – does it run off or need to be squeezed out?

MAIN TEACHING ACTIVITY – PART 1

Talk to the children about ways of finding out the properties of materials. Ask the children to think of properties that could be investigated and how. Work together as a class to complete photocopiable page 106, with information such as that shown in the table on the left.

GROUP ACTIVITIES

1. Tell the children that they are going to plan an investigation into just one of the properties they have looked at on photocopiable page 106. The question they will answer is 'Which material is the… (hardest, strongest, most absorbent)?' You will need to work very closely with each group as they do this. They will need to decide four things: which property to investigate (such as strength or absorbency); what exactly they will test for (perhaps how much force is needed to break something or whether a material absorbs water); how the test will be carried out (perhaps by adding weights or dripping water onto a material); and which materials to test.

MAIN TEACHING ACTIVITY – PART 2

When the children have carried out their planning, bring them back together to discuss how they are going to ensure that the tests they carry out are fair. Discuss the idea of fairness when playing games and apply this to their investigations. (A game is fair if everyone has the same opportunities, for example a team game is fair if the sides are equal and both are playing to the same rules.) Emphasise that for their tests to be fair the children need to treat all the materials the same: if they drip water on materials to test for absorbency they need to drip the same quantity of water on each.

GROUP ACTIVITIES

2. Some groups can carry out their investigation. You may like to use photocopiable pages 59–60 (see Unit 2) for the children to record their results, or for the children to devise their own method of recording their work. At this stage, to ease resource pressures, others can carry out Group activity 3.

3. Ask the children to make carrier bags using the template and instructions on photocopiable page 107. First they should try to decide what makes a good carrier bag. Have some bags available for the children to look at and examine their construction. The children should think about: strength – whether it can carry a heavy load; weight – whether the bag itself is heavy or light; colour – whether it can be coloured (for decoration or advertising); waterproofing – whether it can still be used when it gets wet.

Each group should use just one main material to make the body of the carrier bag, with each group using a different material. They will also need to consider how to attach the sides of the bag together, perhaps using sticky tape, by glueing, or even sewing. Let them test their bags to see which material is the most suitable. Watch out for unprotected toes if the bag breaks and the load (perhaps a big potato) falls out. Encourage the children to try to write a set of instructions telling other people how to make a strong carrier bag.

DIFFERENTIATION

Lower-attaining children will need more support in planning and carrying out the Group activities. Support them with adult supervision wherever possible. Higher-attaining children should be able to work on these tasks with less support and begin to draw some conclusions from their investigations. Encourage these children to justify their choice of material for their carrier bag or why their material was unsuitable (depending on how much choice they had in the material)!

ASSESSMENT

Through scrutiny of the children's work, observation and discussion during the lesson, assess the children's ability to plan and carry out the investigation. Most should be able to carry out the investigation although some support may be needed at the planning stage. What consideration did the children make towards fairness?

PLENARY

Bring the class together before tidying away the groups' investigations so that each group can report to the rest of the class on how they carried out the investigation, their observations and their conclusions.

Conclude the lesson by reinforcing the idea that in choosing appropriate materials to use we need to investigate the properties of possible materials to establish the most appropriate material. The children may describe the 'best' material, but highlight how 'best' is also dependent on purpose.

OUTCOMES

● Know that the properties of materials can be compared by investigation.

● Can plan and carry out a fair test, make predictions and observations and draw conclusions.

LESSON 6

Objective	● To use materials for a specific purpose and to test their suitability for that purpose. ● To identify what scientific questions need to be asked.
Resources	A wide variety of flexible materials such as paper, tissue paper, card, cloth, plastic, scissors, glue, adhesive tape, carrier bags.
Main activity	Ask the children to make a specific item using a particular material, for example an envelope or a small box to keep an item safe. The children should be able to think of a question they need to answer or test to see if their chosen material might be suitable, for example 'What happens to tissue paper when it gets wet?' and thus 'What would happen to an envelope made from tissue paper?', or 'What happens to a paper box when we put a heavy weight on it?' and thus 'Would a paper box protect an egg?' You may like to use photocopiable pages 59 and 60 (see Unit 2), to help the children record their results, or for the children to devise their own ways of recording.
Differentiation	Differentiate by outcome.
Assessment	Through observation and discussion, assess whether or not the children are able to test the appropriateness of the materials used.
Plenary	Bring the children together and share experiences. Draw some conclusions about suitable and unsuitable materials.
Outcomes	● Can use materials for a specific purpose. ● Can test their questions about the material's suitability for that purpose.

LESSON 7

OBJECTIVE
● To know that some materials occur naturally and others do not.

RESOURCES
Main teaching activity: A collection of different natural and manufactured materials, flip chart or board, pens.
Group activities: 1. A copy of photocopiable page 108 for each child, pens, pencils.
2. Clipboards, paper, pens, pencils.

Vocabulary
man-made, manufactured, natural, source

BACKGROUND
There are many ways to group materials. Some groupings are based on the properties of the materials, others are to do with their origins. Materials are often grouped as being 'natural' or 'manufactured' (man-made).

Many years ago, people had access to a very limited range of materials and all of them were natural materials that could be found around them, such as stone and wood. Natural raw materials can be traced to several sources: animals, plants, or the ground ('animal, vegetable or mineral').

Today, while we still use a number of natural materials, we also use a large number of 'man-made' or manufactured materials. These materials are designed and produced to have quite specific properties. For example, plastic is a strong, light and very versatile material that has replaced many natural products. Many materials are manufactured from natural raw materials or derivatives of natural materials. Glass, for example, is manufactured from pure sand.

In the production of objects, materials often go through intermediate stages and are processed as they are turned from a raw material into a finished product. This processing can confuse what is natural and what is manufactured. A wooden chair, for example, is made from the timber of a tree which is sawn into planks; a pullover is made from a ball of wool which previously was the fleece of a sheep.

In summary: 'natural' materials are produced by natural processes, such as raw wool, wood and cotton. What we might call 'processed' materials are usually grouped as natural materials as they are changed physically by humans, although the change does not alter the nature of the material, examples include spun wool and cotton, planks of wood, or cut and finished slabs of stone. 'Manufactured' materials are made by processes that change raw materials into different materials, for example crude oil is used to manufacture plastics and artificial fibres.

INTRODUCTION

Have ready in the classroom a collection of objects made from materials that have been discussed in previous lessons. Talk about the materials, recapping on their properties and uses. Ask: *Could these materials be sorted in a different way to the ways they have been sorted before – not by their properties?*

	NATURAL OBJECT	NOT NATURAL (manufactured) OBJECT
NATURAL MATERIAL	stone plant	wooden chair woollen jumper door
NOT NATURAL (manufactured) MATERIAL		book window pane

MAIN TEACHING ACTIVITY

Look at the collection of materials. Encourage the children to consider the origins of the materials and to think about which ones occur naturally and which have been manufactured. Make a list of natural and manufactured materials.

GROUP ACTIVITIES

1. Distribute copies of photocopiable page 108. Ask the children to work together to make a list of materials and where they come from under the headings on the sheet. Ensure that they record only materials and not objects.

2. Ask the groups to carry out a survey around the classroom to find objects that are made from manufactured materials or natural materials. Use the information and that gained from Group activity 1 to create a Carroll diagram similar to the one above.

DIFFERENTIATION

Lower-attaining children may need extra support in determining whether or not a material is man-made or natural, and may benefit from you providing extra examples. Help will also be needed with drawing and completing the Carroll diagram. Higher-attaining children work with the Carroll diagram to add more examples.

ASSESSMENT

Can the children recognise manufactured materials and naturally occurring materials? Assess their understanding from their ability to sort materials into groups using photocopiable page 108.

PLENARY

Have a quiz in which the children have to find the identity of a mystery material by asking five questions. The respondent can say only 'Yes' or 'No'. The children can use the Carroll diagrams to help them, together with other visual information such as samples of the materials.

OUTCOME

● Can recognise that some materials occur naturally and others do not.

LINKS

Maths: organising data into tables and charts, for example Carroll diagrams.

LESSON 8

Objective	• To be able to compare finished objects with raw materials.
Resources	A selection of raw materials, their corresponding processed materials and finished objects or pictures of these. For example, raw materials could be a sheep's fleece, a tree trunk, or cotton; corresponding processed materials could be a ball of wool, a plank of wood, paper, glass or a reel of cotton; finished objects could be a knitted jumper, a wooden table, a book, a glass vase, a cotton shirt. Also provide secondary sources of information relating to how materials are processed and manufactured.
Main activity	Compare raw materials, processed materials and finished products. Ask the children to sort the materials into related groups, for example a sheep's fleece, a ball of wool and a knitted jumper in one group. They can then present their ideas in pictorial form to show the links and groupings.
Differentiation	Provide lower-attaining children with sets of cards of the three phases of manufacturing to sort into order. More able children can go on to carry out their own independent research looking at how some raw materials are processed and how man-made materials are manufactured, for example how paper or bricks are made.
Assessment	Use the children's work to check that they have an understanding and ability to sort the various items into groups that show raw materials, processed materials and finished products.
Plenary	Share ideas and reinforce the understanding that manufactured items and materials come from natural raw materials.
Outcome	• Can compare finished objects with raw materials.

LESSON 9

OBJECTIVE
• To be able to recognise and describe a range of different rocks.

RESOURCES

Main teaching activity: A selection of different rock samples with their names written on cards. Rock kits containing samples of sandstone, limestone, marble, granite, chalk and slate are available from Hardy Aggregates, Torr Works, East Cranmore, Shepton Mallet, Somerset BA4 4SQ; tel: 01749 880735; e-mail: info@hardy-aggregates.co.uk; website: www.hardy-aggregates.co.uk

Group activities: 1. Hand lenses and magnifiers, paper, pens, pencils; secondary sources of information. **2.** Paper, pens, pencils; secondary sources of information; large sheets of coloured paper, papier mâché 'rocks'.

Vocabulary

chalk, granite, igneous, limestone, marble, metamorphic, sandstone, sedimentary, slate

BACKGROUND

The surface of the Earth – the Earth's crust – is made up from rock, though some of this rock is covered by soil or water.

Rocks are widely used for a variety of building purposes and a walk around any town will give plenty of examples. Towns are often characterised by the colour of the local stone used for their buildings: pink or grey mottled granite, red-brown sandstone, white or yellow limestone. There are many different types of rock that can be identified by looking at factors such as colour, texture and hardness.

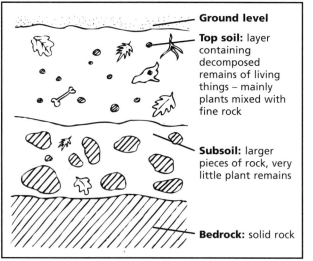

Ground level

Top soil: layer containing decomposed remains of living things – mainly plants mixed with fine rock

Subsoil: larger pieces of rock, very little plant remains

Bedrock: solid rock

Rock is classified according to the way in which it was formed many millions of years ago. Three types of rock make up the Earth's crust. Igneous rocks such as granite were formed from molten or partially molten material during volcanic eruptions and make up nearly 95% of the Earth's crust. Sedimentary rocks such as sandstone and limestone make up about 5% of the Earth's crust and were formed when sediments settled and became compressed. Metamorphic rocks are made from existing igneous and sedimentary rocks that have undergone extreme changes due to heating or pressure – slate, for example, is formed from shale, and marble is formed from limestone or dolorite.

INTRODUCTION

Relate this lesson to the ideas developed in Lesson 7 by asking the children to recall the two groups into which we can classify materials: natural and manufactured. Remind the children that part of one of their tasks was to find out which materials come from under the ground. Ask the children to recall some of these and ask if they can tell you where rocks come from. Discuss whether rocks are man-made or natural, and consider some ways in which they are used.

MAIN TEACHING ACTIVITY

Have available in the classroom a selection of rock samples for the children to look at, touch and experience. Ask the children to describe the rock samples using characteristics such as: size of particles (different visible pieces in the rock's structure) – none, tiny, small, large; shape of particles – angular or smooth and round; colour – black, white, grey, pink, green or yellow for example, and shiny or dull; texture – rough or smooth.

Create a class table of the observations. Now put the name labels with the correct rock samples, and associate the characteristics from the children's descriptions with the rock types.

GROUP ACTIVITIES

1. Using the labelled rocks to reinforce the variety of distinguishing characteristics, ask the children to identify similar small rock samples. Ask them to group the rocks by considering their characteristics. The children can record their work by drawing carefully coloured observational sketches of the rock samples, naming them and, depending on their ability, writing a brief description of one or more of the rock samples.
2. Ask the children to use secondary sources to find out more about the three rock types: igneous; sedimentary; metamorphic. The children can present their findings as a 'Rock factfile' or mounted on to coloured rocks that are either painted stones or papier mâché rocks to form a mountain as a display.

DIFFERENTIATION

Lower-attaining children research some basic facts about one or two rock types. Higher-attaining children research in more detail and find examples of each rock type.

ASSESSMENT

Assess the children's work for evidence of their ability to recognise the samples of the rocks. Most should be able to recognise the majority of the samples having studied the bigger pieces; the most able should recognise them all.

PLENARY

Use the descriptions produced to see if the children can identify the samples from each other's work. Discuss their findings about the three main rock types. Show the children a piece of concrete/aggregate – 'manufactured rock' – and talk about its similarities to natural stone.

OUTCOMES

● Can recognise and describe a range of different rocks.
● Can put rocks into groups.

LINKS

Geography: investigating our local area (in England, QCA *Geography Scheme of Work:* Unit 6).

LESSON 10

Objective	• To know that rocks can be tested for their wear.
Resources	A selection of different rock samples, sandpaper, paper, pens, pencils.
Main activity	Compare rock samples by testing to see how easily they wear. Use hand lenses to observe and sketch the surface of each rock sample. Carry out a 'rubbing test' to compare how easily the samples are ground down: rub each sample ten times with a piece of sandpaper. Try to rub the same place each time and with the same force. Use the hand lenses to carry out a second observation and again record as an observational drawing.
Differentiation	Differentiate by outcome.
Assessment	Through scrutiny of the children's work, observation, discussion and during the Plenary, look for evidence that the children know that rocks can be tested in this way.
Plenary	Ask the children to present their findings and to say which rock sample was the hardest-wearing and which the easiest to wear away. Begin to think about the uses these rocks could be put to.
Outcome	• Can compare and rank rocks according to their ease of wearing.

LESSON 11

Objective	• To know that rocks can be tested for their permeability.
Resources	A selection of different rock samples, water, pipettes, paper, pens, pencils, secondary sources of information.
Main activity	Use a variety of rock samples to test for permeability by dropping small amounts of water onto the samples and observing how quickly the water is absorbed, if at all. Drop five drops of water onto the same place on each sample. Observe and record the results in a table which gives the opportunity for the children to identify the rock samples using secondary sources. After this lesson and Lesson 10, take the children outside. Look around at the local environment for evidence of wear on rocks and stones, for example on carvings on buildings. Speculate on the causes of the wear.
Differentiation	Differentiate by outcome.
Assessment	Look for evidence that the children have been able to carry out the investigation in a fair way.
Plenary	Bring the children together and ask them to share their work with each other. Discuss what the disadvantages of building using very permeable rock would be, for example it may not be weatherproof. You may wish to discuss and demonstrate the effects of water freezing and thawing, for example (the rock surface is broken up).
Outcome	• Can compare and rank rocks according to their permeability.

LESSON 12

OBJECTIVES
- To know there are different kinds of soil.
- To know that there is rock beneath soil.

RESOURCES

Main teaching activity: A piece of rock, some crushed rock, a container of soil; a container of water and a dead plant (a weed); paper, pens, pencils.
Group activities: 1. Soil samples, hand lenses, dishes or shallow trays. **2.** Secondary sources of information.

Vocabulary
bedrock, humus, soil, subsoil, topsoil

BACKGROUND

Soil is a mixture of tiny pieces of rock that have become mixed with decaying plants. This decaying vegetation becomes a substance called 'humus'. The humus sticks all the particles together and absorbs water. This mixture slowly changes and becomes a habitat for living things: plants and minibeasts. Just as there are different rock types, there are also different soil types. The different types of soil are produced depending on the rock types that are underlying the area. As you dig down into the ground, you go through different layers of soil, each slightly different in composition. In Britain, you are likely to find three layers: topsoil, which is the decomposed remains of living things mixed with tiny rock particles; subsoil, which is larger pieces of rock with less decaying plant life; and bedrock, which is the rock from which the soil is made. Each different layer then has different amounts of rock and water in it thus making them different colours and textures.

INTRODUCTION

Take into the classroom a piece of rock, some crushed rock, a container of soil, a container of water and a dead plant (a weed). Ask the children if they can think how these things are all linked. Talk about the possible links that the children suggest.

MAIN TEACHING ACTIVITY

Introduce the idea of how the soil was created. Ask the children to help you to put the items in order to show how soil is made. This should be: rocks become the crushed rocks, to which the decaying plant material and water is added, resulting in the soil. Ask the children to draw a series of illustrations to explain how soil is formed. Remind them of the importance of washing their hands after handling any soil samples.

GROUP ACTIVITIES

1. Ask the children to collect soil samples carefully from the school grounds. Perhaps the children could bring samples from their own gardens. (In an urban area you may need to provide trays of local soils for the children to use.) Ask the children to describe each type of soil and how they differ from those found in the school grounds.
2. Ask the children to use secondary sources to investigate the recognised soil types. Can they find sufficient information to draw an illustration showing the different layers of soil to be found under the ground? This could become a group collage picture.

DIFFERENTIATION

Because of the nature of the activities in this lesson differentiation is largely by outcome.

ASSESSMENT

Through scrutiny of the children's work, assess their level of understanding. All of the children should be able to describe how soil lies on top of rock and most should recognise that there are different types of soil.

PLENARY

Use illustrations to show and talk about how soil can be made up of several different layers of different colours.

OUTCOMES

- Can describe how soil lies on top of rock.
- Can recognise that there are different kinds of soil.

LINKS

Geography: investigating our local area (in England, QCA *Geography Scheme of Work*: Unit 6).

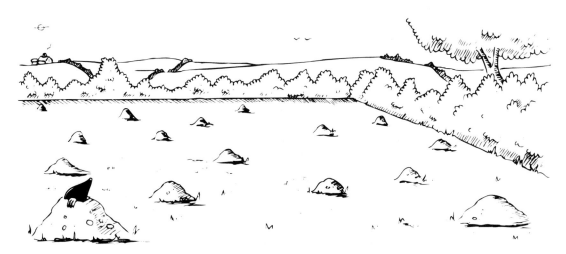

LESSON 13

Objective	● To know that different soils have different-sized particles and different colours.
Resources	Soil samples from Lesson 12, plastic beakers, water, paper, pens, pencils.
Main activity	Use the different soil samples collected from different locations. Put about 5cm of one sample in a clear plastic beaker. Fill the beaker with water, stir, and leave the solution to settle (this may take a couple of days). Different groups of children can look at the different soil samples. As the water clears and the materials settle you should begin to see different layers of particles, with the heavier ones generally settled at the very bottom. Record the results for each soil sample by copying illustrations of a beaker for the children to record their observations on.
Differentiation	Differentiate by outcome.
Assessment	Through discussion and observation, assess the children's ability to compare the particles in the soil. Most should be able to explain the observable differences. Darker soils usually contain more humus; pale, gritty soils may be very sandy, while reddish soils with fine particles tend to be clay-based.
Plenary	Discuss the different layers with the children and compare the contents from the different soil samples.
Outcome	● Can compare soils in terms of particles and colour.

Diagram labels: Humus floating, Clay, Silt, Sand, Stones

LESSON 14

OBJECTIVES

● To know how to compare the permeability of soils.
● To plan and carry out a fair test.

RESOURCES

Main teaching activity: Pictures of rainy days and flooding, soil samples from Lesson 12 plus extra samples, clay and sand, water, beakers, a plastic tray, a timer.
Group activities: 1. Soil samples from Lesson 12 plus extra samples, clay and sand, water, beakers, funnels, filter paper or paper towels, a plastic tray, a timer, paper, copies of photocopiable pages 59 and 60 (see Unit 2), pens, pencils. **2.** Pots, soil samples, cress seeds, copies of photocopiable page 109, paper, pens, pencils.

BACKGROUND

Different soils and sub-soils have different properties: some are fine, some are gritty and open and some are more solid with finer particles that stick together. These different soil types allow the water that falls on them to drain away at different rates. When it rains, you will notice how the water lays longer in some areas than in others. This is often related to the soil type and its permeability (its ability to allow water through). Clay soils, for example, are not very permeable, whereas sand drains quickly.

INTRODUCTION

Talk to the children about rainy days and flooding and show them some pictures. Ask them: *Why do you think the water stays on some surfaces longer than others?*

MAIN TEACHING ACTIVITY

Demonstrate how by pouring water simultaneously through two different soil samples we can show that different soils have different qualities of permeability. Use the clay and sand for the demonstration. Ask the children how they would ensure that your demonstration test was a fair test. Encourage them to say that you should use equal quantities of soil and equal quantities of water. Set the children off planning how to extend this test to investigate the soil samples they have looked at previously.

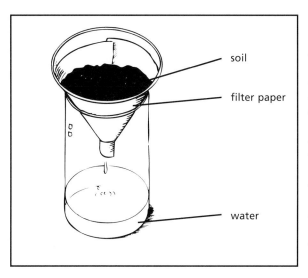

soil

filter paper

water

GROUP ACTIVITIES

1. The children should devise together, with support, a fair test to investigate permeability of soil types. Ensure the children consider what factors will make the investigation a fair test. The test should involve pouring equal amounts of water over equal quantities of soil and timing how long it takes for the water to drain through, or how much water drains through in a given time. On this or a future occasion, the children should carry out their tests on the soil samples. The children could record their findings in a table format using photocopiable pages 59 and 60 as a basis for the report of their findings.
2. Distribute photocopiable page 109 and ask the children to follow the instructions carefully. They should plant cress seeds in two different types of soil and care for them both equally well. A record of their work can be kept on a simple storyboard.

DIFFERENTIATION

This task could be used as a means of assessing the children's ability to carry out a fair test so the differentiation should be by outcome.

ASSESSMENT

Scrutiny of the children's work and your questioning will help you to assess the children's ability to plan and carry out a fair test. Ask questions such as: *Did you use the same amount of water each time? Why? Did you use the same amount of soil? Why? Can you explain what you were trying to find out?*

PLENARY

Give children the time to look at each other's work and to share their findings. Reinforce the concept of permeability and ask the children how they could improve areas where water does not drain away very quickly. Explain how plants need the right amount of water – neither too much (waterlogged soil is cold and airless) nor too little.

OUTCOMES

● Can compare the permeability of soils.
● Can plan and carry out a fair test.

LINKS

Unit 2, Lessons 11–13: plants' need for water and water transport.

LESSON 15

OBJECTIVES
● To assess the children's knowledge and understanding of materials and their uses.
● To assess the children's knowledge and understanding of rocks and soils.

RESOURCES

Introduction: Objects brought from home (less familiar than the usual classroom items).
Assessment activities: 1. Copies of photocopiable page 110, pens, pencils. **2.** Copies of photocopiable page 111, pens, pencils.

INTRODUCTION

Ask the children to bring in one simple object from home (a letter home may ensure they do not bring valuables to school). Ask them to help you to sort the objects according to the materials they are made from. Discuss alternative groupings. Encourage the children to begin to identify the natural raw materials that are used in some of the objects.

ASSESSMENT ACTIVITY 1

Distribute copies of photocopiable page 110 and ask the children to complete the sheet unaided. The tasks are designed to give the children the opportunity to identify the particular uses for materials used to build houses.

Answers
1.

Part of house	Made from	Why?
Window	glass	strong, transparent, lightweight
Roof	slate or clay tiles	strong, rigid, waterproof
Door	wood or uPVC	strong, rigid, waterproof, can be painted (wood)
Guttering	plastic, wood or iron	strong, light, can be shaped, can be painted
Walls	stone, brick or wood	strong, waterproof, can be shaped
Door handle	brass, plastic or metal	strong, can be moulded, shiny

2. An umbrella made from paper would disintegrate when it rained or tear when it was windy. The material is not strong enough and is not waterproof.
3. A hammer made from glass would shatter when used because glass is too brittle and is not as strong as iron.

Looking for levels
All the children should be able to suggest materials for some of the components listed, and most should be able to give one good reason why each material could be used. Most should also be able to give explanations of what would happen if we use the wrong materials for making objects, and a few should be able to give reasons why.

ASSESSMENT ACTIVITY 2

Distribute copies of photocopiable page 111 and ask the children to complete the sheet unaided.

Answers
1. The brick, drinking glass and jewellery are made from (processed) rock.
2. Three pictures to show uses of rock could include: stone walls, dressed building stone, roads, bricks, glass, walls, monuments and so on.
3. Soil is formed when crushed rock is mixed with humus and the mixture is bound together with water.

Looking for levels
All the children should be able to identify which objects are made from rocks, and most should be able to identify another use of rock. Some will identify more than one other use and some will be able to explain how soil is formed.

PLENARY

Discuss the Assessment activities and address any further misunderstandings. Reinforce the link between rock and how soil is made.

Name _____

Changing materials

Can you remember what happens to materials when you change their temperature? Draw these things in the boxes.

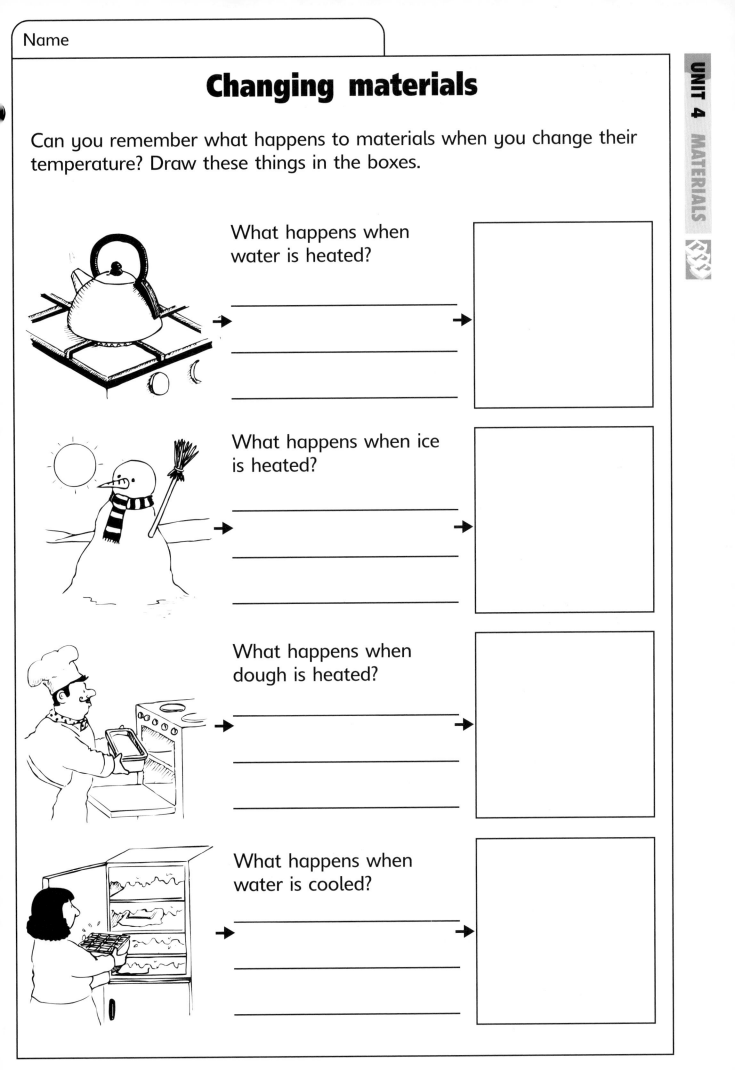

What happens when water is heated?

→ _____
_____
_____ →

What happens when ice is heated?

→ _____
_____
_____ →

What happens when dough is heated?

→ _____
_____
_____ →

What happens when water is cooled?

→ _____
_____
_____ →

Materials

Can you find examples around school of things that are made from each of the materials below?

Remember: a material is the substance something is made from.

Material	Example of its use
Metal	
Wood	
Plastic	
Glass	
Paper	
Stone	
Brick	

Now try to find out what materials these objects in your school are made from. There may be several materials used in making each object.

Object	Materials used
Table	
Chair	
Book	
Pen	
Computer and monitor	
Your classroom	

Name

Properties of materials

Look at the examples of these materials on your table.
Write a list of properties that belong to each one.

Glass	Plastic
Paper	**Wood**
Steel	**Clay**

Name

Investigating properties

How would you investigate these properties of materials? Complete the table. One has been done for you.

Can you add two more properties to test?

Property	Description of material	What could you test?	How could you test it?
Strength	strong/weak	How much force is needed to break it?	Hang weights on it.
Elasticity			
Hardness			
Reflective			
Magnetic			
Absorbency			

Carrier bag template

Copy this template twice onto thin card.

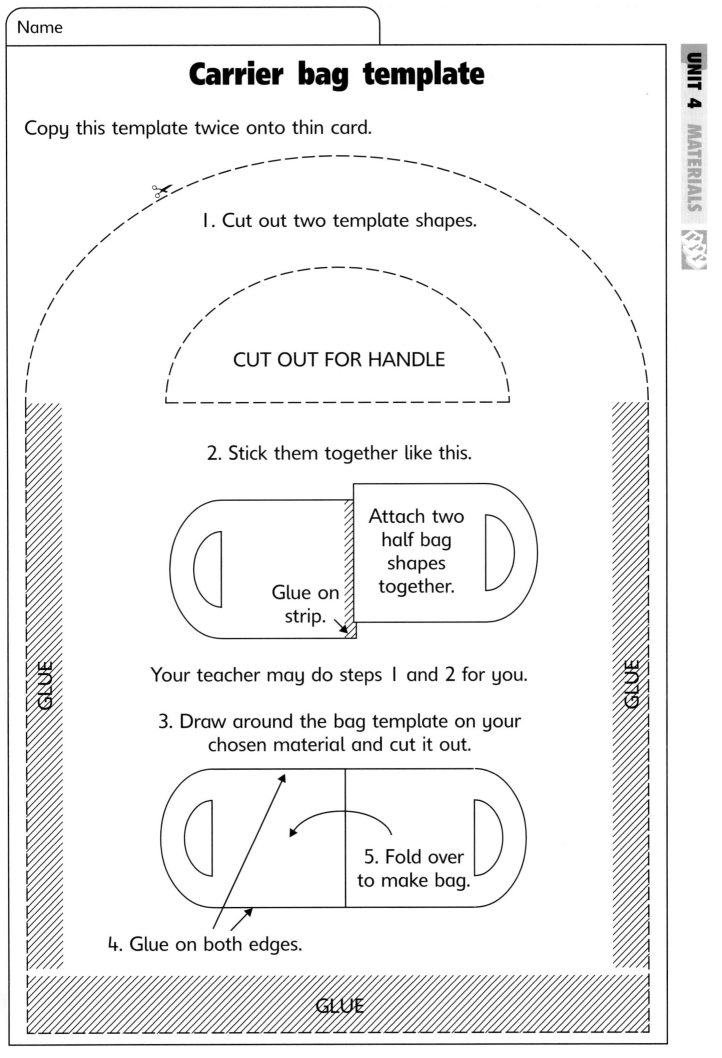

1. Cut out two template shapes.

CUT OUT FOR HANDLE

2. Stick them together like this.

Glue on strip.

Attach two half bag shapes together.

Your teacher may do steps 1 and 2 for you.

3. Draw around the bag template on your chosen material and cut it out.

5. Fold over to make bag.

4. Glue on both edges.

GLUE

GLUE

GLUE

Natural and man-made materials

Where do natural materials come from? See if you can complete this table with examples of materials from each of these sources.

Materials that come from plants

Materials that come from animals

Materials that come from the ground

What sorts of materials are made by people – 'manufactured'?

Materials that are made by people

UNIT 4 MATERIALS

Growing seeds in different soils

You are going to grow some cress seeds in two different soils.
Put different types of soil into each of the two pots. Label them A and B.
Sprinkle the seeds on the soil and gently press them in.
Water the seeds carefully before putting the pots on a window sill.
Make sure you give each the same amount of water.
Draw a storyboard to show what you have done so far.

Keep an eye on the seeds, water them regularly and equally.
Predict in which soil the seeds will grow the best and why.

_____

_____

Draw a storyboard of the pots as the cress grows.

A	A	A
B	B	B

Name

Natural and manufactured materials

1. Look at this picture of a house.

Think about the materials that each part listed below is made from. Say why that material is used for that part.

Part of house	Made from	Why?
Window		
Roof		
Door		
Guttering		
Walls		
Door handles		

Try these questions about what would happen if we used the wrong materials

2. What would happen if we made an umbrella out of paper?

_____

_____

3. What would happen if we made a hammer out of glass?

_____

_____

Natural and manufactured materials

1. Circle the objects that are made from rocks.

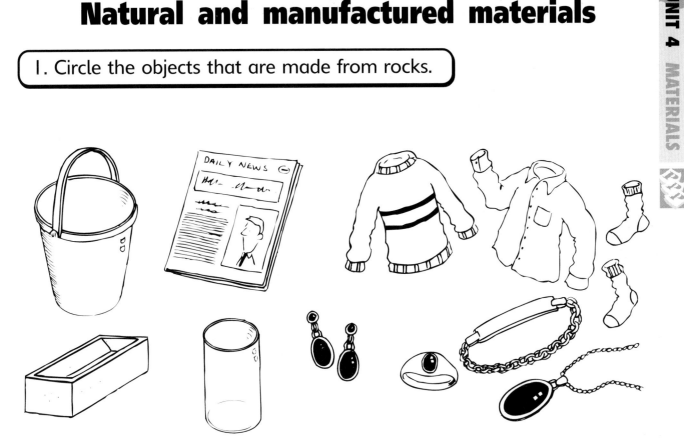

2. Can you think of some more ways that we use rocks?
Draw three pictures.

3. Explain how soil is formed. These words will help you.

humus   **crushed rock**   **water**

_____

_____

Electricity and communication

ORGANISATION (9 LESSONS)

	OBJECTIVES	MAIN ACTIVITY	GROUP ACTIVITIES	PLENARY	OUTCOMES
LESSON 1	● To ask questions that can be investigated scientifically and decide how to find answers. ● To assess and reinforce knowledge of electrical appliances, safety and simple circuits from KS1/P1–3.	Concept mapping.	Drawing concept cartoons. Discussing ideas about electrical safety.	Sharing of concept maps and cartoons.	● Teacher can assess the level of the children in the class. ● Teacher can arrange children in appropriate class groups.
LESSON 2	● To know that electricity can be dangerous and must be treated with great care.	Writing an electrical safety code.	Planning an electrical safety campaign.	Discussion and explanation of the electrical safety code by the children.	● Can recognise the dangers of electricity.
LESSON 3	● To know how to make a simple circuit with a switch.	Making simple circuits.	Making simple circuits with switches. Completing a switch survey.	Sharing findings and reinforcing vocabulary.	● Can make a simple circuit with a switch. ● Can explain how the circuit must be made for the lamp to light.
LESSON 4	● To identify circuits that will not let electricity flow.	Making human circuits.	Looking at broken and complete circuits. Compiling rules for making circuits.	Reinforcing understanding of complete and broken circuits.	● Can identify circuits which will not let electricity flow.
LESSON 5	● To know how to make a simple circuit containing two bulbs.	Making a cat's face light up.		Testing the cat faces.	● Can make a circuit with two bulbs.
LESSON 6	● To know how to make a simple electrical device. ● To know that electricity is used for communicating with sound.	Building a lighthouse.		Demonstrating working models.	● Can make a simple electrical device using a bulb and a buzzer effectively.
LESSON 7	● To recognise and know how to use a buzzer in a circuit.	Making Morse code messages.	Sending Morse code messages with light and sound. Code-breaking.	Demonstrating working models.	● Understand that electricity is important for 20th and 21st century communication. ● Can make a circuit and send a simple message with it.
LESSON 8	● To know that electricity is used for communication systems.	Identifying communication devices. Sending messages.	Identifying communication devices that use electricity. Sending simple e-mails.	Sharing e-mails.	● Can describe a range of ways in which electricity is used in communications.

	OBJECTIVES		ACTIVITY 1	ACTIVITY 2
ASSESSMENT 9	● To assess the children's knowledge and understanding of the language of simple electrical circuits. ● To assess the children's knowledge and understanding of the use of electricity in communicating.		Completing a crossword.	Letter-writing to inventors.

LESSON 1

OBJECTIVES

● To ask questions that can be investigated scientifically and decide how to find answers.
● To assess and reinforce knowledge of electrical appliances, safety and simple circuits from KS1/P1–3.

RESOURCES

Main teaching activity: Large sheets of paper, pens or pencils.
Group activities: 1 and 2. Paper, pens, pencils, drawing materials.

BACKGROUND

In Key Stage 1/Primary 1–3, the children will have been given opportunities to find out about uses of electricity, particularly everyday electrical appliances in the home and at school and their safe use. They will also have learned about simple series circuits, including the use of switches, and about the dangers of electricity. In addition the children should be able to construct and make drawings of simple working circuits and explain why some circuits work and others do not. This unit reinforces these concepts, extending the children's knowledge and understanding of electrical safety and electrical circuits, and introduces how we use electricity for communication. The assessment task detailed below is designed to ascertain the level of the children's prior understanding of electricity from their previous work and thus to enable you to arrange the children into groups appropriate to your school setting.

INTRODUCTION

Briefly remind the children that they have already carried out some work on electricity in KS1/ P1–3. At this stage, avoid giving too many details, as this may have some influence on the effectiveness of the assessment process.

MAIN TEACHING ACTIVITY

Explain that the activity the children are going to carry out is to draw concept maps and concept cartoons. Ask them to try to remember everything they have learned about electricity and to think about all the things they know about electricity, then ask them to write the word 'electricity' in the centre of their page and to write down all the things they can think of about that are connected with electricity.

GROUP ACTIVITIES

1. When the children have completed their concept maps, ask them to choose one idea from which to create a concept cartoon that will show the idea in greater detail, for example how a light bulb and battery are connected in a circuit. Note that in the illustration of children's drawings below only d) shows a correctly completed circuit.
2. Ask the children to write down their ideas about electrical safety and their thoughts about the dangers of electricity.

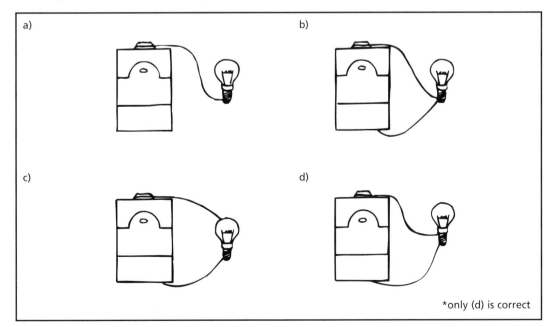

a)

b)

c)

d)

*only (d) is correct

DIFFERENTIATION

Prompt lower-attaining children's thinking with the use of key words. Encourage higher-attaining children to join concepts that are directly related to each other on their concept maps.

ASSESSMENT

In this initial assessment lesson, look for evidence of the children's understanding of electrical circuits and how they are made. Most children should have some understanding and be able to make a simple circuit. Some will also have developed an understanding of safety. Use this information to inform your planning so that children's alternative understandings can be addressed and their thinking moved on.

PLENARY

Bring the children together to share their concept maps and cartoons, and draw one large class concept map.

OUTCOMES

● Teacher can assess the level of the children in the class.
● Teacher can arrange children in appropriate class groups.

LESSON 2

OBJECTIVE

● To know that electricity can be dangerous and must be treated with great care.

RESOURCES

Main teaching activity: A copy of the 'Firework code' or similar safety code of practice enlarged on the flip chart or OHP; one or more household electrical appliances.
Group activity: Art materials; access to graphics and paint packages on the class computer.

PREPARATION

Prepare a bank of key words for lower-attainers – see Vocabulary.

Vocabulary

current, dangerous, electric shock, electricity, electrocution, voltage

BACKGROUND

Electricity is an important part of modern life and as such is very much taken for granted by most people, both adults and children alike. Children use electrical equipment every day often without a second glance, yet do not always acknowledge the dangers of electricity. Therefore, it is very important to re-emphasise, with progressively more detail and explanation, the correct use and potential dangers of the misuse of electricity. While electricity is invisible, its effects are there to be seen by everyone and its dangers should not be underestimated. The misuse of electricity can lead to electric shocks, burns and even death. Mains electricity should be treated with respect and children alerted to the dangers of

interfering with this source of energy. (This is reiterated in every electricity unit in the *100 Science Lessons* series.) There are a number of clear rules that everyone should adopt with regards to electricity:
- Never poke anything into mains sockets.
- Always switch sockets off before unplugging appliances.
- Never interfere with electrical equipment or attempt to dismantle it while still plugged in.
- Never handle electrical equipment with wet hands.
- Never take mains equipment into the bathroom.
- Avoid using faulty appliances, have them checked by a qualified electrician.
- Never overload sockets.
- Never play with electricity.
- Never play near electrified railway lines.
- Play well away from high-voltage overhead power lines.

In school, the safest way to investigate electricity is by using 1.5V cells or batteries. However, it is clearly important that the children realise that a battery is only relatively safe and that even if batteries are misused (for example, by causing a short circuit) the connecting wires can get very hot and may cause a burn.

INTRODUCTION

Ask the class: *Can you name things that are powered by electricity? What types of appliance do you have at home… for example in your kitchen, your living room and your bedroom? What about here in school? Which appliances do you use regularly that are powered by electricity?* Write a list of these appliances, and discuss who uses which ones.

Ask the class to think about the electricity that powers the appliances. Let the children brainstorm ideas about what electricity is like. Their ideas, which should be encouraged, will reflect their level of understanding and may include descriptions related to: sound – 'It is silent', 'I can sometimes hear it' (humming sub-stations and crackling cables); smell – 'It does not smell'; visibility – 'It is invisible', 'I can sometimes see electricity moving' (lightning); effects – 'It makes things go', 'It warms things up', 'It cools things down'; origins – 'It comes from a battery', 'It comes out of the wall', 'It is energy'.

While not all the ideas will be accurate, it is important in this task that you avoid saying specifically to the children that they are wrong.

MAIN TEACHING ACTIVITY

Using the electrical appliances that you have available as illustration, lead the children on to thinking about mains electricity being very powerful and dangerous. Talk about the dangers of abusing mains electricity and its consequences.

Begin to compile an 'Electrical safety code' together. Present the 'Firework code' or other safety code as an example. The 'Electrical safety code' can be presented as a combination of text and appropriate illustrations, either with the children working individually or, after putting together a class code, one group producing it for display using the computer or drawing materials.

GROUP ACTIVITY

In their groups, the children should use their 'Electrical Safety Code' as the basis on which to plan a safety campaign. The campaign may consist of:
- Posters: designed to be eyecatching with a simple, clear message, or maybe a series of posters which each contain just one statement from the code.
- Leaflets: illustrating the code in an imaginative and entertaining way. These could be produced on a computer using art or desktop publishing software.
- Drama: a short sketch that illustrates what could happen if you do not follow the code, or a safety talk presented by the children.

DIFFERENTIATION

Lower-attaining children may need support with developing the 'Electrical safety code'. Prepare a word bank for them to use. Alternatively they could present their rules pictorially. Higher-attainers should be encouraged to extend the number of rules in their code. Can they think of ten different rules?

ASSESSMENT

Look at the 'Electrical safety code' each child has devised and their involvement in the Group activities. Do these demonstrate that the child understands and recognises the key messages to communicate about the dangers of electricity?

PLENARY

Bring the children back together before the end of the lesson in order that individuals can explain one item from their code to the class and groups can present their drama and so on.

The Group activities could be used as part of an associated class assembly. Display the posters, present the drama and hand out copies of the leaflets to all those present.

OUTCOME

- Can recognise the dangers of electricity.

LINKS

PSHE: developing a healthy, safer lifestyle.

LESSON 3

OBJECTIVE

- To know how to make a simple circuit with a switch.

RESOURCES

Main teaching activity: Batteries, battery holders, bulbs, bulb holders, switches, cables, crocodile clips.
Group activities: 1. Paper and pencils. **2.** Copies of photocopiable page 125, pens, pencils.

Vocabulary

batteries, battery holders, circuit, crocodile clips, lamp holders, lamps, motor, switches, wire

BACKGROUND

For electricity to flow, a number of components need to be arranged in such a way that they make a complete circuit. This circuit will consist of a conductive material and a source of electrical energy. The circuit may also include a device that uses electricity. In the primary classroom these components are invariably things like batteries, bulbs, buzzers, bells, motors and wire. In any circuit there are sometimes occasions when the devices (bulbs, bells) are not required to operate continuously. For both safety and convenience, it is not appropriate to disconnect the battery each time the current needs to be cut off. An alternative is to use a switch. A switch is quite simply a means of making and breaking the circuit. When the switch is closed (or 'on'), the circuit is complete and electricity can flow. When the switch is open (or 'off') the circuit is broken and electricity does not flow. There are a number of different types of switch and each serves a different need but all fulfil the same function. These include:

- toggle switches – normal, fixed-position on/off switch
- push switches – the sort used as a bell push, which only remain on when pressure is applied
- pressure switches – used in burglar alarms and respond to the application of pressure
- light-sensitive switches – used in security lighting and respond to the intensity of light
- temperature-sensitive switches – make and break the circuit depending on the ambient temperature as in a thermostat
- tilt switches – make a complete circuit when they are moved.

(There are opportunities and guidance on making and using switches of these types in *100 Science Lessons: Year 4/Primary 5* and further in *Year 6/Primary 7*.)

INTRODUCTION

Gather the children so they can all see the components you have available. Include batteries, battery holders, bulbs, buzzers, bells, a motor, crocodile clips and wire. Ask them to identify each one for you and explain what it is used for in school science.

MAIN TEACHING ACTIVITY

Without demonstration, ask the children to volunteer to come out and help to make the bulb light up using the equipment available. Ask the children to explain what has been done and what the arrangement is called (a circuit). Discuss the need for a complete circuit. Show the children a switch, and ask someone to try to put it into the circuit.

GROUP ACTIVITIES

1. The children can record their work in words and pictures showing the circuit. Ask them also to include an explanation of what must happen for the bulb to light.
2. Distribute copies of photocopiable page 125 and ask the children to think about the different types of switch they come across both at home and at school. Some examples include:

rocker switches for lights, sockets, vacuum cleaners, table lamps; pull switches (with strings) in bathrooms; dimmer switches for lights and volume controls on TV and audio equipment; push switches for PCs, printers, doorbells, TV and audio equipment.

DIFFERENTIATION

Many children will be able to present their work largely unaided. Prepare a writing frame to help lower-attainers present their work, with headings such as: 'We were trying to _____', 'We used _____', 'Our circuit looked like this _____', 'We used a switch to _____'

ASSESSMENT

Through observation and checking their written work, assess whether the children understand how to construct a simple circuit with a switch.

PLENARY

Come together to share findings and reinforce new vocabulary. Recap the essentials of building a complete circuit with a switch to control its operation.

OUTCOMES

- Can make a simple circuit with a switch.
- Can explain how the circuit must be made for the lamp to light.

LESSON 4

OBJECTIVE

- To identify circuits that will not let electricity flow.

RESOURCES

Main teaching activity: Sufficient small balls to allow one per child.
Group activities: 1. Six prepared circuits labelled 1 to 6 (see Preparation); a copy of photocopiable page 126 on a clipboard with a pencil for each child. **2.** Paper, pens, pencils; a computer with word-processing or desktop publishing software.

PREPARATION

Use classroom components to make six circuits – some complete and working, others that are not complete, for example: no bulb, no battery, switch left open, wires not connected or wires wrongly connected and so on. If possible, display them on separate tables.

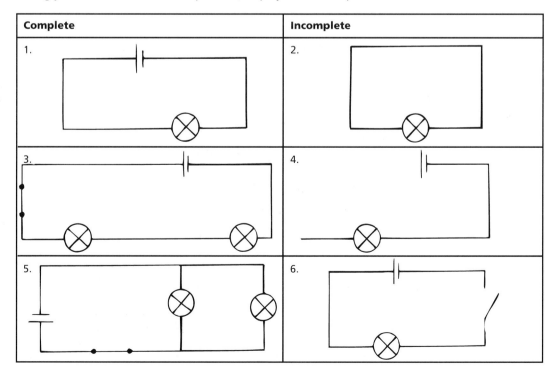

Vocabulary

battery, break, bulb, bulb holders, buzzer, circuit, connection, mains, switch, wire

BACKGROUND

For electricity to flow, a complete circuit of conductive material and a source of electrical energy is required. The circuit may also include a device that uses electricity. If the circuit is broken, then the flow of electricity is interrupted and any devices fail to function. While a switch of some description is generally used to control the flow of electricity around the circuit – a controllable break – there are other reasons why the electricity may not flow. These include: incomplete circuits; incorrect circuits; faulty bulbs or buzzers; flat batteries; the inclusion of insulators in a circuit.

INTRODUCTION

Begin by reinforcing the work carried out during the previous lesson when the children made circuits. Discuss what is needed for electricity to flow and for bulbs or buzzers to operate.

MAIN TEACHING ACTIVITY

Ask the children to stand in a circle. Each child needs to hold a small ball and must start passing them clockwise together on your command. Tell them you will act as a battery to keep things moving, dropping each ball received into a container and taking out and passing on another. Tell the children that the passing of the small balls around the circle represents the flow of the electricity around a circuit. Ask one child to turn sideways and not to pass on the balls – this person represents a break in the circuit or a switch and has stopped the flow of electricity. Likewise, you could break the circuit and interrupt the flow by not having a complete circle and so on. Try to replicate one or two of the circuits you have produced for the Group activities.

GROUP ACTIVITIES

1. Set out your selection of prepared circuits that have been numbered 1 to 6 as a circus of activities. Distribute copies of photocopiable page 126 on clipboards and ask the children to move around, in groups, looking at each circuit. Give them a set time for this and rotate the groups at intervals. They should discuss with each other and predict whether or not each of the circuits will allow electricity to flow, recording their prediction on the photocopiable page; then test the prediction and record their findings.
2. Ask the children to write and illustrate a list of 'Rules for making circuits', which might include things such as: 1. Ensure the ends of the wires are bare. 2. Make good connections. 3. Use a good battery. 4. Use a good lamp. 5. Ensure switches are working and turned on. Some children could use the computer to present their work.

DIFFERENTIATION

Differentiate the task by using simpler circuits for lower- attaining children, and more complex circuits with higher-attaining children.

ASSESSMENT

The children should complete the photocopiable page accurately and correctly with understanding of the concept.

PLENARY

Bring the children together to discuss which of the six circuits would or would not allow electricity to flow and to explain why. Reinforce the concept of complete circuits allowing electricity to flow.

OUTCOME

● Can identify circuits which will not let electricity flow.

LESSON 5

Objective	● To know how to make a simple circuit containing two bulbs.
Resources	Batteries, battery holders, lamps, lamp holders, cables, crocodile clips, paper clips, card.
Main activity	Talk about 'illuminations': pictures made with lights. Using the ideas from earlier lessons, the children could, in groups, make a cat's face that has eyes that light up. Copy a cat 'mask' on to card (preferably black). Let the children cut out the face, and colour it if appropriate. Cut out holes for the eyes. The children should then insert two lamps in a circuit and push them through the eye holes in the mask. Make sure the children realise that no animal's eyes really light up – they only ever see by reflected light. Cat's eyes shine in the dark because they are good reflectors. Other spooky variations on this idea would be good for a Hallowe'en display, or to make constellations with more bulb 'stars' in a black paper sky.
Differentiation	Lower-attainers make a circuit with two bulbs to light up the eyes. Higher-attainers make a circuit with more bulbs in a background of their own devising.
Assessment	Through observation and the completion of a working example assess if the outcome has been met.
Plenary	Gather the children together to share completed faces and to test them out.
Outcome	● Can make a circuit with two bulbs.

LESSON 6

Objectives	● To know how to make a simple electrical device. ● To know that electricity is used for communicating with light and sound.
Resources	Batteries, battery holders, lamps, lamp holders, buzzers, switches, cables, crocodile clips, plastic bottles, a copy of *The Lighthouse Keeper's Favourite Stories*, art materials.
Main activity	Read a story from *The Lighthouse Keeper's Favourite Stories* by Rhona and David Armitage, (Scholastic). Talk about electricity powering our means of visual communication, for example signs and traffic lights. Set the children a small group challenge: *Can you build a working model of a lighthouse that has a visual warning – it shines a light – and an audible warning – a fog horn?* 　Introduce the buzzer, if necessary. Talk about other electrically powered warning sounds such as the fire alarm at school. 　The model can be built from small plastic bottles and painted in appropriate colours. The light and buzzer can be controlled by means of a switch.
Differentiation	Use small, mixed-ability groups so that each child has a specific task and so lower attainers can be supported, giving them some sense of success.
Assessment	Observe during the building process: are the children thinking systematically and working collaboratively? Question them during the Plenary and scrutinise the working models. *How did you light up your model? How does a light help people? Can you explain how you made your lighthouse have a buzzer as well as a light? How do you control your signals?*
Plenary	Ask the children to demonstrate the working models and to explain how their lighthouses operate.
Outcome	● Can make a simple electrical device using a bulb and a buzzer effectively.

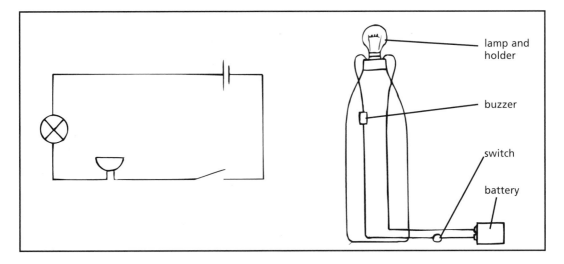

LESSON 7

OBJECTIVES

● To know that electricity is used for communicating with sound.
● To recognise and know how to use a buzzer in a circuit.

RESOURCES

Main teaching activity: A copy of the Morse code (see photocopiable page 127) enlarged on the flip chart or OHP.
Group activities: 1. Batteries, battery holders, lamps, lamp holders, buzzers, switches, cables, crocodile clips, torches, mirrors, copies of photocopiable page 127. **2.** Copies of photocopiable page 128, pens, paper.

PREPARATION

Have ready sufficient resources for the children to work in small groups of two or three.

Vocabulary

buzzers, communication, lights, Morse code

BACKGROUND

We communicate with each other in very many ways which include the use of signs and symbols, the written word, the spoken word, and visual arts like pictures, objects and drama.

The number and diversity of ways in which electricity is being used for communicating is steadily on the increase as new technologies become more and more widespread. The use of electricity in communications started many years ago as the telegraph system was developed and lighthouses began to move from candle power to electrical power. Whilst these are very different ways of communicating, they are both none the less a means of passing a message to people. The telegraph system uses the Morse code; so, util recently, did the communications between ships. The Morse code consists of groups of dots and dashes (shorts and longs), each representing a letter or number.

INTRODUCTION

Ask the children to think of ways in which they can communicate with each other. Include things like speaking, writing, sending signals using flags, smoke or mirrors and by tapping a sound.

Play 'Chinese whispers'. Talk about how communication is a two-way process and that to communicate we need to understand what people are saying. Ask the children to think of other times when we fail to communicate with each other, which might include: when someone is not listening; when we cannot see the other person; when the weather is poor or when there is a breakdown in a system.

MAIN TEACHING ACTIVITY

Sometimes we need to communicate with each other in private. Ask the children to think of different ways in which we could communicate with other people secretly, that is, in code. Introduce the idea of people communicating using codes and the idea of Morse code. Explain the Morse code system and how messages can be sent using a series of dots and dashes. Circuits with switches are very good for codes that can be communicated through a series of on/off switching.

Ask the children to think how they could very simply send a message. Using a large version of the code to follow, clap out one of the most well-known Morse code messages: ...−−−... (three dots, three dashes, three dots, meaning SOS). Then try something simple like your class name, your school, town or village. When the children have grasped the idea, ask one or two to tap out their own names using Morse code. The other children will need to listen carefully and check that the coded messages are correct.

Discuss with the children how they could send a Morse code message to someone so far away that they could not hear the claps. Introduce the idea of using light, such as a torch light or mirror. Talk also about the limitations of this. Ask the children to think about the equipment they would need in order to be able to send and receive Morse code messages over a much further distance, where they could neither see nor hear the sender of the message, for example things like electrical circuits containing bells, buzzers and lights which extend over some distance.

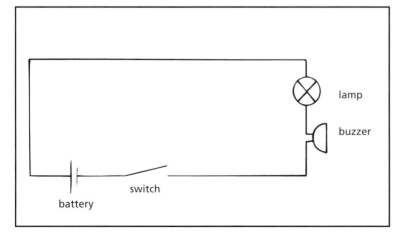

lamp

buzzer

switch

battery

GROUP ACTIVITIES

1. Distribute copies of photocopiable page 127 showing the Morse code. Working in small groups the children should try to send a message using a torch, a mirror, a simple switched circuit with a bulb, a simple switched circuit with a buzzer or a simple switched circuit with a bulb and buzzer. The children should take it in turns to write and send a short message, which the others can receive and interpret. They should record their ideas in words or pictures.

2. Distribute copies of photocopiable page 128 and ask the children to try to crack the codes. The first one is quite simple and also has a simple message to decipher: 'Hello. What is your name?' For the second code, a = 1, b = 2 and so on until z = 26. The message is: 'Never play with electricity.' The children should finish the sheet by devising their own code. Lower-attaining children should devise a simple code and send a short message, whereas higher-attainers should devise a more sophisticated code and send a longer message.

DIFFERENTIATION

Ask lower-attainers to send a simple message in Morse code using either light or sound and higher-attainers to send a simple message in Morse code using both light and sound.

ASSESSMENT

Assess the children's ability to make a complete circuit through observation and questioning. During the lesson observe the children to assess their ability to identify a message that you might send them. Ask them also to send you a predetermined message.

PLENARY

Ask some of the children to send a message to the class while others identify the message. Discuss the 'best' method – what does 'best' mean here? Mention the drawbacks of such a system of communicating, particularly speed, accuracy and reliability.

OUTCOMES

● Understand that electricity is important for 20th and 21st century communication.
● Can make a circuit and send a simple message with it.

LINKS

ICT: manipulating sound (see QCA *Information Technology Scheme of Work for Year 3:* Unit 3B).

LESSON 8

OBJECTIVE

● To know that electricity is used for communication systems.

RESOURCES

Main teaching activity: A selection of pictures cut from magazines and catalogues of electrical goods such as computers, TVs, radios, telephones and so on.
Group activities: 1. A selection of pictures, magazines and catalogues of computers, TVs, radios, telephones and so on; large sheets of plain paper, pens and pencils, scissors, glue, scrap newspaper (to protect tabletops from glue). **2.** A computer with Internet access to send e-mails.

PREPARATION

Prepare two or three pictures to use as an illustrative resource (backed onto card with Blu-Tack fixings). Ensure you have appropriate e-mail facilities and someone to send messages to (perhaps someone else in school or a link school in another part of the country or overseas).

Vocabulary

communication, computer, devices, e-mail, fax, Internet, radio, telephone, television

BACKGROUND

In the 1830s Samuel Morse, inventor of the Morse code, invented a printer to send and receive messages on his electric telegraph system. Since then the way we communicate has been ever-changing. In 1876, Alexander Graham Bell invented the telephone, a system that retains the same basic principles today although the technology has obviously advanced. By 1888, we were seeing the first radio communications when Heinrich Hertz sent and received radio waves in his laboratory. In 1896 Guglielmo Marconi visited England where he established radio as a means of communication, although it was not until 1906 that the first radio broadcasts were made. Scottish TV pioneer John Logie Baird was born in 1888 and it was in 1926 that he first demonstrated his television system. It would be many years before the system was perfected and television became popular. The rest, as they say, is history.

The advances in technology during the 20th century continued as we saw the advent of satellite and microwave communications, video phones, fax machines and computers. In today's changing world the methods of communication that we use are becoming faster and faster and increasingly sophisticated: e-mail and the mobile phone, for example. The modern methods of communication that children are experiencing and that are becoming an integral part of everyday life are all dependent upon electricity. These methods of communication include: television – the broadcast media and its increasing interactivity; radio – the broadcast media and short wave radio communication systems; telephone – voicemail, faxes; computers – e-mail, the Internet, online shopping and so on.

INTRODUCTION

Recap on the disadvantages of the Morse code buzzers and flashers the children made last lesson. Ask them to think of any other means of communicating in which electricity is used, apart from lights and buzzers. Record the children's ideas and display with them some of your prepared pictures. Discuss the Background information.

MAIN TEACHING ACTIVITY

Having identified a range of ways in which electricity is used in communication, explain to the children that they are going to consider how we use these items to communicate. Show the children some of the illustrations or photographs you have prepared from magazines, discuss them and ask the children to give some details of how we communicate using that particular device (for example, with a telephone the method is by dialling numbers and talking, and with a computer the method is through e-mail by tapping the keys on the computer keyboard.)

GROUP ACTIVITIES

1. On a large sheet of plain paper, children glue three or four of your prepared pictures (or cut out and glue their own), or draw their own illustrations, and give written descriptions of how we communicate using each particular device.
2. Ask the group to compose a simple message about the importance of electricity in a communication system that can be sent by e-mail to someone else, perhaps in another school or to someone on your school network who can respond with a reply.

DIFFERENTIATION

Lower-attaining children will complete the activity with cut-outs and a few words. Higher-attaining children will want to draw their own ideas, described in greater detail, and will write a more complex e-mail message.

ASSESSMENT

Look at the children's work for clear identification of devices using electricity and an ability to explain how we communicate with them. Are the children proficient at using e-mail?

PLENARY

Share with each other the e-mails which the children wish to send. Reinforce the part that electricity plays in the effective use of the devices identified and hence our ability to communicate rapidly and reliably worldwide. Recall the previous day's 'world news' from TV or newspapers, for example.

OUTCOME

● Can describe a range of ways in which electricity is used in communications.

LINKS

ICT: e-mail (see QCA *Information Technology Scheme of Work for Year 3:* Unit 3E).

ASSESSMENT

LESSON 9

OBJECTIVES

● To assess the children's knowledge and understanding of the language of simple electrical circuits.
● To assess the children's knowledge and understanding of the use of electricity in communicating.

RESOURCES

Assessment activities: 1. Copies of photocopiable page 129 for each child, pencils. **2.** Paper, pencils, pens

INTRODUCTION

Begin the Assessment activities by reminding the children of all the activities they have done recently about electricity.

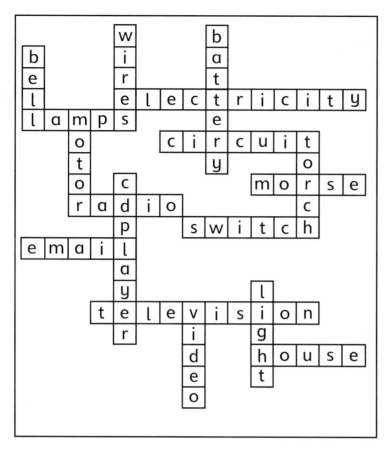

ASSESSMENT ACTIVITY 1

Distribute copies of photocopiable page 129. Tell the children that this crossword is to see what they have learned and uses all the new words they have met recently in science. Allow them time to complete the puzzle individually. You may wish to tell the children that you want to find out what they have understood and that it is important to complete the sheets individually. Beware that the children's literacy skills, rather than their achievement in science, may be a limiting factor here, so verbal responses and/or the support of an adult scribe may be valuable for some less literate children. You will need to collect these in order to mark them effectively.

Answers

1. used in circuits to make a ringing sound (or similar explanation). 2. wires. 3. battery. 4. makes a lamp light up (or similar explanation). 5. lamps. 6. motor. 7. what we call an arrangement of batteries, bulbs and wires (or similar explanation). 8. can be used to flash a message to a friend (or similar explanation). 9. Morse. 10. CD player. 11. radio. 12. switch. 13. e-mail. 14. television. 15. electronic recorded moving pictures (or similar explanation). 16. and 17. light house.

Looking for levels

Assess the children's work on photocopiable page 129 for levels of understanding of electricity and its uses. The children's crossword definitions will be indicative of their understanding. Use your judgement to decide whether or not they show a good level of knowledge and an ability to explain, for example, what makes a circuit.

ASSESSMENT ACTIVITY 2

Write the names and the inventions of the following people on the board or flip chart: Samuel Morse – Morse code; Guglielmo Marconi – radio; Alexander Graham Bell – telephone; John Logie Baird – television; American engineers – computer. Ask the children to write a letter to one of these people explaining how their invention is now used and how we communicate in the 21st century. Ask the children to begin the letter 'Dear Mr…' The children could, for example, write about how we use computers today and how there are many people with home PCs or about how we can now watch live TV pictures not just from the other side of the world but from space.

Answers

For Assessment activity 2, again, verbal responses and/or the support of an adult scribe may be valuable for some less literate children.

Looking for levels

The content of the letters for Assessment activity 2 will give some indication of the children's knowledge of how these devices are now used. Look for examples of uses and an understanding of how we communicate using this equipment.

PLENARY

Discuss the Assessment activities and address any misconceptions still held by the children.

Name

Switches

There are many different types of switches. Here are a few that you might have seen at school or at home.

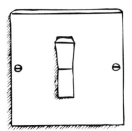
Rocker switch

Pull switch

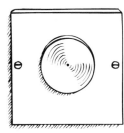
Dimmer switch

Push switch

Think about where you have seen these types of switches used. Look around your classroom and think about your house, then fill in the table below. Two examples are shown for you.

Where seen?	Electrical equipment	Type of switch
Classroom	Lights	Rocker
Home	CD player	Push switch

Have you seen any other switches that are different from these? Draw them here, then see if you can find out what they are called.

Name

Circuits

Look at the circuits drawn below.

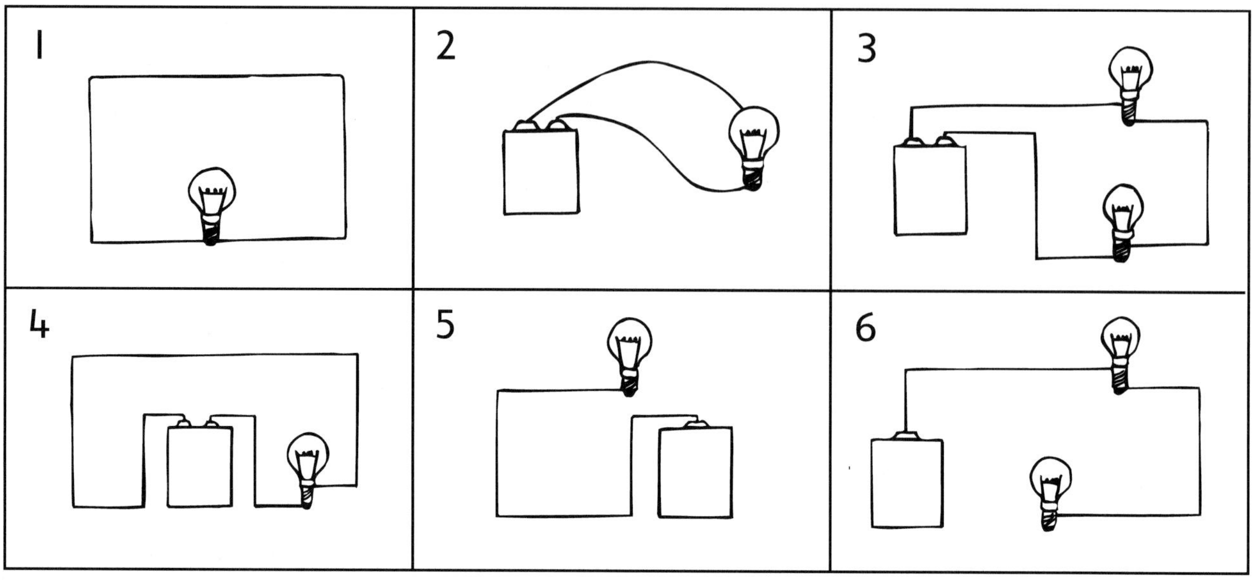

1	2	3
4	5	6

Will each circuit allow electricity to flow?
Fill in your predictions with a tick ✓ in the Yes or No box.

Circuit	Predictions		Test	
	Yes	**No**	**Yes**	**No**
1				
2				
3				
4				
5				
6				

Now check. Do the circuits allow electricity to flow around them?
Tick Yes or No in the Test part of the table.

Complete this sentence.

For the bulbs to light, I needed to make a _____ so that the

_____ can _____ from the _____

around the _____ to the _____ .

Morse code

Here is the Morse code.
Can you clap your name in Morse code? Try it for your friends.

A •—	**K** —•—	**U** ••—	**1** •————
B —•••	**L** •—••	**V** •••—	**2** ••———
C —•—•	**M** ——	**W** •——	**3** •••——
D —••	**N** —•	**X** —••	**4** ••••—
E •	**O** ———	**Y** —•——	**5** •••••
F ••—	**P** •——•	**Z** ——••	**6** —••••
G ——•	**Q** ——•—		**7** ——•••
H ••••	**R** •—•		**8** ———•••
I ••	**S** •••		**9** ————•
J •———	**T** —		**10** —————

Using the available equipment devise three ways of sending messages using Morse code. Describe your three ideas using words or pictures.

Try to send a simple message to your friends in each way.
Which of your methods do you think is best? Why?

Name

Code breaker

The Morse code is just one way of sending a secret message.
It's easy to devise a code – here are two for you to crack.

The first code is done for you, but what is the message?

a	b	c	d	e	f	g	h	i	j	k	l	m	n	o	p	q	r	s	t	u	v	w	x	y	z
z	y	x	w	v	u	t	s	r	q	p	o	n	m	l	k	j	i	h	g	f	e	d	c	b	a

s	v	o	o	l		d	s	z	g		b	l	f	i		m	z	n	v	?

Write your reply here in code.

Now try to read the message by cracking this code.

14	5	22	5	18	16	12	1	25	23	9	20	8	5	12	5	3	20	18	9	3	9	20	25

Fill in the code.

a	b	c	d	e	f	g	h	i	j	k	l	m	n	o	p	q	r	s	t	u	v	w	x	y	z

Try to make up a code of your own. Send a friend a message and ask them to try and crack the code.

Electricity and communication

Here are some words and some meanings. Fill in the missing words and meanings. Then fit all the words into the grid below.

	Word	Clue
1.	bell	
2.		These are used to join the components in a circuit.
3.		This is a source of electricity.
4.	electricity	
5.		These are used to give us light.
6.		This uses electrical energy to make things turn.
7.	circuit	
8.	torch	
9.		This is a type of code.
10.		We use this to listen to music on compact disc.
11.		Marconi invented this.
12.		Use this to control the flow of electricity.
13.		A means of sending a message using a computer.
14.		We watch this for fun and learning.
15.	video	
16, 17.		This warns ships of rocks.

Magnets and springs

ORGANISATION (13 LESSONS)

	OBJECTIVES	MAIN ACTIVITY	GROUP ACTIVITIES	PLENARY	OUTCOMES
LESSON 1	● To ascertain the children's current knowledge of forces and motion from their work in KS1/P1–3.	Concept mapping.	Drawing concept cartoons. Looking at magnetic and non-magnetic materials.	Sharing ideas and asking questions.	● Teacher can assess the level of the children in the class. ● Teacher can arrange children in appropriate class groups.
LESSON 2	● To know that there are forces between magnets which push and pull. ● To make observations.	Looking at the poles of magnets.	Completing a worksheet on magnets. Looking at magnets and their properties. Investigating repulsion and attraction in magnets.	Agreeing a general rule for the attraction and repulsion properties of magnets.	● Can demonstrate how a magnet is attracted and repelled by another magnet. ● Can make observations.
LESSON 3	● To know that some materials are magnetic and others are not. ● To be able to make observations and comparisons.	Testing materials for attraction by a magnet.	Testing different types of metal for magnetic attraction. Researching magnetic attraction in metals.	Comparing results and research.	● Can recognise magnetic and non-magnetic materials.
LESSON 4	● To know that magnets have uses.	Looking at the uses of magnets.	Using secondary sources to explore uses of magnets. Writing a 'Guide to...' the uses of magnets.	Drawing conclusions about the range of uses of magnets.	● Can describe a range of uses of magnets.
LESSON 5	● To know that magnets can be tested for strength. ● To be able to plan and carry out a fair test.	Planning an investigation to test the strength of magnets.	Investigating the strength of magnets. Making magnets.	Discussing findings and feedback on ensuring a fair test was carried out.	● Can consider what makes a fair test. ● Can use simple equipment safely. ● Can describe their observations using scientific vocabulary.
LESSON 6	● To know that springs and elastic bands exert forces.	Brainstorming knowledge of springs.	Experiencing and describing a selection of springs and elastic bands. Looking at the direction of the forces exerted by springs and elastic bands.	Demonstration of push and pull forces in springs.	● Can recognise the pushes and pulls made by springs. ● Can recognise the forces exerted by a stretched elastic band.
LESSON 7	● To know that springs are used in a variety of ways.	Completing a survey of springs.		Sharing of survey findings.	● Can describe how springs are used in a variety of ways.
LESSON 8	● To investigate the forces exerted by springs and elastic bands.	Designing and making a simple ballista.		Demonstration by the children.	● Know that an elastic band can exert a force. ● Can recognise that a force acts in a particular direction.
LESSON 9	● To know that the force exerted by an elastic band depends on how much it is stretched. ● To make observations, measure in standard measures and to draw conclusions from results.	Using simple catapults to project a missile.	Investigation using a flat board catapult into the relationship between stretch and the force exerted by an elastic band. Making a simple paddle boat.	Children's explanation of their findings and the relationships.	● Can describe the relationship between the amount an elastic band stretches and the force that it exerts. ● Can make observations, measure in standard measures and draw conclusions from results.

ORGANISATION (13 LESSONS)

	OBJECTIVES	MAIN ACTIVITY	GROUP ACTIVITIES	PLENARY	OUTCOMES
LESSON 10	● To know that elastic bands exert forces that can be used to drive things along.	Making cotton reel vehicles.		Holding a 'Cotton reel grand prix'.	● Can recognise that elastic bands exert forces that can be used to drive things along.
LESSON 11	● To know that energy can change forms.	Looking at stored and movement energy.	Completing a worksheet on energy transfer. Designing and building a model which shows energy change.	Demonstrating models.	● Can recognise that energy can change forms. ● Can recognise that stored and electrical energy can be changed into movement energy.
LESSON 12	● To know that heat is a form of energy and it may be supplied by several sources. ● To know that energy can change forms.	Looking at uses of heat energy.	Identifying sources of heat energy and its uses.	Sharing ideas about how heat energy is used.	● Can recognise that heat is a form of energy. ● Can recognise different sources of heat energy. ● Can recognise different applications of heat in everyday life.

	OBJECTIVES	ACTIVITY 1	ACTIVITY 2
ASSESSMENT 13	● To assess the children's knowledge of the properties of magnets, types of forces and the uses of springs.	Describing bar magnets and attraction and repulsion.	Identifying pushes and pulls and the uses of springs.

LESSON 1

OBJECTIVES

● To ascertain the children's current knowledge of forces and motion from their work in KS1/P1–3.

RESOURCES

Main teaching activity: Flip chart or board, pens.
Group activities: 1 and 2. Large sheets of paper, pens, pencils.

BACKGROUND

In Key Stage 1/Primary 1–3 the children will have had the opportunity to become familiar with some of the basic principles of magnets in that they will have used magnets when investigating the properties of some materials. They will probably not have used or considered magnets in terms of a force which can make something move, stop or change direction or shape.

INTRODUCTION

Begin the lesson by talking to the children about work they will have covered in Key Stage 1/ Primary 1–3. Explain that they will be building on what they learned then and discovering a little more about forces.

MAIN TEACHING ACTIVITY

The children should work in small groups to develop a concept map of forces and, in particular, ways of making things move and stop. They should express all their ideas and knowledge about the subject and then attempt to join their ideas with lines and arrows to produce a map. A large class concept map can be drawn using the groups' ideas. Some of the key ideas, which are relevant to Key Stage 1/Primary 1–3 will include: forces make things move; forces can make things go faster, change direction or slow down; there are many types of force including friction, pushes, pulls, gravity and magnetism; and magnets attract some materials but not others.

GROUP ACTIVITIES

1. Ask the children to draw a concept cartoon to show that magnets attract certain materials, that magnets do not attract some materials, that magnets can attract each other, and that magnets have uses.

2. Write two headings on the board or flip chart: 'Attracted by magnets' and 'Not attracted by magnets'. Ask the children to copy the headings and write the names of as many materials that they can think of in each column, giving very careful consideration to their choices.

DIFFERENTIATION

Prompt lower-attaining children's thinking when compiling the concept map. Encourage higher-attaining children to annotate their concept cartoon in detail.

ASSESSMENT

In using the Group activities look for evidence that the children have some understanding of forces, motion and magnetism. Most children will know that pushes and pulls make things move and most should be able to recognise that some materials are attracted by magnets while other materials are not. It is unlikely any will have connected the two and understood that magnets exert forces, although they may suggest that magnets can make things move.

PLENARY

Share ideas and encourage the children to begin to formulate their own questions about what they think they would like to find out about.

OUTCOMES

- Teacher can assess the level of the children in the class.
- Teacher can arrange children in appropriate class groups.

LESSON 2

OBJECTIVES

- To know that there are forces between magnets which push and pull.
- To make observations.

RESOURCES

Introduction: A magnetic travel game.
Main teaching activity: A selection of bar magnets of different strengths, preferably one or more per child.
Group activities: 1. The magnets from the Main teaching activity, photocopiable page 147.
2. Strong, thin thread; pieces of polystyrene (for example from packing, cut into pieces big enough to sit a magnet on); trays of water.

PREPARATION

Check the magnets are sufficiently magnetic! School magnets are often damaged and hence demagnetised.

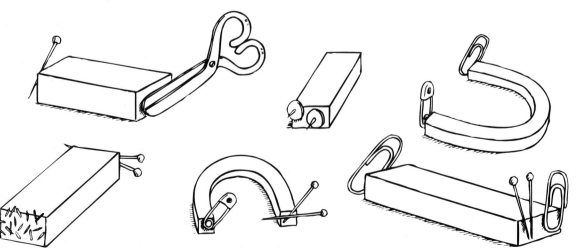

Vocabulary
attract, magnet, magnetism, north, poles, repel, south

BACKGROUND

It is difficult to provide a definition of magnetism other than to say that magnetism is a force that attracts certain materials to it. Iron, cobalt, nickel and their alloys such as steel and alnico are all attracted to magnets, whereas all other materials do not have any magnetic attraction.

Magnetism, unlike most other forces except gravity, can work from a distance. A force is a push or a pull: it can make something slow down, speed up or change direction or shape. Magnetism can do just that. Since magnets come in different strengths their effects can be similarly different. A strong magnet can be effective over a much greater distance or through much thicker non-magnetic materials. Magnets of the same strength can, like all equal forces, counterbalance each other: if you placed a piece of iron between two magnets of equal strength the iron would remain stationary. If on the other hand one magnet was brought closer, its magnetic force would have a greater effect and the iron would move.

Every magnet, whatever its shape, has a north pole and a south pole. It is at these poles that the magnetic force is concentrated. When the poles of the two magnets are brought together, like poles (two north poles or two south poles) repel each other, and unlike poles (a north pole and a south pole) attract.

Magnets can be made by bringing iron into close contact with a magnet, by stroking it with another magnet or by inducing magnetism with a current of electricity. Heating, hammering and banging magnets can cause the domains to become jumbled again and so the material will lose its magnetism. It is important then that magnets are treated carefully, not dropped or damaged, and because magnetic properties are used in televisions, cassette tapes and computer floppy disks it is also important to keep these well away from the effects of magnets.

The Earth itself acts like a huge bar magnet. Perhaps confusingly, the Earth's geographic North Pole is magnetically a south pole. This is because the Earth's magnetic north pole attracts the north poles of magnets – because unlike poles attract, it must be that the Earth's magnetic north is really a south-seeking pole. It must also be remembered that the geographic North Pole and the magnetic north pole are not at the same point on the Earth.

INTRODUCTION

Begin the lesson using a children's travel game (many use magnets to hold the pieces on) or magnetic letters and numbers as a visual aid to encourage the children to begin to think about magnets. Ask them why the letters appear to stick on the board and why the pieces on the travel game have not fallen off. Most should be able to tell you that they are magnets or magnetic. Ask the children if they can think of the words we use when a magnet 'sticks'. Introduce the words 'attract' and 'repel' (although we shall see that repel in magnetic terms has a more active effect than simply 'not sticking').

MAIN TEACHING ACTIVITY

Distribute magnets to the children and ask them to tell you about the magnets they have. Talk about and introduce the idea that there are two ends to a magnet called poles. These poles, indicated by N and S, are the north and south poles of the magnet. Ask the children to work in pairs to see what happens when these poles are brought together. Ask them to try like poles and unlike poles. Discuss the outcomes before moving on to complete photocopiable page 147.

GROUP ACTIVITIES

1. Distribute copies of photocopiable page 147 and ask the children to read through the sheet with you, and then complete it by exploring with the magnets. If resources are short, let the children work in pairs or fours with two magnets.

2. Let the children investigate repulsion and attraction further. Different groups could try suspending a magnet so that it spins freely, then bringing another magnet towards it. Repeat at each end of the magnet. They could also try floating a magnet on a small piece of polystyrene in a tray of water. Again bring the poles together in different combinations.

In each case, the children should observe what happens and attempt to answer: *Which direction does the magnet point when allowed to move freely? Can you make up a general rule based on what you have found out about magnets repelling and attracting?*

DIFFERENTIATION

Lower-attaining children could record their findings diagrammatically. Higher-attaining children can go on to record their findings in writing.

ASSESSMENT

Mark the children's work for evidence of understanding. The diagrams should indicate that like poles repel and unlike poles attract.

PLENARY

Bring the children together to discuss the activities during the lesson and for them to share with each other their ideas for a general rule about repulsion and attraction. Attempt to come to an agreed statement that can be used to reinforce the aims of the lesson, such as: 'When we brought two ends of magnets together that were the same they repelled each other.' and 'When we brought two ends of magnets together that were different they were attracted to each other.' Use the work carried out during the Group activities to reinforce these statements.

OUTCOMES

- Can demonstrate how a magnet is attracted and repelled by another magnet.
- Can make observations.

LESSON 3

OBJECTIVES

- To know that some materials are magnetic and others are not.
- To be able to make observations and comparisons.

RESOURCES

Main teaching activity: A collection of different magnetic and non-magnetic materials (in trays), magnets.
Group activities: 1. A collection of objects as for the Main teaching activity, magnets, large sheets of paper, pens, pencils. **2.** Secondary sources of information.

PREPARATION

Gather the materials and magnets together and have these to hand.

Vocabulary

attract, magnet, magnetised, magnetism, north, poles, repel, south

BACKGROUND

Some materials cannot be made into magnets and similarly are neither attracted to nor repelled by them. Magnets attract metals, but not all metals. Be aware that in carrying out investigations into which materials are attracted by a magnet and which are not, it is important to remember that the only materials attracted are iron, steel, nickel and cobalt. Some objects may be made out of an alloy, which contains large amounts of iron. Some coins, for example, are magnetic because of this, while others have less or no iron and so are not magnetic. Similarly, things which you may think should not be attracted to magnets may have a coating under which is steel. So not everything may be as it seems.

The area around a magnet that experiences the effects of the magnetic force is called the 'magnetic field'. While the magnetic field cannot be seen, its effects can. By using iron filings or a plotting compass it is possible to see the extent of the magnetic field. This force exerted by a magnet is used widely (see Lesson 4) but, as we have already seen, its effects can only be felt by certain materials.

INTRODUCTION

Revise magnets repelling and attracting. Ask the children if they can tell you what sort of materials (or objects, such as the fridge) magnets are attracted to. Compile a list of suggestions on the board. Talk about the difference between 'repulsion' (a push away) and 'non-attraction' (no reaction). Tell the children that in this lesson they will be finding out about materials that are magnetic and those that are not.

Materials attracted by magnets	Materials not attracted by magnets*
iron steel nickel cobalt	brass tin aluminium wood water plastic

*This list could be added to with the names of very many other materials.

MAIN TEACHING ACTIVITY

Write the headings 'Attracted by magnets' and 'Not attracted by magnets' on the board or flip chart. Distribute large sheets of paper, the magnets and selections of various materials/objects. Ask the children to test each item to see if it is attracted to the magnet or not. This could be done in groups, as a circus, or each child's results collated on to a large sheet of paper using the headings you have written. Provide each group of children with a tray containing the necessary resources (see above). These trays could be different and passed around after a given time. Each child in the group could have a responsibility, such as object selector, material identifier, predictor, tester, recorder. The children could change responsibilities so that each gets a 'turn'.

GROUP ACTIVITIES

1. Distribute further large sheets of paper. The children should investigate further items in the classroom and around school. This time, however, they should concentrate specifically on items that are metal or appear to be metal. Children record their thoughts about the objects that are and are not attracted by the magnet.

2. The children could use secondary sources to try to research which metals are attracted by magnets and which are not. Aluminium and tin cans are good examples.

DIFFERENTIATION

Lower-attaining children concentrate on testing materials for attraction to magnets, higher-attaining children extend their work to research into magnetic/non-magnetic metals.

ASSESSMENT

Looking at the children's work will give a good indication of whether the children have learned that some materials are attracted by magnets or not. Discussion during the Group activities will support this judgement.

PLENARY

Bring the children together and discuss the list they have made. Compare it with the lists written earlier. Those who have been researching metals could feed back their findings.

OUTCOME

● Can recognise magnetic and non-magnetic materials.

LINKS

Unit 5: Materials.
Unit 6, Lesson 4.

LESSON 4

OBJECTIVE

● To know that magnets have uses.

RESOURCES

Main teaching activity: Flip chart or board, pens; examples of objects that use magnetism to work, preferably that can be taken apart to expose the magnet, such as electric bells, motors, loudspeakers; an old cassette recorder and/or computer disk drive (try car boot sales).
Group activities: 1 and 2. Paper, pens, pencils; secondary sources of information such as books, videos, CD-ROMs or the Internet.

PREPARATION

Ensure that the secondary resources are available and contain appropriate information. Search for suitable websites.

Vocabulary
burglar alarms,
compasses,
door latches,
metal detectors,
telephones,
vending machines

BACKGROUND

Magnets and the characteristics and properties of magnetism are used in a wide variety of ways all around us, though the children are unlikely to recognise many of them. The children need only to know that these items use magnets, not all the science of how – keep it simple.

Bells, motors and loudspeakers use electricity to make magnetism. In an electric bell, a magnet attracts the bell clapper. Another major use of magnetism is in the recording of data. Magnetic tape is used in tape recorders where patterns are applied to the tape by the tape head. On replay, this magnetic patterned tape causes an electrical signal in the head that then reproduces the sound. Data on computer hard and floppy disks is recorded in the same way. (CD-ROMs are different, however, and are recorded and reproduced using a tiny laser beam.) Other uses of magnets include: burglar alarms, telephones, door latches, vending machines, metal detectors, moving large quantities of iron and steel, separating materials, compasses.

INTRODUCTION

Reinforce the concepts covered so far. Ask the children if they can think of any uses for magnets. If they have difficulty, show them again your magnetic travel game, or magnetic letters.

MAIN TEACHING ACTIVITY

Show the children any resources you have collected together: an electric bell, a (classroom) motor, or an old loudspeaker. Show the children that these all have magnets in them to make them work. Talk about floppy disks and cassette tape and how they use magnets to record data. Highlight the dangers of putting magnets near such items. (You will lose the data stored on the disk or tape.) Begin to compile a list of uses for magnets.

GROUP ACTIVITIES

1. Ask the children to write down all the uses of magnets you have discussed and then to add more from any available secondary sources of information.
2. Tell the children to go on to use the secondary sources to investigate one or two uses of magnets in more detail according to their abilities. They could present their findings as an information sheet or poster as a 'Guide to…' the uses of magnets.

DIFFERENTIATION

Lower-attaining children may need support in making their list. Higher-attainers should be able to undertake some independent research which could be presented with annotated diagrams.

ASSESSMENT

The children's posters will indicate their level of understanding. All the children should be able to find some uses for magnets.

PLENARY

Come back together and discuss the uses that the children have found. Draw a conclusion about the use of magnets in terms of being widespread – if hidden – and very important in a range of everyday objects.

OUTCOME

- Can describe a range of uses for magnets.

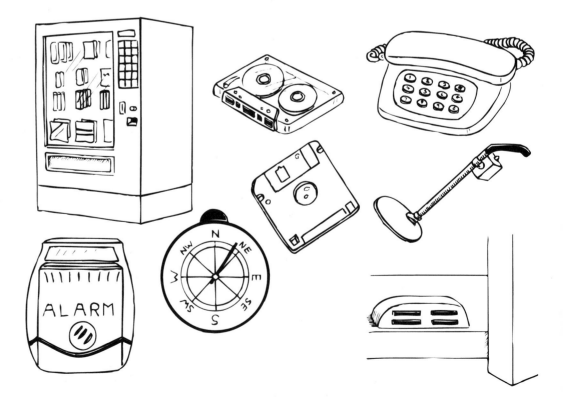

LESSON 5

OBJECTIVES
● To know that magnets can be tested for strength.
● To be able to plan and carry out a fair test.

RESOURCES
Main teaching activity: Paper, pens, pencils.
Group activities: 1. Bar magnets, horseshoe magnets, paper clips, paper, card, cloth, writing and drawing materials. **2.** Bar magnets, steel pins or nails, paper clips.

Vocabulary

horseshoe magnet,
bar magnet

BACKGROUND
Magnets come in different strengths depending on what they are made from, how they are magnetised and how they are kept. Not all magnets are the same: iron is usually easier to magnetise, but loses its magnetism much more quickly and is used to form temporary magnets. Steel, however, retains its magnetism much better and is used to make permanent magnets. More expensive magnets are likely to last longer than cheaper ones, but if magnets are not treated with care they will lose their magnetism. The incorrect storage, heating and hitting of magnets will all cause damage.

Strong magnets can attract other magnetic materials over larger distances, through non-magnetic materials and through a vacuum. The strongest area of the magnetic field is at the poles; the area down the length of, say, a bar magnet is generally much weaker.

INTRODUCTION
Remind the children that last lesson they were looking at how magnets have a wide variety of uses. Ask the children if they think, therefore, that all magnets are the same. Talk about magnets being of varying sizes and strengths. Ask the children if they can think of a fair way to test a magnet to find out how strong it is. Collect suggestions.

MAIN TEACHING ACTIVITY
Together, plan an investigation to test the strength of the magnets you have. The children could look at: the number of paper clips which can be attracted in a line; whether the size of the magnet affects its strength; which are stronger – horseshoe or bar magnets; how close something needs to be to a magnet before it is attracted; the thickness of materials through which a magnet can attract, for example, layers of paper, card or cloth.

The class could work in groups to plan their investigations into one of these different factors. Write on the board or flip chart a writing frame to help the children with the format and to direct their thinking under the following headings: 'My question'; 'What I will do to find the answer'; 'What I will need'; 'What I think will happen'. Highlight making this a fair test. They should record thus: for 'My question' they write down what they are trying to find out; for 'What I will do to find the answer' they write down how they are going to carry out the investigation; for 'What I will need' they draw or write down all the things they will use; and for 'What I think will happen' they predict what they think may happen.

GROUP ACTIVITIES
1. In groups, the children should carry out their investigation, recording their work as they go along under headings such as: 'This is what I did', where they record how they carried out their test; 'This is what I found out' where they should draw up a table for results something like the one shown below; and 'This is what I now know' where they should write down what they have learned from this investigation. Write these headings on the board or flip chart for children to copy if need be.

2. Ask the children to use a bar magnet and a steel nail or needle to create a new magnet. (Make at least twenty strokes in the same direction with a magnet to magnetise the nail.) The group can test the new magnet's strength.

Type of magnet	Number of paper clips

DIFFERENTIATION
In this lesson the children could work in mixed-ability groups with the higher-attainers supporting the lower-attainers with differentiation by outcome.

ASSESSMENT

Review the children's reports of their investigation, looking for their ability to plan and carry out the investigation and for their understanding that magnets can be tested for strength. Do they understand what they have done that makes this a fair test?

PLENARY

Discuss with the children the investigation they have carried out. Ask the children to explain what they have done, what they have found out and how they ensured a fair test.

OUTCOMES

- Can consider what makes a fair test.
- Can use simple equipment safely.
- Can describe their observations using scientific vocabulary.

LESSON 6

OBJECTIVE

- To know that springs and elastic bands exert forces.

RESOURCES

Main teaching activity: Flip chart, paper, pens.
Group activities: 1. A collection of springs and elastic bands (for example, from the inside of ballpoint pens, from an old clock, from machinery, from an old push-chair or pram). **2.** Springs, elastic bands, copies of photocopiable page 148.

Vocabulary

elastic band, exert, force, pull, push, spring

BACKGROUND

Forces exist all around us. A force acting on an object or body can make the object move, speed up, slow down, change direction, and can change the shape of the object.

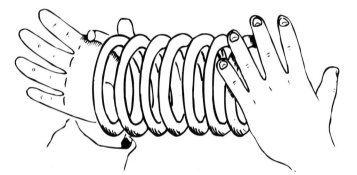

There are several different types of forces, the two we are concerned with here are stretching and compression. The children will have already looked at forces in terms of push and pull, so these can now be introduced in terms of a stretching force being the same as a pull, and a compression force being the same as a push.

Springs of varying sizes have an equally varying range of uses, from the tiny spring in a ballpoint pen to the suspension springs on large vehicles, but all work in the same way. When a mass is hung from a spring, the force of gravity pulling on the mass pulls the spring and causes it to stretch. The spring itself can support this weight because it in turn exerts a pull force on the mass. This pull in the spring is called tension.

The opposite of stretching, in this sense, is compression. When a spring is compressed, a force is exerted by the spring on whatever is causing the compression and at the same time the mass compressing the spring is also exerting a force on it. For example, if you were to sit on a sprung chair your mass, together with gravity, would exert a downward force on the springs causing them to compress. At the same time, the springs would be exerting an upward force on you. When the two forces are equal you stop sinking into the chair and remain still: the upward force from the springs is effectively supporting you.

Springs, then, can exert two forces: a stretching force and a compression force. Elastic bands are slightly different. Springs stretch and compress because of the way the material has been shaped – the material the spring is made from only stretches to a limited extent. However, some materials do stretch rather more and still return to their original size when the force on them is removed. These materials are said to be elastic. While the spring may be said to have elastic properties, its material does not stretch as much as, say, rubber. A rubber band is very elastic and will stretch when a force is exerted upon it. When the force is removed it will return to its original shape. This is not compression since the material is merely returning to its original shape. If you try to exert a compression force upon a rubber band you would not succeed since there is no useful or significant opposite force.

INTRODUCTION

Begin the lesson by looking at a simple retractable ballpoint pen. Ask the children if they know how the pen refill clicks in and out. Take it apart to investigate. Show the children the spring, ask them what it is and what they think it does.

MAIN TEACHING ACTIVITY

Elicit from the children what they know already about forces. They should know in simple terms that a force is a push or a pull (or a twist or a squash, maybe), can make an object move, and then change speed and/or direction, and can change the shape of an object.

Talk about how springs can be used with a push or pull and that when we push or pull a spring we are exerting a force on it. Discuss also that the spring itself is exerting a force: this is easily felt pushing back when a spring is squashed. Ideas can be collated onto a simple class concept map on a large sheet of paper or the board.

GROUP ACTIVITIES

1. Distribute a selection of springs to the children for them to look at and handle. Ask them to pull and push the springs and to describe the direction of the force on their hands. The children should record their work with comments such as: 'When I stretch the spring, I feel a pull on my hand' or 'When I push the spring, it pushes on me'. Remind the children to take care when using springs – overstretched springs may break and could injure.

2. Distribute copies of photocopiable page 148 and read through it together. Explain the tasks to the children. Say that for every force, not just in springs, there is a force the opposite way. The sheet asks them to mark on the diagrams the direction of the forces exerted by themselves and by the spring. As an extension activity some children could repeat this with elastic bands and decide why it would be difficult to repeat the push test.

DIFFERENTIATION

Lower-attaining children should use only springs in the Group activities and may need assistance in developing appropriate vocabulary to explain their findings. Higher-attaining children use springs and elastic bands in the Group activities and use more explicit scientific vocabulary to explain the forces exerted.

ASSESSMENT

Discuss with the children their experiences of pushing and pulling the springs and elastic bands; try to encourage them to describe what they felt and to explain what is happening. Listen for use of appropriate vocabulary that shows understanding and knowledge of the exertion of a force. Looking at the children's work will also give an indication of understanding if the children have been able to mark the direction of the forces correctly on the worksheet.

PLENARY

Bring the children together at the end of the lesson and recap on the Group activities. Ask the children to demonstrate both types of force – pushes and pulls – and to begin to discuss how these forces are used.

OUTCOMES

- Can recognise the pushes and pulls made by springs.
- Can recognise the forces exerted by a stretched elastic band.

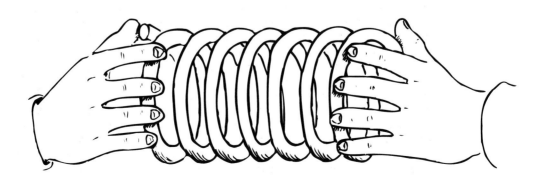

LESSON 7

Objective	• To know that springs are used in a variety of ways.
Resources	A collection of objects with springs, access to other parts of the school, secondary sources of information.
Main activity	Carry out a survey of your classroom or school to find as many uses for springs as you possibly can. You might find springs in doors, pens, spring balances, clocks and watches. Choose one of the uses for springs and examine it in more detail. Find out and record in words and pictures how the spring works, what it does and what would happen if it was not there. Does this spring use a push or a pull to perform its function?
Differentiation	Lower-attaining children concentrate more on identifying uses for springs. Higher-attainers move more quickly on to what function the spring performs.
Assessment	Assess the children's understanding through discussion with them during the survey. Can they identify a number of different uses?
Plenary	Bring the class together to share findings and discuss how many uses people have found. Ask: *Can anyone explain the function of the spring?* (for example, in a ballpoint pen it causes the refill to retract.)
Outcome	• Can describe how springs are used in a variety of ways.

LESSON 8

Objective	• To investigate the forces exerted by springs and elastic bands.
Resources	A variety of pieces of wood, elastic bands, simple hand tools, glue, safe missiles.
Main activity	Design and make a simple ballista that will project a missile in a particular direction. In projecting the missile, the children should understand that the force required to move the missile is being exerted in a particular direction. The ballistas could be tested and a challenge match arranged to see which group's device can project a missile the furthest, most accurately, or the highest. Apart from the concept of the direction of the force there is also the possibility of investigating variables that affect the performance of the device: weight of missile, pull back on the sling, angle of release of the missile. 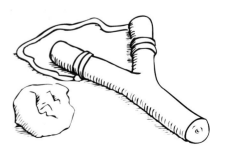
Differentiation	Lower-attainers make a simple catapult device. Higher-attainers investigate the trajectory of the missile.
Assessment	During construction and testing ask the children to explain what they are doing and look for the use of appropriate language and an ability to explain how the forces are acting on the missile.
Plenary	Bring the class together and test the ballistas under a challenge situation. Discuss the notion of the force being exerted and it acting in a particular direction, such as sending the missile towards its target.
Outcomes	• Know that an elastic band can exert a force. • Can recognise that a force acts in a particular direction.

LESSON 9

OBJECTIVES

● To know that the force exerted by an elastic band depends on how much it is stretched.
● To make observations, measure in standard measures and to draw conclusions from results.

RESOURCES

Main teaching activity: Simple toy catapults, projectiles.
Group activities: 1. Flat board catapults (one per group – see Preparation), toy cars, rulers, photocopiable page 149. **2.** Thin balsa wood, simple hand tools, nails, card, elastic bands, a water trough (guttering).

PREPARATION

Make flat board catapults to project your toy cars similar to that shown opposite:

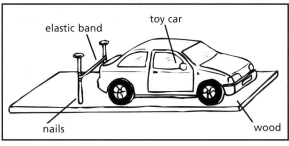

BACKGROUND

Vocabulary
exert, force, measurement, prediction

Most materials will stretch to some extent when a force is applied to them. The 'elasticity' of a material is the extent to which it will return to its original size and shape following the application of a force to it. English inventor and scientist Robert Hooke (1635–1702) is best remembered for his work on elasticity. Hooke found that the stretch (in an elastic band, for example) is directly proportional to the added load, up to a certain point. Clearly if you were to continue adding masses, there will come a point where the elastic band will no longer return to its original size and shape when the mass is removed. At this point the material is said to have reached its extent of elasticity and will remain in a deformed state. This principle clearly has it uses, mainly in weighing equipment.

Materials like steel, iron, copper and concrete have very little elasticity, while a material like rubber (or more usually plastic these days), is very elastic.

INTRODUCTION

Begin the lesson by recapping the learning from previous lessons, asking the children to tell you all they can about forces. Ask the children to recall the work they have done using elastic bands and how they exert a force upon objects to make them speed up, slow down or move in a particular direction. Ask the children to think of ways that this idea is used – give hints along the lines of Robin Hood's bow and the use of medieval ballistas to lead the discussion into catapults. Ask the children if they know how a bow and arrow works and how someone like Robin Hood was able to get his arrows to travel over great distances. Tell the children that they are going to use simple catapults to see who can send something over the greatest distance. Remind the children of the dangers of catapults and stress that they must not fire at anyone.

MAIN TEACHING ACTIVITY

Sit the children in a horseshoe shape, behind the catapults, and fire the toys away from the group. Using a number of simple catapults, the sort available cheaply from many toy shops, carry out a challenge to see who can catapult an object the furthest distance. During this time talk to the children about the fairness of this as a scientific investigation. Would this be a good way to accurately measure the effect of pulling the elastic back further in order to send the projectile further?

Ask the children to consider all the factors that determine the distance that the projectile will travel. Variables may include: the angle of projection; the strength of the person; the mass of the projectile. These are all factors that will affect the trajectory of the projectile. Ask the children to think of a way of limiting these variables and of testing to see if the force exerted by an elastic band has an effect on the distance a projectile will travel. A flat board catapult will go some way to addressing some of these variables.

GROUP ACTIVITIES

1. Ask the children to work in groups of four to use the flat board catapult to investigate the relationship between the amount an elastic band stretches and the force that it exerts by catapulting a toy car along a surface. They should predict what they think will happen before using the flat board catapult to help them determine the distance the elastic is stretched and the distance the car travels.

This equipment and the careful measuring of the retraction should mean that a fair test can be carried out without uncontrollable variables. During the investigation the children should record their results on a copy of photocopiable page 149 and then complete the questions.

2. Make a simple paddle boat using balsa wood. Investigate the relationship between the number of turns of the paddle and the distance travelled. Test them in a long trough of water – a section of guttering is ideal.

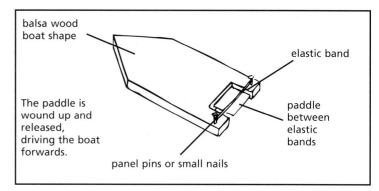

balsa wood boat shape

elastic band

The paddle is wound up and released, driving the boat forwards.

paddle between elastic bands

panel pins or small nails

DIFFERENTIATION

Lower-attaining children may require support to measure how far back the band is pulled the distance the car travels, and to formulate their explanations for the photocopiable page. They may not be able to express this in writing so you may wish to ask them some appropriate questions while they are carrying out the investigation.

ASSESSMENT

Scrutinise the children's work for evidence of understanding. Are they able to explain what happens when the elastic band is pulled back further? (The force exerted is greater.)

PLENARY

Discuss the investigation with the children and the conclusions they have come to. Ask some of them to explain their understanding of the relationship between the amount the elastic band stretches and the force that it exerts. They can demonstrate its effect with their flat board catapult: 'The further I pull the band back, the further the car travels, so the bigger the force that I am making must be.'

OUTCOMES

● Can describe the relationship between the amount an elastic band stretches and the force that it exerts.
● Can make observations, measure in standard measures and draw conclusions from results.

LESSON 10

Objective	● To know that elastic bands exert forces that can be used to drive things along.
Resources	Cotton reels, elastic bands, spent matches, a candle.
Main activity	Use cotton reels and elastic bands to make an elastic-band-powered vehicle. Thread an elastic band through the cotton reel, anchoring it at one end with a piece of match. At the other end, wax the cotton reel or thread a bead onto the elastic. Next, insert a match through the elastic band and wind it up until secure. Continue to wind before allowing the elastic band to unwind and drive the vehicle forward. Test the vehicle to see how many turns are needed to make the vehicle move. Remind the children not to under- or over-wind the elastic band. The children can present their findings in an appropriate way – written, diagrammatically or verbally.
Differentiation	Differentiate by outcome.
Assessment	Through looking at the children's findings, observations and by discussion, establish if the children have understood that it is the elastic band exerting a force that drives the vehicle. Ask questions such as: *What made the toy car move? Why did it stop?*
Plenary	Ask the children to demonstrate their investigation and to explain the forces that started and stopped their cotton reel vehicles. Hold a 'Cotton reel grand prix'.
Outcome	● Can recognise that elastic bands exert forces that can be used to drive things along.

half matchstick as anchor for other end of elastic band

cotton reel

elastic band

LESSON 11

OBJECTIVE
- To know that energy can change forms.

RESOURCES

Main teaching activity: Springs and elastic bands.
Group activities: 1. Photocopiable page 150, pens, pencils **2.** Model-making materials, tools, glue, Lego or similar construction sets.

Vocabulary
chemical, electrical, heat, light, movement, nuclear, solar, sound, stored

BACKGROUND

In everyday conversation the meaning attached to the word 'energy' is often different from that used in the scientific world. 'Energy' does not make things move – forces do. We cannot see or feel energy itself; we can only observe its effects. Energy is needed to make objects move, speed them up, change their direction, heat them up and so on, but these are all manifestations of energy being transferred from one thing to another. For example, when you play on a pogo stick, energy is moved from you into the spring of the stick. Energy, therefore, cannot be created or destroyed; it can only be moved from place to place and can come in a number of forms: heat (thermal) energy, sound energy, solar (Sun) energy, nuclear energy, kinetic (movement) energy, light energy, electrical energy, chemical energy; stored (potential) energy. These and others can be reduced to two forms: stored (potential) energy, for example a stretched spring or elastic band has stored energy and when the energy is released it can make objects move; and movement (kinetic) energy, for example a spring or elastic band moves as it is released.

INTRODUCTION

Begin the lesson by having a brainstorming session, in groups, about energy: *What is it? Where does it come from? What forms does it come in?* Any ideas should be considered. Collect the children's ideas together and come to some agreement. Talk to the children about energy being needed in order to make things move, change speed or direction and to heat things up: *Can you name any different types of energy?* They may need prompting. Try to come up with a list of different forms of energy that includes: heat energy (thermal energy), sound energy, Sun energy (solar energy), light energy, electrical energy, nuclear energy (the children may have heard about this through 'green' TV, but without much actual understanding) and chemical energy (the children may suggest 'food energy').

MAIN TEACHING ACTIVITY

Ask the children if they know where all this energy comes from. Introduce the idea that we cannot create or destroy these energy forms; we can only change them from one to another. Give some examples: electrical energy can be changed to heat energy in an electric fire or to light in an electric lamp; movement energy can be changed to sound energy by banging a drum; wind and water movement energy can be changed to electrical energy.

Ask the children to think of further examples. Talk in simple terms about the ideas of stored and movement energy. Use a spring or elastic band to demonstrate by saying that if you stretch a spring and hold it still or pull back a catapult there is some energy in that spring or elastic band, and because it is just there and not causing movement we call it stored. When we release the spring or elastic band the energy causes movement so we call that movement energy.

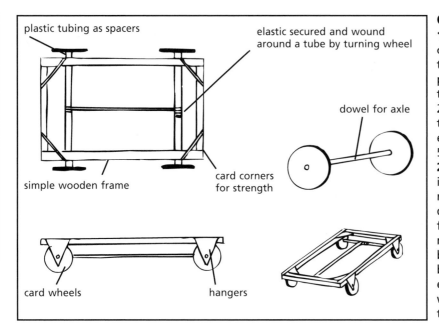

plastic tubing as spacers

elastic secured and wound around a tube by turning wheel

dowel for axle

simple wooden frame

card corners for strength

card wheels

hangers

GROUP ACTIVITIES

1. Distribute copies of page 150 for the children to complete. The children have to identify the energy changes taking place. The answers to the examples on the sheet are: 1. electrical to sound; 2. electrical to heat; 3. light (from Sun) to light (from electricity); 4. stored energy to sound and movement; 5. wind (movement) to light.

2. Ask the children to design (and make, if you have sufficient and suitable resources) a simple model vehicle that demonstrates the change in energy from stored or electrical energy into movement energy. The vehicle could be battery-powered so the change would be from electrical energy to movement energy, or powered by an elastic band which would be stored energy changed to movement energy.

DIFFERENTIATION

Lower-attaining children may need to discuss the photocopiable page with an adult helper. Higher-attaining children may well get on to making models from their designs, but lower-attainers may benefit from manipulating the resources available to try to build a vehicle, or could simply follow the instructions provided in a kit to make a vehicle displaying the energy changes.

Be careful not to limit the children's practical experience of science by their limited design skill.

ASSESSMENT

Look at the children's completed photocopiable pages for evidence of understanding of energy changes and an ability to identify the types of energy that can be changed. Through observation and discussion, assess whether the children can recognise that stored or electrical energy can be changed into movement energy. Ask, for example: *What sort of energy is in the battery? What type of energy is making the vehicle move?*

PLENARY

Bring the children together to demonstrate models and reinforce the concept of energy change.

OUTCOMES

- Can recognise that heat is a form of energy.
- Can recognise different sources of heat energy.
- Can recognise different applications of heat in everyday life.

LINKS

Unit 1, Lessons 2 and 3.

LESSON 12

OBJECTIVES

- To know that heat is a form of energy and it may be supplied by several sources.
- To know that energy can change forms.

RESOURCES

Main teaching activity: Flip chart or band and felt-tipped pen.
Group activities: 1. Copies of photocopiable page 151, pencils and pens. **2.** Paper, pens, pencils.

BACKGROUND

- **Energy sources:** nearly all the energy used on Earth can be traced back to the Sun. All the fossil fuels that we use – coal, oil and gas – were formed many millions of years ago from plants,

trees and animals that grew using energy from the Sun. Heat energy is released and transferred when fuels are burned. This energy can be transferred and put to a number of uses, including cooking, generating electricity, keeping warm and driving vehicles.

● **Energy transfer:** energy cannot be created nor can it be destroyed but it can, however, be transferred when we perform an activity. The energy can be converted from one form into another. If we consider what happens when a stone is fired from a catapult, we can see an example of how energy is transferred from its kinetic to its potential form and back to kinetic again. As the elastic is drawn back, there is movement (or kinetic) energy used in stretching it. As the catapult is held, the energy is stored in the elastic (potential energy). Releasing the elastic allows movement again (kinetic energy), pushing the stone and transferring this kinetic energy into the stone. The stone travels at speed from the catapult, still using kinetic energy and the elastic comes to rest because it has transferred all its energy to the stone. You can of course trace these energy transfers back further towards their ultimate source.

● **Heat energy:** heat is also a form of energy and it too can be transferred. It can also be created as a result of an energy transfer, when coal, oil, gas or wood are burned and when movement takes place, such as friction. The more energy that is required and which we use in carrying out a task (such as running), the more energy is transferred into heat energy.

INTRODUCTION

Remind the children about the work they have done on stored and movement energy and recall the thoughts they have about different types of energy.

MAIN TEACHING ACTIVITY

Talk in simple terms to the children about heat being a form of energy. Ask the children to talk about the many different ways in which we use heat energy. Use a flip chart or board to record 'Uses of heat'. Discuss with the children the fuels that produce our heat energy. Again brainstorm ideas about heat energy sources.

GROUP ACTIVITIES

1. Distribute photocopiable page 151 for the children to complete. They are asked to identify the means we have of using heat energy and the sources of fuel used to produce that energy.
2. Ask the children to think of a number of different activities that require them to use energy, such as walking on the level, walking up and down stairs, running slowly, running quickly and so on. They should try out some of these simple movements to see how warm they feel after each exercise. They could record their results in a table using simple terms that describe how they feel, such as: 'I did not feel any different', 'I felt quite warm', 'I felt very warm', 'I felt hot'.

DIFFERENTIATION

Lower-attaining children should find one or two examples of where our heat comes from. High-attainers go on to find more examples and some which are less obvious.

ASSESSMENT

Assess the children's work for understanding and by having a quiz.

PLENARY

Share ideas about the sources of heat energy and how different forms of exercise requiring us to use more energy produce more heat in us.

OUTCOMES

● Can recognise that energy can change forms.
● Can recognise that stored and electrical energy can be changed into movement energy.

LINKS

Unit 1, Lessons 2 and 3.

LESSON 12

OBJECTIVE

● To assess the children's knowledge of the properties of magnets, types of forces and the uses of springs.

RESOURCES

Assessment activities: 1. Copies of photocopiable page 152, pens, pencils. **2.** Copies of photocopiable page 153, pens, pencils.

INTRODUCTION

Begin the Assessment activities by reminding the children of some of the activities they have done recently without going into too much detail.

ASSESSMENT ACTIVITY 1

Distribute copies of photocopiable page 152 which the children should complete individually. Encourage the children to think carefully about their work on magnets and assure them that there is nothing new on the worksheet.

Answers

1. The children's picture of the bar magnet should include the poles marked with N and S for north and south.
2. When the poles are the same the magnets will repel each other, and when the poles are different they will attract each other.
3. Six uses of magnets could include: bells, burglar alarms, telephones, door latches, vending machines, metal detectors, moving large quantities of iron and steel, separating materials and compasses.

Looking for levels

For Assessment activity 1, all of the children should be able to draw a bar magnet with most of them being able to label the poles. Most should be able to explain that like poles repel and unlike poles attract, as should they be able to identify some uses of magnets. Higher-attaining children will be able to identify a greater number of less obvious uses such as magnetic tape and floppy disks.

ASSESSMENT ACTIVITY 2

Distribute copies of photocopiable page 153, which the children should complete individually. Again encourage the children to think carefully about their work on forces and springs and assure them that there is nothing new on the worksheet. For lower-attaining children, you may wish to add a word list to the photocopiable page from which the children can choose the missing words before completing the page.

Answers

For the first section of photocopiable page 153 accept any sensible object which uses springs and is either pushed or pulled. The words to complete the sentences are: 1. force, 2. spring, 3. elastic band, 4. push, 5. pull, 6. exert, 7. speed up; slow down, 8. pushing.

Looking for levels

For Assessment activity 2, all of the children should be able to identify uses of springs and most should be able to say whether those uses involve pushes or pulls. Most children should be able to complete sentences 1 to 3, with some able to complete them all.

PLENARY

Discuss the Assessment activities, perhaps allowing an element of self-marking before discussing any misconceptions the children may still have.

Magnets

Draw and colour a diagram of a bar magnet.
Colour one end red and the other end blue.
Mark N at the red end and S at the blue end.

Complete these sentences

N stands for _____. S stands for _____.

The ends of the magnet are called the _____.

Bring the ends of two bar magnets close together.
    Bring N to N. What do you notice?
    Bring S to S. What do you notice?
    Bring N to S. What do you notice?
Draw a diagram to show what happens each time.

Magnets	Diagram	What happened?
N to N		
S to S		
N to S		

Springs

Use springs to test for their push or pull.
Push the spring together from both ends.
Draw red arrows to show the direction of your force. Draw blue arrows to show the direction of the force of the spring.

Push

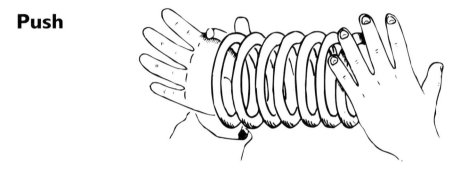

Pull the spring gently from both ends.
Draw red arrows to show the direction of your force. Draw blue arrows to show the direction of the force of the spring.

Pull

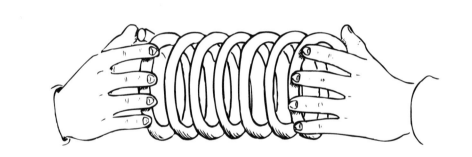

Now try the pull test with a rubber band. Draw what you see below.

Why would it be difficult to repeat the push test with the rubber band?

_____

_____

Name

Testing a rubber band

You will need a flat board catapult, a toy car, a ruler, a tape measure and a flat clear surface. Catapult the toy car along the flat surface. Draw a diagram here.

What do you think will happen if you pull the rubber band back further?

_____

Test your prediction by measuring the distance you pull the rubber band back and the distance the car travels.

Pull back on rubber band (cm)	Distance car travelled (cm)

What happens as you pull the rubber band back further?

_____

Is this what you predicted would happen?

_____

Explain why this happens.

_____

_____

_____

Energy

Energy can change forms from one type of energy to another. Can you identify the types of energy in these pictures?

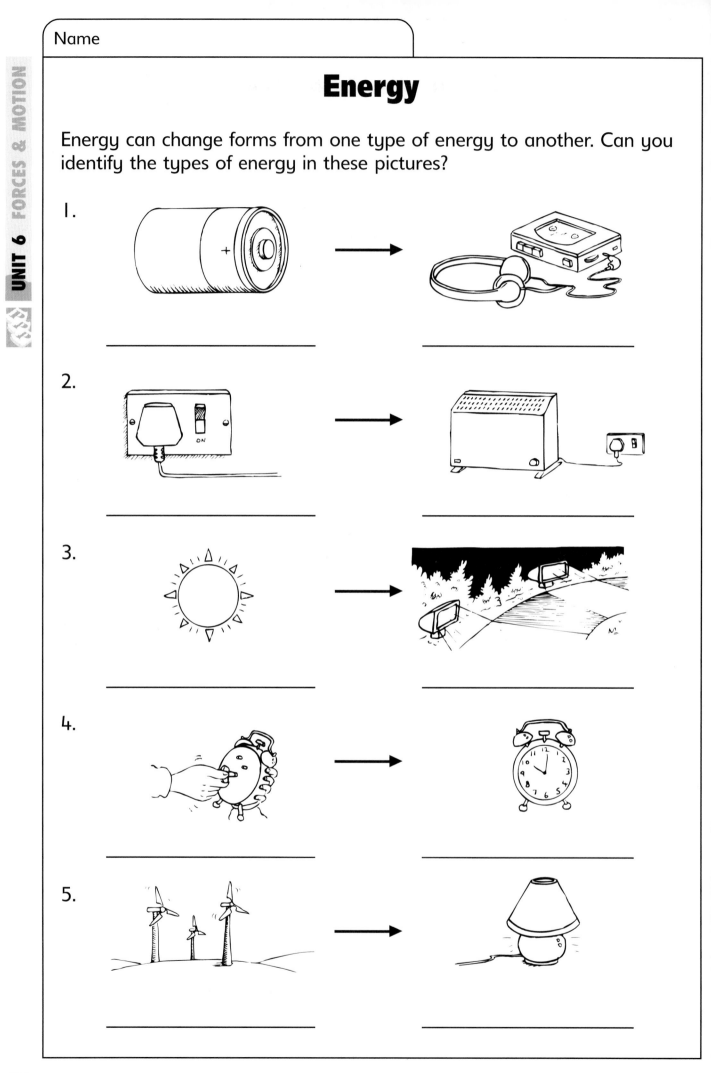

1.

2.

3.

4.

5.

Where do we get our heat from?

Think about all the times we need heat.
Complete this table to show the ways in which heat is supplied and its sources.

In the classroom		Around school	
How it comes to us	Source fuel	How it comes to us	Source fuel

At home		Outside	
How it comes to us	Source fuel	How it comes to us	Source fuel

Think about all these sources of heat energy. Where does the energy come from in the first place?

UNIT 6 FORCES & MOTION

Magnets and springs

1. Draw a picture of a bar magnet. Show what is usually written at the ends.

What happens when two magnets are brought together? Draw sketches to help explain your answers.

2. a) When the poles are the same:

_____

_____

_____

b) When the poles are different:

_____

_____

_____

3. Write down six uses of magnets.

_____   _____   _____

_____   _____   _____

Magnets and springs

Write down or draw all the things you can think of that use springs. Say whether the spring is being pulled or pushed.

Object	Pull or push?

push	force	spring	slow down
pushing	exert	speed up	pull	elastic band

Complete these sentences.

1. A push or a pull is called a _____.

2. A coil of metal used to make things move is called a _____.

3. A loop of rubber or elastic
   used to make things turn round is an _____ _____.

4. A compression force is a _____.

5. A stretching force is a _____.

6. Springs _____ forces.

7. Forces can make things _____ _____ or _____ _____.

8. A catapult uses _____ forces to project a missile through the air.

UNIT 7

Sources and effects

ORGANISATION (14 LESSONS)

	OBJECTIVES	MAIN ACTIVITY	GROUP ACTIVITIES	PLENARY	OUTCOMES
LESSON 1	● To ascertain the children's levels of understanding of light and how shadows are formed.	Concept mapping.	Looking at uses of light. Letting light through.	Formulating questions.	● Teacher can assess the children's level of understanding of light and shadows. ● Teacher can arrange children in appropriate class groups.
LESSON 2	● To know that when light from the Sun is blocked by an object a shadow forms.	Looking at how shadows are formed.	Casting shadows, observation and recording. Completing a worksheet looking at shadow formation.	Discussion and reinforcement of how shadows are formed.	● Can recognise that a shadow forms when sunlight is blocked.
LESSON 3	● To know that when light from sources other than the Sun is blocked, shadows are also produced.	Using a variety of light sources to cast shadows.	Completing a worksheet on how shadows are formed. Survey of light sources.	Reinforcing shadow formation and size.	● Can recognise that light from a range of sources produces shadows. ● Can describe how the shape and size of the shadow varies with the position of the light source.
LESSON 4	● To use the fact that when light is blocked, shadows are produced.	Making shadow puppets using different materials.		Making a puppet show and reinforcing the concept of shadow creation.	● Can recognise that light from a range of sources produces shadows. ● Can describe how the shape and size of the shadow varies with position of the light source. ● Can use knowledge of shadows.
LESSON 5	● To know that there is a wide range of colours that can be seen.	Looking at the colours of the spectrum and colour collections.	Completing a worksheet on colour, and pictures and collage work of the spectrum.	Reinforcement of the colours of the spectrum.	● Can recognise the colours in the spectrum.
LESSON 6	● To know that colours are used for decoration and to give messages in the natural world.	Using secondary sources to investigate how animals use colour.		Sharing research with each other.	● Can describe how plants and animals use colours.
LESSON 7	● To know that colours are used for decoration and to give messages in the man-made world. ● To know that colour and light are important in road safety.	Looking at the messages different colours give us, including traffic light sequences.	Looking at the many uses of colour in road safety and giving descriptive illustrations.	Looking at colour families.	● Is aware that humans use colour to send messages. ● Can describe the use of colour in road safety. ● Can describe the use of light in the local environment, for example for road safety.
LESSON 8	● To ascertain the level of the children's understanding of how sounds are made including quiet and loud sounds.	Concept mapping.	Completing a worksheet on making sounds. Sorting sounds using Venn diagrams.	Feedback and addressing misconceptions.	● Teacher can assess the level of the children in the class.
LESSON 9	● To know that there is a wide variety of sound sources. ● To be able to plan a fair test, make observations and judgements. ● To be able to draw conclusions.	Looking at natural and non-natural sound sources.	Carrying out a school sound survey. Describing sounds.	Identifying quiet and noisy areas around school.	● Can recognise sound sources. ● Can understand that humans are responsible for making, and so controlling, much noise. ● Can plan a fair test, make observations and judgements. ● Can draw conclusions.

ORGANISATION (14 LESSONS)

	OBJECTIVES	MAIN ACTIVITY	GROUP ACTIVITIES	PLENARY	OUTCOMES
LESSON 10	● To know and see that sound is produced when objects vibrate.	Circus of activities.		Sharing experiences of activities.	● Know that sound is produced when objects vibrate.
LESSON 11	● To know that of the many sounds around us at any one time some are loud, some are soft/quiet, some are high- and others are low-pitched. ● To distinguish these different types of sound.	Looking at ways of producing high- and low-pitched sounds.	Completing a sound survey and a loud and soft sounds worksheet.	Children demonstrate and explain how high- and low-pitched sounds are produced.	● Can recognise loud and soft sounds. ● Can recognise high and low pitched sounds.
LESSON 12	● To know that the pitch of a sound can be changed: raised or lowered.	Circus of activities looking at pitch.		Sharing the results of the activities.	● Know that the pitch of a sound can be raised or lowered.
LESSON 13	● To know about some of the uses of sound.	Using secondary sources to investigate the uses of sound.		Sharing of investigations.	● Know about some of the uses of sound.

	OBJECTIVE	ACTIVITY 1	ACTIVITY 2
ASSESSMENT 14	● To assess the children's level of understanding of the sources and effects of light and sound.	Completing a worksheet assessing shadows, light sources and uses of light.	Completing a worksheet assessing sources and uses of sound.

LESSON 1

OBJECTIVE
● To ascertain the children's levels of understanding of light and how shadows are formed.

RESOURCES
Main teaching activity: Flip chart or board, large sheets of paper, pens, pencils.
Group activities: 1. Paper, pencils, pens, colours, large sheets of coloured paper, scissors.
2. A copy of photocopiable page 169 for each child, pens, pencils.

BACKGROUND
From their work in Key Stage 1/Primary 1–3 the children should be able to recognise that light is needed to see and that 'dark' is the absence of light. They should know that the Sun is our main source of light, but that there are other light sources. They should recognise that different materials let varying amounts of light pass through, and should also be able to explain that shadows are formed when light is blocked. They may also know that light is a form of energy (but this is not a curriculum requirement throughout the UK). This first section of Unit 7 looks at light; the second section (from Lesson 8 onwards) at sound.

INTRODUCTION
Begin the lesson by talking to the children about the work they have covered in Key Stage 1/ Primary 1–3 on light. Ask the children to begin to think about what they can recall about light. Ask questions such as: *Where does light come from and how do we use it?* Explain that they will be building on what they already know and discovering a little more about light.

MAIN TEACHING ACTIVITY
The children should work in small groups on developing a concept map of light. They should express all their ideas and knowledge about the subject and then attempt to join their ideas with lines and arrows to produce a map. A large class concept map can be drawn on a flip chart or board using the groups' ideas.

GROUP ACTIVITIES

1. Ask the children to discuss the uses of light, such as to illuminate buildings, torches, warning lights or to show an appliance is working. Share out the ideas among the groups and ask each child to draw a picture and write a paragraph highlighting one use of light. The children should then present their work in an imaginative way. They could stick all the 'uses' onto a giant cut-out of a lamp, stick them on smaller individual lamps to make a string of lamps or make a catalogue.

Allows light through	Allows some light through	Allows no light through
Clear glass	Newspaper	Card
Water	Oil	Wood
	Cloth	Metal
	Curtains	

2. Distribute copies of photocopiable page 169 and ask the children to complete it unaided. The tasks are designed to assess the children's understanding of how light can pass through some materials and not others, thus creating shadows. The answers are that if you shine a torch at a clear drinking glass, the light would pass through the glass; and if you shine a torch at a book, the light would not pass through and a shadow would be formed.

DIFFERENTIATION

Because these tasks are designed to assess understanding, differentiation is by outcome.

ASSESSMENT

Through observation, discussion, and scrutiny of work, assess the children's understanding of the uses of light, how shadows are cast and how light passes through some materials and not others. All the children should be able to name some uses of light; most should also be able to say that only some materials allow light through. Some children will be able to describe how shadows are formed.

PLENARY

Share ideas and encourage the children to begin to formulate their own questions about what they think they would like to find out about.

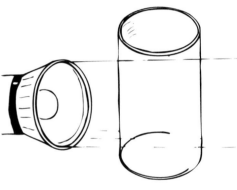

OUTCOMES

● Teacher can assess the children's levels of understanding of light and how shadows are formed.
● Teacher can arrange children in appropriate class groups.

LESSON 2

OBJECTIVE

● To know that when light from a source such as the Sun is blocked by an object, a shadow forms.

RESOURCES

Main teaching activity: An OHP, various opaque objects.
Group activities: 1. A sunny day, paper, pencils. **2.** Copies of photocopiable page 170, pens, pencils.

Vocabulary

block, light source, shadows, Sun

BACKGROUND

The Sun is the 'source' that gives us most of our light and our heat. Light is a form of energy. It is transmitted by electromagnetic waves that, like other forms of energy, we cannot see. What we *can* see are the objects on which light falls.

Light travels in straight lines and at a tremendous speed – 3000 000km per second. In fact, nothing travels faster. Despite its speed, it can travel only through certain materials. When it meets the surface of a material, light can either be transmitted (allowed to travel through, such as with glass), absorbed (as in a black surface) or reflected (as with a mirror, but also by all the objects we can see). It is reflected light that travels to our eyes that produces an image on our retina, thus allowing us to see objects.

Because some light is usually reflected from an object, and because light cannot travel around corners, the area behind an object comes into shadow. A shadow therefore is simply an area from which light is blocked. Clearly there is usually some light reaching that area otherwise behind, say, a building there would be complete darkness. Usually this is light reflected from other objects. Shadows are strictly areas of less light rather than no light at all.

INTRODUCTION

Begin the lesson by asking the children to think about walking down the street on a dark night where the main source of light is the street lighting. What is the one thing that always follows them along that street, that some people are frightened of, but is harmless? Discuss (scary) shadows and the children's experiences of shadows.

MAIN TEACHING ACTIVITY

Ask the children if they know how shadows are made. Use the light from an OHP to demonstrate how shadows are formed. Use an object and explain that the light is being blocked when it reaches the object, hence the darker area behind. Ask the children to think about where most of our light comes from and therefore gives most of our shadows. Discuss the Sun as being a major light source and, if appropriate, that light is actually another form of energy.

GROUP ACTIVITIES

1. In the playground, and working in groups, the children should make shadows while other members of their group observe and record their observations as sketches. Ask the groups to observe and record their shadows at different times during the school day (perhaps each break time may be possible). What, if anything, do the children think will be different?
2. Distribute photocopiable page 170 to the children and explain the task. This sheet asks questions about the way in which shadows are formed, so it may be useful to have your demonstration from the Main teaching activity available for them to refer to. The final section asks the children to draw a picture of the Sun and a shadow that it may cast. At this point it is worth reinforcing the importance of **never** looking directly at the Sun.

DIFFERENTIATION

Differentiate by outcome.

ASSESSMENT

Mark the children's work for evidence of an understanding of how shadows are formed. The questions and diagrams should reflect the knowledge that a shadow is formed when light from the Sun or other light source is blocked.

PLENARY

Discuss with the children how shadows are formed, asking them to explain shadow formation in their own words. Look at the pictures of the Sun and shadows that the children have drawn. Reinforce understanding of the concept that when an object blocks the Sun's light a shadow is cast. If the children draw a Sun with rays coming from it, use that to illustrate the concept that the object blocks the Sun's rays, even though we cannot see the rays as such.

OUTCOME

● Can recognise that a shadow forms when sunlight is blocked.

LINKS

Unit 6, Lessons 11 and 12: forms of energy and energy transfers, including heat and light.

LESSON 3

OBJECTIVE

● To know that when light from sources other than the Sun is blocked, shadows are also produced.

RESOURCES

Main teaching activity: Candles, torches, a computer screen.
Group activities: 1. Copies of photocopiable page 171, pens, pencils. **2.** Clipboards, paper, pens, pencils.

Vocabulary

light source, Sun

BACKGROUND

It is a common misconception that seeing involves something being emitted from our eyes like we are some superhero! Another is that the Moon and planets, for example, are light sources. They are not. They can be seen because they reflect light from the Sun. We can see objects because light is reflected from them, which comes from a light source such as:
● the Sun – the light from the Sun supplies us with our daylight and also heat energy; the light energy from the Sun is also used by plants to make their food (photosynthesis)
● an electric light – electricity passes through the filament in the light bulb which heats up so much that light is emitted
● a candle – chemical energy is released by the burning of the candle wax which causes heating, and when the fuel becomes white hot the candle produces a light.

All light sources can produce shadows, but their intensity will vary depending on the strength and intensity of the light source. The intensity of a shadow can be varied by moving the object casting the shadow nearer or further away from its light source. The shadow also loses its definition, but gains in size as the object is moved nearer to the light source – this happens because more reflected light is able to fall in the shadow. Similarly the intensity and sharpness of shadows is affected by the intensity of the light source. On a bright sunny day shadows are very sharp and distinct, whereas on an overcast day when the light is diffused by clouds the shadows are far less distinct.

INTRODUCTION

Ask the children if they can think of or remember any other sources of light apart from the Sun. Compile a list of these on the board. Discuss briefly the concept of needing light to be able to see anything, whether it is the light from the Sun or elsewhere, and that we see because light bounces off (is reflected from) objects and enters our eyes.

MAIN TEACHING ACTIVITY

Use a variety of light sources so the children can see that shadows will be cast by any light source. A candle, torch and computer screen can all be used and will produce shadows of varying quality and intensity. Ask the children to think about what will happen as the light source is moved nearer and further away from an object. Demonstrate with the help of the children.

GROUP ACTIVITIES

1. Distribute copies of photocopiable page 171 and ask the children to complete the sheet based on the things they have just seen and talked about.
2. Carry out a survey around school of the many and varied different light sources to be seen. The children can present their findings as a 'We spy' booklet of light sources, such as desk lamps, an OHP or a computer monitor.

DIFFERENTIATION

Allow higher-attaining children to use the objects from the Main teaching activity when they complete Group activity 1. Encourage lower-attaining children to present their light source survey findings with additional background information.

ASSESSMENT

Check that the children have been able to identify a number of other light sources and that their diagrams show that when a light source comes nearer an object the shadow becomes larger. Aim only for a general understanding here – the children will explore this more systematically in future years.

PLENARY

Use an OHP as a light source for the children to demonstrate their understanding of light sources and shadow sizes by making shadow puppets with their hands. Encourage them to use their knowledge from this lesson to add feeling to their shadows by varying their sizes.

OUTCOMES

● Can recognise that light from a range of sources produces shadows.
● Can describe how the shape and size of the shadow varies with the position of the light source.

LINKS

Unit 8, Lessons 2–4: Shadows from the Sun.

LESSON 4

Objective	● To use the fact that when light is blocked shadows are produced.
Resources	Craft materials with varying light-blocking qualities, small garden canes, dowel, glue or tape, a light source such as an OHP, a screen (for example, a wooden frame covered with tracing paper).
Main activity	Talk about traditional shadow puppetry, for example in Asian culture, where shadow puppets are sometimes used to tell the traditional legends of the gods at festival time. Demonstrate how the shadows are made. Show the children how to make their own shadow puppets. The puppets can then be manipulated by the children to tell an existing story, or they could devise one of their own.
Differentiation	Differentiate by outcome.
Assessment	During the Main activity, talk to the children about their shadow puppets and the materials they are using. Ask them which materials cast better shadows than others and why. See if they know what they need to make effective shadow puppets.
Plenary	Bring the children together and allow them time to present their shadow puppet stories.
Outcomes	● Can recognise that light from a range of sources produces shadows. ● Can describe how the shape and size of the shadow varies with the position of the light source. ● Can use knowledge of shadows.

screen   shadow puppet   light source

LESSON 5

OBJECTIVE
● To know that there is a wide range of colours that can be seen.

RESOURCES

Main teaching activity: Soundtrack recording of Andrew Lloyd Webber's musical *Joseph and the Amazing Technicolour Dreamcoat*, children's story Bible (optional).
Group activities: 1. A small collection of objects that are one particular colour, copies of photocopiable page 172, pens, pencils. **2.** Paper, painting equipment, collage materials, glue, scissors.

PREPARATION

Set up a 'colour display' of objects that are one particular colour – perhaps you have a school colour that you could use as a basis for this.

BACKGROUND

Vocabulary

red, orange, yellow, green, blue, indigo, violet, spectrum

We are able to see things around us when light from a light source reaches an object, hits it, is reflected and enters our eyes. But what about seeing colour? The light that is all around us is 'white', but it is accepted that it is made up from seven colours. Together, these colours are called the 'spectrum'. They are: red, orange, yellow, green, blue, indigo and violet. We can see these colours split apart in a rainbow, where red is on the outside and the rest follow in this order, in bands, to the violet on the inner edge.

In this spectrum of light, there are three 'primary' colours: red, green and blue. It is important to remember that the primary colours of light and the primary colours of paint are different. Different rules apply to mixing light compared to mixing paint.

When white light hits, for example, a blue object, the red and green elements of the white light are absorbed by the object. The blue light is reflected into our eyes by the pigments in the object, and we see a blue object. The same applies to the other primary colours. If the object is a mixture of colours, then the colour pigments in the object reflect some of the constituent colours and absorb the rest.

INTRODUCTION

How many colours can you see in the classroom? What is your favourite colour? Carry out a quick and simple survey of favourite colours.

MAIN TEACHING ACTIVITY

Talk about how we may wear clothes in our favourite colours. Introduce and play the song 'Joseph's coat' from *Joseph and the Amazing Technicolour Dreamcoat*. Tell the children that Joseph's story is in the Bible as is Noah's, and something else that is multicoloured appears in that story – the rainbow. You may like to read the end of the Noah story to the children. Ask them to name the colours of the rainbow. Teach them to remember the colours in order using a mnemonic such as: Richard Of York Gave Battle In Vain.

You may wish to explain, very simply, how we see colour.

GROUP ACTIVITIES

1. Give out copies of photocopiable page 172 for the children to complete. Encourage different groups to make different colour collections on their own of items from around the classroom.
2. Paint a picture or make a collage of a rainbow. The children could also make up new versions of the 'ROYGBIV' mnemonic as the centrepiece for a display of work from the following lessons.

DIFFERENTIATION

Differentiate by outcome.

ASSESSMENT

Look for evidence in the children's completed photocopiable pages that they are able to name the colours of the spectrum and correctly complete the cloze procedure.

PLENARY

Ask some of the children to share their work with the class. Reinforce the concept of a range of colours and knowledge of the colours of the spectrum. Listen to new versions of the 'ROYGBIV' mnemonic. You may like to read more of the stories of Noah or Joseph to round off this lesson.

OUTCOME

● Can recognise the colours in the spectrum.

LINKS

RE: Biblical stories of Noah and Joseph.
PSHE: coping with jealousy and bullying.
Art: colour recognition and colour mixing.

LESSON 6

Objective	● To know that colours are used for decoration and to give messages in the natural world.
Resources	Secondary sources of information, such as books, CD-ROMs and so on; art materials.
Main activity	Use secondary sources to investigate colours in nature, how animals and plants use colour as a warning, as camouflage or as a means of attracting another of the same species. The children could work in small groups and present their findings with art work to add to a class display. Provide a background of green art paper leaves, where green bugs can hide. Let the children make 'blot' butterflies, but discuss what colours they should use to give warnings (red = 'I'm not nice to eat'; yellow and black = 'I sting'), or to attract a mate (the peacock's greens and blues, for example). Emphasise the symmetry of the patterns, too.
Differentiation	Lower-attaining children could research one specific item, perhaps camouflage or warnings. Higher-attaining children could try more complex research that investigates a range of animals, plants and uses of colour, and uses a range of media to present findings, such as images from the Internet.
Assessment	Look for evidence of an understanding of how plants and animals use colour for camouflage, attraction or warning.
Plenary	Ask the children to share their findings and allow an opportunity for the children to read and look at each others' work.
Outcome	● Can describe how plants and animals use colours.

LESSON 7

OBJECTIVES

● To know that colours are used for decoration and to give messages in the man-made world.
● To know that colour and light are important in road safety.

RESOURCES

Main teaching activity: Flip chart or board, road safety posters, pictures of emergency vehicles, copies of photocopiable page 173, pens, pencils.
Group activities: 1. Paper, pencils, colours. **2.** Large sheets of paper, decorating paint charts, painting equipment.

PREPARATION

Display the posters and pictures where the children can see them easily.

BACKGROUND

As in nature, humans often use colour to send messages. We paint our homes in certain colours to create particular atmospheres: green is said to be calming, whereas blue is generally considered cold. The colour of the clothes we wear sends messages: they may indicate what sort of person we may be or even which football team we support. But certain colours have particular associations: red we associate with danger, fire engines and a warning to stop; green we associate with nature, the environment and traffic lights telling us it is safe to go; colours are 'adopted' by certain organisations and sections of our society.

Vocabulary

amber, danger, green, red, reflective, safe, traffic

On the roads, make great use of colour and light. Not only do we use lamps to light the streets, but also to control the traffic (see the DoT *Highway Code* for more information), and for vehicles to signal when they are manoeuvring or stopping. Pedestrians too may wear appropriate clothing to warn of their presence. Many children who walk to and from school wear coats with reflective patches or armbands, and people working on the roads wear bright reflective jackets in orange, bright green or yellow.

INTRODUCTION

Begin by asking the children how they travelled to school this morning. Introduce some elements of road safety. Ask the children how they keep themselves safe on the roads, particularly when it is dark. Encourage them to consider street lighting, crossing at pelican crossings (the green man), and wearing reflective clothing or armbands.

MAIN TEACHING ACTIVITY

Discuss with the children how colour and light are very important in road safety. Red is often used as a warning colour to tell people that there is danger ahead; green is used generally as a sign that things are safe. Amber is used as a warning that danger may lie ahead. Make a list of examples on the flip chart, one of these should be traffic lights. Ask the children if they know the colours that are used in traffic lights. Tell them the sequence of traffic light changes, and what each one means. Distribute photocopiable page 173 and allow the children time to complete it. The children will have to recall the sequence of traffic lights, which should be: red; red and amber together; green; amber; red.

GROUP ACTIVITIES

1. Ask the children to think about colour use outside in the local environment. Ask them to draw a picture of a street scene and to mark on as many uses of colour and light as possible. In particular, they should indicate how light and colour are used in road safety, including: traffic lights, street lighting, emergency vehicles, reflective clothing, road signs, cat's eyes, roadside barriers and markers. Alternatively, this could be a collaborative display, with the children drawing and cutting out their individual contributions to stick on to a group or class scene.
2. Ask the children to think about colour use inside the home. Give out some decorating paint charts and ask the children to look at variations in colour among the colour groups. Ask the children to choose one colour family and to create their own paint chart. Each chart should have about six blocks of colour and the children should give each an appropriate name. Encourage systematic mixing, with the children adding white or black to a starting hue.

DIFFERENTIATION

Lower-attaining children may need support in sequencing the changes in traffic lights. Higher-attaining children should be able to work unaided, and you may wish to delete the word bank and reference to it before you copy the page.

ASSESSMENT

Have the children been able to indicate appropriate uses for colour and light in road safety, and/or other human situations?

PLENARY

Reinforce the importance of colour and how certain colours send out certain messages: red for danger and green for safety. Have a quiz where one child gives a traffic light colour or colours and another has to give the sequence that either follows or comes before it.

OUTCOMES

● Is aware that humans use colour to send out messages.
● Can describe the use of colour in road safety.
● Can describe the use of light in the local environment, for example for road safety.

LINKS

Unit 5, Lessons 6–8: using lights for communication.

LESSON 8

OBJECTIVE

● To ascertain the level of the children's understanding of how sounds are made including quiet and loud sounds.

RESOURCES

Main teaching activity: Flip chart or board, pens, cassette recorder and tape.
Group activities: 1. Copies of photocopiable page 174, pens, pencils. **2.** Magazines, large sheets of paper, glue, scissors.

BACKGROUND

From their work on sound in Key Stage 1/Primary 1–3, the children should already have some understanding that sounds are made in a variety of ways. They should also know how to make sounds using different objects and materials and have some knowledge that sounds get fainter as they travel away from their source.

INTRODUCTION

Begin by talking to the children about a 'mystery'. Describe 'sound' without naming it, and ask the children to guess its identity. Use phrases such as: *It is invisible; It can be beautiful; It can be awful; It is all around us; Some people do not experience it; We all make it; Some of us make too much of it.*

MAIN TEACHING ACTIVITY

Talk to the children about sound, and ask them to brainstorm words that are in some way related to sound. They could be words that describe sounds, how sounds are made or feelings about sound. Record these on the flip chart before completing a concept map to help link the children's ideas together to give a body of understanding. As an alternative, or in addition, why not make an audio concept map? Record the children as they explain the links they are making between the words collected.

GROUP ACTIVITIES

1. Distribute copies of photocopiable page 174. Ask the children to work through the sheet by themselves.
2. Ask the children to cut pictures from magazines to make a collection of things that make loud and soft sounds. Draw a Venn diagram to sort them into groups and make a poster of the results. Higher-attaining children may be able to sort the objects into three groups, since some objects may be capable of producing both loud and soft sounds.

DIFFERENTIATION

When completing Group activity 2, lower-attaining children could sort objects into two groups and higher-attaining children could sort into three groups.

ASSESSMENT

Most of the children should be able to contribute to the concept map with some knowledge and understanding of sound sources. Most children should be able to complete the Group activities and know how sounds are made, with an understanding of loud and quiet.

PLENARY

You may wish to use the Plenary to discuss the questions and to allow the children to initially mark their own or another child's work. During this time, you can begin to pick up and address any misconceptions the children may still have from the previous year's work.

OUTCOME

● Teacher can assess the level of the children in the class.

LINKS

Unit 6, Lesson 11: energy can change forms.

LESSON 9

OBJECTIVES

- To know that there is a wide variety of sound sources.
- To be able to plan a fair test, make observations and judgements.
- To be able to draw conclusions.

RESOURCES

Main teaching activity: A flip chart or board, pens.
Group activities: 1. Simple plan of the school, clipboards, pens, pencils. **2.** Paper, pens, pencils.

PREPARATION

Copy a plan of the school for each child or group.

Vocabulary

detect, hear, loud, noisy, quiet, sound, transmit, vibrate

BACKGROUND

Sound plays an important part in our lives. It enables us to communicate with each other, and gives music and the spoken word to enjoy. Sound originates from very many different sources – some natural, some made by human activity or intention. But whether it is pleasant or unpleasant, all sounds are produced, transmitted and detected in the same way. All sound sources produce their sounds by causing a vibration.

INTRODUCTION

Begin the lesson by playing some music, banging about, singing, opening and shutting doors and generally making a great deal of varied noise. Suggest it's a little noisy in the classroom and ask the children to suggest where all the sounds are coming from – own up to it being you! Tell the children that they are going to be thinking about and listening for sounds.

MAIN TEACHING ACTIVITY

Ask the children to close their eyes for one minute and to listen very carefully for all the sounds they can hear. Compile a class list of those sounds. Ask the children to think of where all these sounds were coming from and they will soon begin to realise that there is a wide variety of sources of sound. Highlight that these 'sources' can be divided into those that are natural and those that are made by human actions, events or inventions. Talk about the sounds the children like and those they do not. Introduce Group activity 1. Tell the children to imagine they are 'Sound consultants' who have been called in to school to carry out a 'Sound survey'. Their task is to walk around the school, in groups, inside and/or outside on a 'Sound survey walk'.

Natural sound sources	Description of the sound
Dog	Barking to communicate

Not natural sound sources	Description of the sound
Trumpet	Music

GROUP ACTIVITIES

1. The children should mark on a map the locations and types of sounds that they hear as they walk around. They should prepare a 'Sound consultants' report' to be presented at the end of the survey.
2. The children remaining in class while the 'Sound consultants tour the school can make two lists identifying a variety of sound sources and describing the sound that is produced. These sounds can be divided into 'natural' (such as birds, animals, humans, the weather and so on) and 'not natural' (such as machinery, music, doors banging and so on).

DIFFERENTIATION

Lower-attaining children can draw the sound sources and choose words from a word bank of descriptive words to describe the sounds. Higher-attaining children can write down the names of the sound sources and use more descriptive language in describing the sounds.

ASSESSMENT

Have the children been able to identify a variety of sound sources? Expect a good range, with perhaps ten examples in each section for higher-attaining children. Can the children offer any judgements about the noises around school – should there be talking in the 'Quiet reading area'? Why? Why not?

PLENARY

Ask each group of 'Sound consultants' to present their findings from the sound survey walk. Encourage them to draw conclusions from their data (the completed maps). *Can you see where the quiet areas are? What goes on there? Where are the noisy areas? What is the source of most of the sound?* Ask: *If you were to carry out the survey at different times of day would your findings be the same or not?* (Consider the playground at break time and during assembly time.) Point out that one survey (or experiment) may not be enough for scientists to get the whole picture. Emphasise the importance of carrying out a fair test and being able to make judgements based on the evidence collected.

Explain that loud sounds are produced when more energy is expended in their production, for example hitting a drum hard produces a louder sound than gently tapping it.

OUTCOMES

- Can recognise sound sources.
- Can understand that humans are responsible for making, and so controlling, much noise.
- Can plan a fair test, make observations and judgements.
- Can draw conclusions.

LINKS

Literacy: non-fiction writing.

Objective	● To know and see that sound is produced when objects vibrate.
Resources	A guitar or a violin, cymbals, tuning forks, a dish of water, paper, a drum, a drumstick, combs, tissue paper, boxes, elastic bands.
Main activity	Set up a circus of simple activities for the children to experience that will reinforce their understanding that sounds are produced when objects vibrate. Some ideas include: watching musical instruments vibrate when played (such as a cymbal or a guitar or violin string); tapping a tuning fork and then listening to the sound before placing the tip of the tuning fork on the surface of a dish of water; spreading torn-up paper shreds on the skin of a drum, then gently tapping the drum and observing the paper; making a comb and paper kazoo; make a simple rubber band guitar using a small box and elastic bands.
Differentiation	Differentiate by outcome.
Assessment	Through observation and discussion during the lesson, assess the children's understanding of sound being made by vibrations.
Plenary	Ask the children to share one of the activities with rest of the class and to explain the vibrations they can see or feel.
Outcome	● Know that sound is produced when objects vibrate.

LESSON 11

OBJECTIVES

● To know that of the many sounds around us at any one time some are loud, some are soft/quiet, some are high- and others are low-pitched.
● To distinguish these different types of sound.

RESOURCES

Main teaching activity: A selection of tuned and untuned percussion instruments and recorders or other pitched instruments; access to a piano where the strings can be exposed (you don't have to be able to play it!)
Group activities: 1. Sound maps from Lesson 7, clipboards, paper, pens, pencils. **2.** Copies of photocopiable page 175, pens, pencils.

PREPARATION

Collect together the instruments, and arrange to take the top off the piano to view the strings.

BACKGROUND

Vocabulary
high-pitched, loud, low-pitched, quiet, volume

In the last lesson the children looked at changes in loudness or volume. 'High' and 'loud' do not mean the same thing. 'Pitch' and 'volume' are often confused: pitch is to do with the frequency of the sound waves, whereas volume is to do with their size. When the vibrations in the air produced by a sound source are very rapid, the pitch of the sound is said to be high; when the vibrations are slow the pitch is said to be low.

Volume or loudness depends on amplitude – that is, the height of the sound wave. The greater the amplitude, the louder the sound. For example, if you pluck a guitar string it will vibrate at a certain frequency or speed. If you pluck the string harder (that is, pull it back further), it will still vibrate at the same frequency, but it will vibrate in a higher plane, and therefore the sound will be louder.

INTRODUCTION

Begin the lesson by beating a drum, first softly and gradually louder: it's guaranteed to get the children's attention!

MAIN TEACHING ACTIVITY

Allow the children to try some of the unpitched percussion instruments. Ask the children to think about what the differences are between the sounds produced when someone hits an instrument hard and when another hits it gently.

Introduce the concept of loud and soft sounds and how they are produced. Use the piano to demonstrate again how the volume can be varied. Play the same note gently and with greater force. Ask the children if it is possible to change the sound in another way. Invite someone to demonstrate that the sound can be changed by playing different keys. Show the strings of the

Place	Sound	Pitch: high/low	Volume: soft/loud

piano to explain to the children how the pitch of a sound changes depending on the thickness and length of the string. Recap by explaining that high- and low-pitched sounds are produced by objects of different sizes, and loud and soft sounds are produced by putting more effort into the production of the sound.

GROUP ACTIVITIES

1. Ask the 'Sound consultants' to revisit the same areas of the school as before with the sound maps they produced during their earlier visit (the previous lesson), but this time using a colour-coding system to mark on their maps if the sounds are high-pitched, low-pitched, loud or soft. You should highlight that they need to go at the same time too! Clearly some of these observations will be subject to personal judgement: what is 'soft' to one person may be 'loud' to another. The children should discuss with each other their judgements of the sound and agree on the quality values of the sound. Their findings could also be collated on a grid.

After the walk the children should analyse their findings, adding to their previous report to highlights areas in and around school where the sounds are high-pitched, low-pitched, loud, soft, or combinations of volume and pitch.
2. Distribute copies of photocopiable page 175 for the children to complete.

DIFFERENTIATION

Lower-attaining children may need help to begin to analyse the sound survey results.

ASSESSMENT

Check to ensure that the children's answers show that they recognise the difference between volume and pitch.

PLENARY

Bring the children together and ask the groups to give an updated report on their sound survey. Ask them to explain how loud and soft sounds are produced and how high- and low-pitched sounds are produced.

OUTCOMES

● Can recognise loud and soft sounds.
● Can recognise high- and low-pitched sounds.

LESSON 12

Objective	● To know that the pitch of a sound can be changed: raised or lowered.
Resources	Jam jars, rigid plastic piping, boxes, elastic bands, pitched percussion instruments.
Main activity	Carry out an investigation into pitch and how the pitch of a sound can be varied. The children could begin to develop an understanding of the relationship between the length of a vibrating object and the pitch of sound it gives off. This could involve using: jam jars filled with different amounts of water; different lengths of rigid plastic piping to hit; varying the length of an elastic band stretched over a box; looking at pitched percussion instruments such as a xylophone or chime bars. Some of these could be teacher-led demonstrations, followed by a circus of activities for the children to experience altering the pitch of a sound.
Differentiation	Differentiate by outcome.
Assessment	Through observation and discussion during the lesson, assess the children's understanding of pitch.
Plenary	Discuss with the children their experiences from the activities and reinforce the idea that pitch can be varied by varying the size of the vibrating object.
Outcome	● Know that the pitch of a sound can be raised or lowered.

LESSON 13

Objective	● To know about some of the uses of sound.
Resources	Secondary sources of information.
Main activity	Ask the children to use their experience and secondary sources of information to find out as much as they can about how we use sound. If this lesson follows a break and your school uses bells, introduce the lesson in this context as a use we make of sound. Other uses include entertainment, communication, or as a warning. Consider also the natural sound we hear and look at how birds and animals use sound as a means of communication and warning.
Differentiation	Differentiate by outcome.
Assessment	Through scrutiny of the children's work, assess the level of their understanding about the uses of sound. Most children should be able to identify some, with higher-attainers identifying a wider and more complex range.
Plenary	Bring the children together to share and discuss their findings. Ask for examples of how we use sounds.
Outcome	● Know about some of the uses of sound.

LESSON 12

OBJECTIVE
● To assess the children's level of understanding of the sources and effects of light and sound.

RESOURCES
Assessment activities: 1. Copies of photocopiable page 176, pens, pencils. **2.** Copies of photocopiable page 177, paper, pens, pencils, drawing materials.

INTRODUCTION
Begin the Assessment activities by having a vocabulary quiz. Either give a word or phrase and ask for the definition or give a definition and ask for the word or phrase. Words to use could include: shadow, spectrum, light source, the colour red, loud, soft, pitch.

ASSESSMENT ACTIVITY 1
Distribute copies of photocopiable page 176 to test the children's understanding and let them complete it individually. The test would be best marked yourself, although you may wish the children to mark each other's.

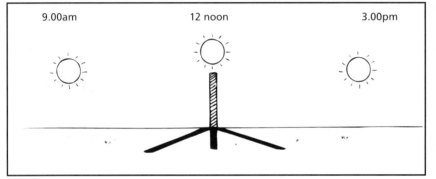

Answers
1. The children should draw pictures similar to those shown on the left.
2. Accept any four light sources, such as: the Sun, a candle, an electric lamp, a fire or a TV screen. Do not accept reflected light such as the Moon as a light source.
3. The colours of the rainbow in the correct order are: red, orange, yellow, green, blue, indigo, violet, with red on the outside of the rainbow.

Looking for levels
Look for a good understanding of the concepts covered and the ability to correctly answer the questions on photocopiable page 176. All the children should be able to answer questions 2 and 3. Some will be able to answer question 1 correctly – look for shorter shadows at 12 noon. Most children should be able to answer question 4.

ASSESSMENT ACTIVITY 2
Distribute copies of photocopiable page 177 and ask the children to look very carefully at it. Ask the children to colour (in one colour, see below) all the objects that are sources of sound. Then they should write about some of the sound sources, thinking about how the sound is made, whether it is a loud or soft sound, whether it is a high- or low-pitched sound, and whether that sound has a use or not, for example communicating or entertaining.

As an extension activity the children could colour (in a different colour) the light sources shown in the same picture. Again, they could write an explanation of the light sources, their uses and benefits.

Looking for levels
All of the children should be able to identify the sound sources in the picture. Most should be able to write about those sound sources, with the higher-attainers being able to write a more complex explanation.

PLENARY
You may wish to review the unit with the children and go through any misconceptions that the children may still have.

Light

Some materials allow light through, some do not allow any through, and some allow only a little light through. Complete these sentences.

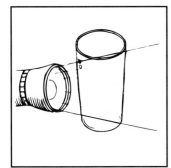

If you shone a torch at a clear drinking glass the light would

_____

_____.

If you shone a torch at a book the light would

_____

_____.

Can you sort these things into the correct column?

clear glass   oil   newspaper   card   wood
metal   water   frosted glass   cloth   curtains

Allows light through	Allows some light through	Allows no light through

Add some more of your own to each column.

Me and my shadow

What is a shadow?

_____

_____ .

How are shadows formed?

_____

_____ .

What do you need to make a shadow?

_____

_____ .

Draw a picture to help you with your answers.

Draw a picture of the Sun, the Earth's main light source, and a shadow of yourself.

Light sources

A torch is a light source. All light sources can be used to produce shadows. Describe what happens when you use a torch to investigate shadows. What happens when you move the torch nearer to the object?

Make a drawing in the space below.

Torch   **Object**   **Shadow**

_____

_____ .

What happens when you move the torch further away from the object?

Make a drawing in the space below.

Torch   **Object**   **Shadow**

_____

_____ .

Colour

orange   violet   rainbow   red   colours   light
indigo   seven   green   yellow   blue

Complete these sentences. Choose the correct words from the word bank above.

We are able to see things because of _____.

We can see the _____ of things because light is made up

from _____ colours.

The colours can be seen in a _____.

The colours are _____, _____, _____,

_____, _____, _____, _____.

Draw a rainbow and put the colours in the right order.

Colour on the roads

Colours are often used to give us a message or an instruction. Complete these sentences. Choose the correct words from the word bank.

> **a warning**   **dangerous**   **safe**

Red is often used to indicate that something is _____.

Green is often used to indicate that something is _____.

Amber is often used to indicate _____.

Now think about how traffic lights work. Can you remember the sequence in which the lights shine? Colour these traffic lights.

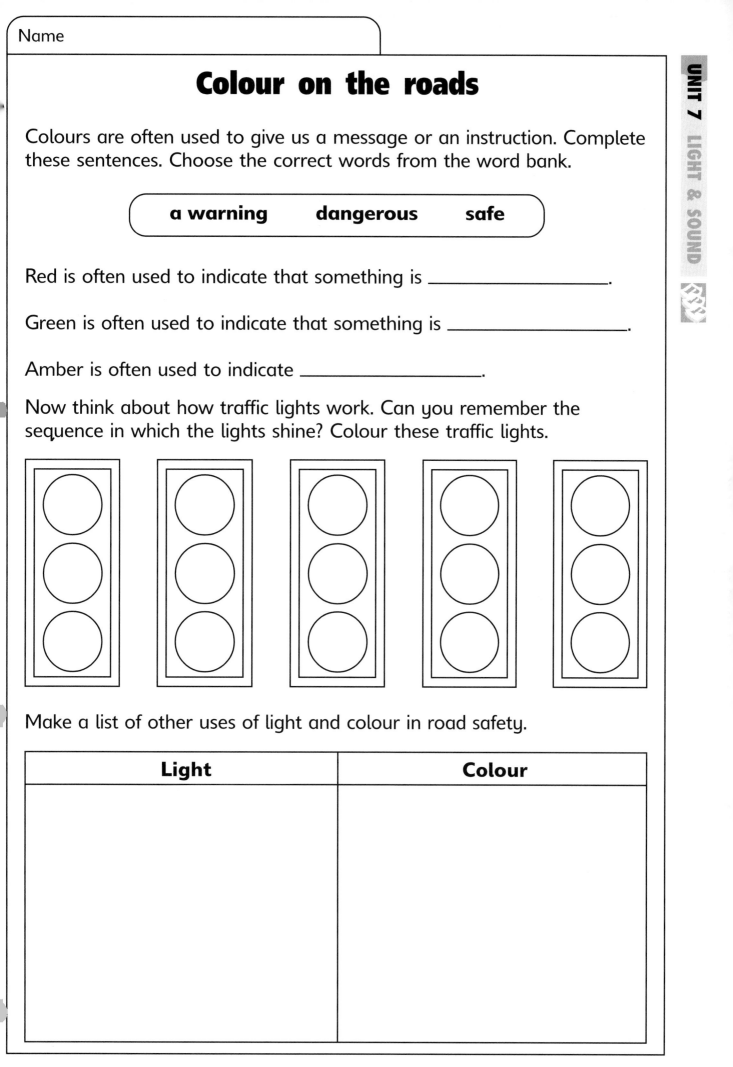

Make a list of other uses of light and colour in road safety.

Light	Colour

Name

Making a sound

How do you think you could make a sound with these objects? Choose the correct word from the word bank below.

> blow   bang   shake   pluck

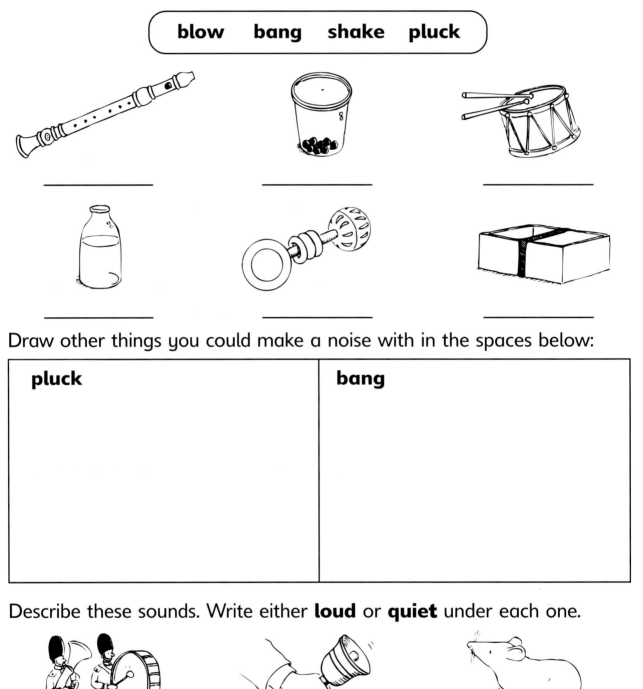

_____   _____   _____

_____   _____   _____

Draw other things you could make a noise with in the spaces below:

pluck	bang

Describe these sounds. Write either **loud** or **quiet** under each one.

_____   _____   _____

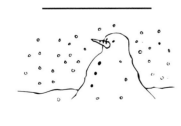      

_____   _____   _____

Loud and soft sounds

The sound of an explosion is loud. The sound of a whisper is soft. Other sounds are in between.

1. In the playground make a loud sound and a soft sound.
Complete these sentences.

I made a loud sound by _____

_____ .

I made a soft sound by _____

_____ .

2. Ask a friend to make a loud sound, then move away from the sound.
Describe what happens.

3. Devise a way of making a soft sound more easily heard at the other end of the playground. Draw or write about it.

4. Can you think of any uses for loud sounds? Write or draw four ideas.

UNIT 7 LIGHT & SOUND

Sources and effects

1. Draw the shadows cast by the post at 9.00am, 12 noon and 3.00pm.

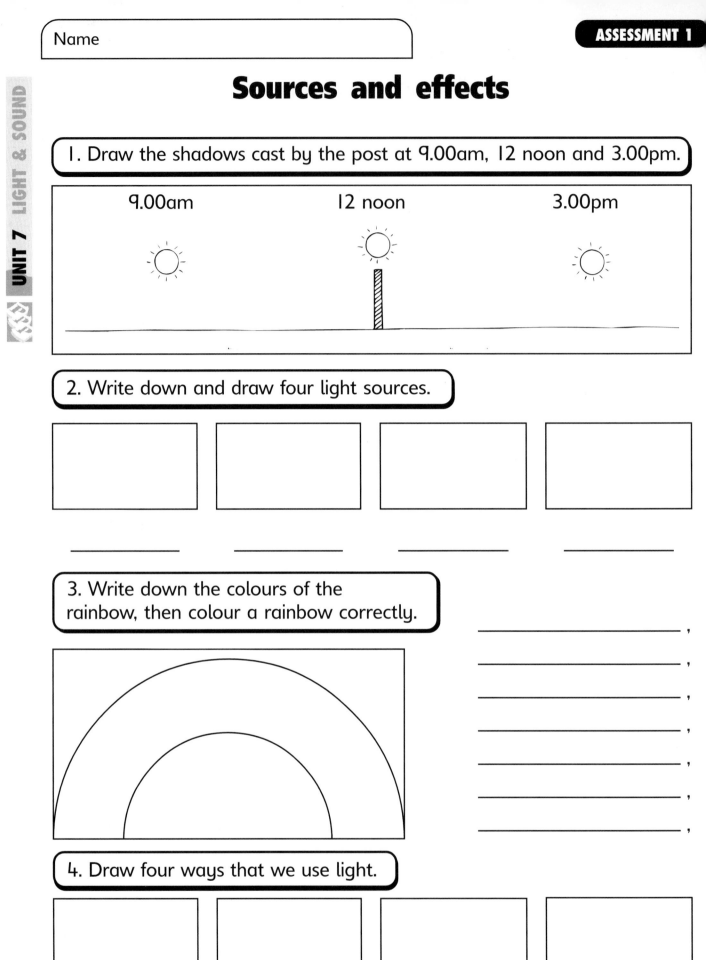

9.00am   12 noon   3.00pm

2. Write down and draw four light sources.

3. Write down the colours of the rainbow, then colour a rainbow correctly.

_____,

_____,

_____,

_____,

_____,

_____,

_____,

4. Draw four ways that we use light.

Sources and effects

The Sun and shadows

ORGANISATION (9 LESSONS)

	OBJECTIVES	MAIN ACTIVITY	GROUP ACTIVITIES	PLENARY	OUTCOMES
LESSON 1	● To ascertain the levels of the children's knowledge of light and dark in relation to sunlight from their work in KS1/P1–3.	Concept mapping.	Completing a 'day and night' worksheet. Investigating light sources.	Sharing ideas and formulating questions.	● Teacher can assess the level of the children in the class. ● Teacher can arrange children in appropriate class groups.
LESSON 2	● To know that shadows are formed when objects block light from the Sun.	Explanation of how shadows are formed.	Worksheet on shadows. Looking at shadow formation.	Reinforcing ideas about shadows.	● Can describe how shadows are formed when objects block light from the Sun.
LESSON 3	● To know that shadows of objects in sunlight change during the course of the day.	Observing and drawing shadows.		Looking at observations and drawing conclusions about how shadows change.	● Can observe, record and understand how the shadows of objects change during the course of a day.
LESSON 4	● To know that the shape and position of a shadow change at different times of day. ● To know that the shape and position of a shadow can be measured at different times of day and the results displayed graphically to show a relationship. ● To be able to measure in standard measures and present results in tables and bar charts.	Measuring the length of shadows cast by a rounders post at intervals throughout the day.		Sharing findings and addressing misconceptions.	● Can measure in standard measures and present results in tables and bar charts.
LESSON 5	● To know that the Sun appears to follow a curved path across the sky every day.	Observing and recording the path of the Sun.	Making a sunshine recorder to plot the path of the Sun on paper. Researching the Sun.	Looking at an outline drawing of the path of the Sun and describing it.	● Can describe the shape of the path of the Sun across the sky.
LESSON 6	● To know that the Sun appears to follow a curved path across the sky every day.	Relating results from previous investigations to see the relationship between the Sun's position and shadow length.		Discussing findings.	● Can describe the shape of the path of the Sun across the sky.
LESSON 7	● To know that the path of the Sun across the sky is due to the movement of the Earth, not the movement of the Sun. ● To understand that the Sun is at the centre of the Solar System and that the Earth orbits it.	How the Earth and other planets orbit the Sun.	Completing a worksheet looking at the relationship between the Sun and the Earth. Researching the Solar System using secondary sources.	Demonstration of modelling. 'Guess the planet' quiz.	● Can explain why the Sun appears to move across the sky even though it stays in the same position in space relative to the Earth. ● Can understand that the Sun is at the centre of the Solar System and that the Earth orbits around it.

ORGANISATION (9 LESSONS)

	OBJECTIVES	MAIN ACTIVITY	GROUP ACTIVITIES	PLENARY	OUT
LESSON 8	To know that shadows can be used to tell the approximate time of day.	Looking at sundials and how they are used.	Making and using a simple sundial. Completing a worksheet looking at how shadows can be used to tell the time on sundials.	Discussing the effectiveness of sundials.	Can u... tell the appro... time of day.

	OBJECTIVES		ACTIVITY 1	ACTIVITY 2
ASSESSMENT 9	To assess the children's level of understanding of the path the Sun takes across the sky and the relationship between the Earth and the Sun. To assess the understanding of the use of shadows in telling the time.		Completing a worksheet on the position of the Sun in the sky.	Completing a worksheet on sundials.

LESSON 1

OBJECTIVE

- To ascertain the levels of the children's knowledge of light and dark in relation to sunlight from their work in KS1/P1–3.

RESOURCES

Main teaching activity: Large sheets of paper on a flip chart or board.
Group activities: 1. A copy of photocopiable page 190 for each child. **2.** Paper, pencils, pens, drawing materials, pictures of the Sun or sunny scenes cut from magazines, large sheets of paper, glue, scissors.

BACKGROUND

As the centre of our solar system and the provider of almost all of the Earth's light, the Sun is the focus for many activities in this unit. Like all stars, the Sun is an extremely hot place. All of the energy on the Earth comes from the Sun and without it, life here on Earth would quite simply not exist. The sun is some 149 600 000km (93 000 000 miles) away and the light from it takes eight minutes to reach the Earth. The Sun is a sphere of atoms that generates its energy from a nuclear reaction at its core. The temperature at the core is thought to be 14–16 000 000°C (water boils on Earth at 100°C), while the surface is a rather cool 6000°C!

From work previously carried out, you can expect most children to know something about the Sun's relationship with day and night. Through work related to light and shadows the children should have learned that the sun is just one of many sources of light and that darkness is the absence of light (see also Unit 7, page 154). They may also have learned something about the relationship between the Sun and the seasons.

INTRODUCTION

Begin the lesson by talking to the children about work they will have covered in Key Stage 1/ Primary 1–3. Explain that they will be building on what they learned then and discovering a little more about the Earth.

MAIN TEACHING ACTIVITY

Ask the children to give you words that are in some way connected with the Sun. Make a list of suggestions on the board, a flip chart or an OHP, recording key words and phrases. Look for contributions from as many children as possible. In discussion with the children, try to link some of the words together to form a concept map that will indicate their level of understanding.

GROUP ACTIVITIES

1. Distribute copies of photocopiable page 190 and ask the children to complete it without working together; highlight that you want to find out what they each know individually.
2. Ask the children to think of as many light sources as they can. Tell them to make a list of light sources and use pictures to make a group collage.

DIFFERENTIATION

Because this is largely an assessment lesson, differentiation will be by outcome. For higher-attaining children you may wish to delete the word bank before copying page 190, while for lower-attaining children, you may wish to add further sentence starters, or scribe for these children while they describe their answers.

ASSESSMENT

Most children should have a good grasp of the concepts covered in Key Stage 1/Primary 1–3; however, some will not, and may continue to hold misconceptions such as that the Sun literally rises and sets or goes behind a cloud, that at night the Sun has gone to Australia, or that the Moon emits light. This activity will help to identify these misconceptions.

PLENARY

Share ideas and encourage the children to begin to formulate their own questions about what they think they would like to find out about.

OUTCOMES

- Teacher can assess the level of the children in the class.
- Teacher can arrange children in appropriate class groups.

LINKS

Unit 7, Lessons 2 and 3.

LESSON 2

OBJECTIVE

- To know that shadows are formed when objects block light from the Sun.

RESOURCES

Main teaching activity: An OHP or torch, various objects with which to make shadows.
Group activities: 1. Copies of photocopiable page 191 for each child, pens, pencils. **2.** Paper, pens, pencils, drawing materials.

Vocabulary

Sun, shadows, cast, sunlight, long, short

BACKGROUND

When light from the Sun reaches an object on Earth, it is not always able to pass through the object. Materials that let most of the light through are said to be transparent; those that let a little of the light through are translucent, and those that let none at all through are opaque. It is this last group which tend to form the best shadows. A shadow from the Sun is never still, unlike those made by many other light sources. Since the Earth is constantly moving in relation to the Sun, shadows cast by objects lit by the Sun change shape continually from sunrise to sunset. Of course, the Sun does not actually move at all.

Shadows first thing in the morning and late in the evening are longer because of the angle of the Sun's light to the Earth: the Sun appears much lower in the sky at these times. As the day progresses towards midday, the shadows become shorter as the Sun apparently 'climbs' higher in the sky to its peak. The same situation occurs on a seasonal basis, too: shadows at midday in summer are much shorter than those at midday in winter, again due to the apparent path of the Sun across the sky.

INTRODUCTION

Begin by giving the children a number of statements that will lead to the identification of a mystery thing – a shadow. When they think they know the answer, the children should write it down secretly. The statements could be: *This thing can change shape. It can appear and disappear instantly. It can be anywhere, at any time. Its shape can change before your eyes. It does not have any colour. One of these can follow you around. Sometimes they can be scary. Sometimes they can be useful. They can move, but they are not alive. Without light, they simply do not exist.*

MAIN TEACHING ACTIVITY

When the children have the answer, begin to talk a little about how shadows are formed. Encourage the children to think about the Sun and the shadows cast when the light from the Sun is blocked by objects. Using a light source, for example an OHP or torch, demonstrate shadow-making with a variety of different-shaped objects (see Unit 7, Lessons 3 and 4 for ideas).

Ask the children if they have ever noticed what happens to shadows during the day. Many will already have noticed that shadows 'move' position as the Sun appears to move across the sky, and that the shadows change their size and shape. Using the light source show how, as an object moves across in front of a light source, not only is a shadow cast, but that the shadow moves as the object moves.

GROUP ACTIVITIES

1. Distribute copies of photocopiable page 191 which asks the children to match shadows with the objects that cast them.
2. Ask the children to explain in writing and diagrams how shadows are formed. Their work should go on to explain how the Sun's shadows change during the day.

DIFFERENTIATION

Prepare a vocabulary list for lower-attaining children to use as they write about shadows. Ask higher-attaining children for more accurate, detailed explanations.

ASSESSMENT

Mark the written work and worksheet for evidence that the children have developed their understanding of how and why shadows change during the day. Can they explain what happens to the shadows? (They change size and position.)

PLENARY

Bring the children together to look at their findings from the Group activities and to reinforce the concept of changing shadows.

OUTCOME

● Can describe how shadows are formed when objects block light from the Sun.

LINKS

Unit 7, Lessons 2–4.

LESSON 3

Objective	● To know that shadows of objects in sunlight change during the course of the day.
Resources	A sunny day, paper, pencils.
Main activity	During the day the shadows of various objects, cast by the Sun, change. Ask the children to work with a partner. At regular intervals throughout the day, they should stand in the playground; one child should cast a shadow while the other partner observes and draws the shadow cast. Ensure that the children observe each other.
Differentiation	Differentiate by outcome.
Assessment	Through discussion with the children and scrutiny of their sketches ensure that the children understand that the shadows change in two ways: position and size.
Plenary	Look at each other's records and try to draw conclusions about how the shadows have changed – not just their position, but the length of the shadows cast as the day progresses.
Outcome	● Can observe, record and understand how the shadows of objects change during the course of a day.

LESSON 4

Objectives	● To know that the shape and position of a shadow change at different times of day. ● To know that the shape and position of a shadow can be measured at different times of day and the results displayed graphically to show a relationship. ● To be able to measure in standard measures and present results in tables and bar charts.
Resources	Wooden posts (rounders posts and stands), metre rulers or measuring tapes, paper, graph paper, access to a computer.
Main activity	Use pieces of wood fixed vertically (rounders posts in stands would be ideal), to cast shadows on the playground. Leave them in the same place all day where they will not be disturbed. At regular intervals throughout the day (hourly on the hour, or some other convenient regular time), observe the shadows of the posts. The children should measure and record the length of their post's shadow and tabulate the results in a simple chart. They should then use this information to draw a bar graph that will show how the shadow length shortens towards midday.

Time	Length of shadow
9.00	
10.00	
11.00	
12.00	
13.00	
14.00	
15.00	

Differentiation	Lower-attaining children could use computer software to draw a simple bar chart, or make a cut out of the shadow each hour and stick these on the wall to make a 'living' graph by the hour. Add a scale and title to the resulting display. Higher-attaining children use computer software to produce a variety of graphs.
Assessment	Assess the children's work for evidence of their ability to collect the relevant data and present information as a clear graph.
Plenary	Share findings, look at each other's graphs and draw conclusions. Try to correct any misconceptions still held about how and why shadows change during the day.
Outcome	● Can measure in standard measures and present results in tables and bar charts.

LESSON 5

OBJECTIVE
● To know that the Sun appears to follow a curved path across the sky every day.

RESOURCES
Main teaching activity: Clipboards, paper, pencils.
Group activities: 1. Sheets of paper, pencils, dowel, pots of sand, Plasticine. **2.** Paper, pencils, secondary sources of information.

PREPARATION
Gather the resources together, and make a demonstration model.

Vocabulary
arc, curved, Earth, rotation, sky, Sun, sunrise, sunset

BACKGROUND
The Sun is at the centre of our Solar System. The planets, of which Earth is just one, travel around the Sun, each in a different orbit. The Earth's orbit takes 365.25 days, which we call one year. Because of the effective loss of one quarter day every year we add an extra day into our calendar every four years, in a leap year.

At the same time as the Earth is orbiting the Sun, it is rotating about its own axis. The time taken for this to occur is 24 hours or one day. At any time, only half of the Earth is being lit by the Sun – the other half is turned away and is, therefore, in darkness. As the Earth rotates, the half of the Earth in darkness changes. This is the change from night to day. Daytime begins as the Sun appears to rise. Of course, it does not actually rise; it is simply our perspective of it as we rotate. The Sun then begins its apparent journey across the sky. The path this apparent journey takes varies depending on where you are on Earth and on the time of year. In Britain, the Sun appears to rise in the eastern sky and set in the western sky, passing on its journey through the southern sky. The path it takes is always the same general symmetrical curve or arc. The Sun is at its highest in our southern sky around midday (but this varies depending on GMT or BST). There are a number of differences in the seasonal paths that the Sun takes. In summer, the Sun appears to rise north of east and set north of west, thus if you were in the Arctic you would experience a period when the Sun did not appear to set at all, it would simply travel around the sky. In winter, the converse applies as the Sun appears to rise south of east and set south of west. There are in fact only two days when the Sun appears to rise over Britain due east and appears to set due west: 21 March and 21 September. Both are mid-way between the longest and shortest days, when the Sun rises and sets at its earliest and latest respectively.

While we still talk about the Sun rising and setting and about it travelling through the sky, it is worth reminding the children that the Sun is not moving, but that the Earth is rotating.

INTRODUCTION
Remind the children of the work they have done previously and their observations of how shadows change. Look at the shape of their charts.

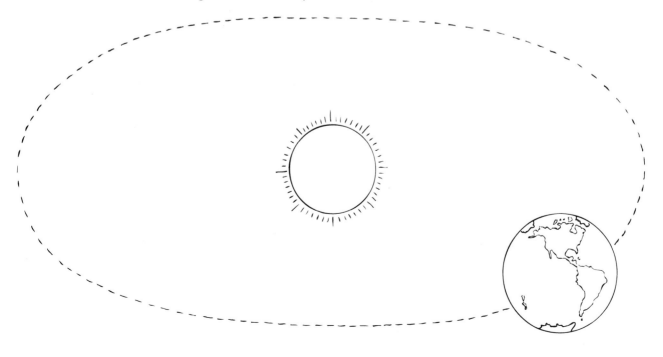

MAIN TEACHING ACTIVITY

Early in the day, take the children outside and ask them to draw the general outline of the scene from where they are standing in the playground. Without looking directly at the Sun, they should also mark on the position of the Sun relative to the objects in their outline drawing. As they mark on the position of the Sun, they should also record alongside it the time of the observation.

Back inside, tell the children that throughout the day they are going to carry out observations of the position of the Sun in the sky. Ask them to predict where they think the Sun will be in one hour. After one hour, return to exactly the same spot and observe the position of the Sun now. Were the children's predictions correct? Continue this pattern of observation and prediction hourly throughout the day, recording each time on their outline drawing.

Safety: continue to stress the importance of not looking directly at the Sun, but simply observing its general location relative to their drawings.

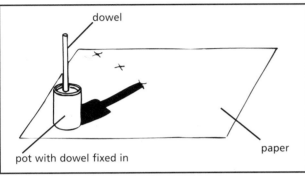

dowel

pot with dowel fixed in

paper

GROUP ACTIVITIES

1. Each group should fix a small length of dowel into a pot of sand to make a small 'sunshine recorder'. Stand the pots on sheets of paper and position them on a sunny window sill. At regular intervals throughout the day, one of the children should record the position of the end of the shadow. When seen together this will indicate the path taken by the Sun across the sky. The points could be joined in a curve to give a more accurate representation of the path. Similarly, more frequent observations and points of reference will make the task easier.

2. The children should use secondary sources to carry out some research to strengthen their background knowledge of the Sun. Their findings could be presented on a large Sun cut from coloured paper.

DIFFERENTIATION

Differentiate by outcome.

ASSESSMENT

Through observation and discussion with the children throughout the day assess their understanding of the path the Sun takes across the sky. Ask the children to explain what they are doing and to describe the shape of the path that they have plotted.

PLENARY

Use the children's outline drawings to look at the path of the Sun. Reinforce the concept that this path is only apparent and that in reality it is the Earth that is moving.

OUTCOME

● Can describe the shape of the path of the Sun across the sky.

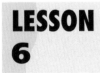

LESSON 6

Objective	● To know that the Sun appears to follow a curved path across the sky every day.
Resources	Information from previous lessons.
Main activity	Relate the results from the activities in Lessons 4 and 5 to come to some conclusions about the relationship between the position of the Sun in the sky and the length of shadows cast. Encourage the children to see that when the Sun appears to be lower in the sky, the shadows are longer and that when it is high in the sky, the shadows are shorter.
Differentiation	Differentiate by outcome.
Assessment	Look for evidence of the ability to describe the path of the Sun.
Plenary	Discuss the findings of the children and their conclusions. Reinforce the children's knowledge and ability to describe the path of the Sun across the sky and how the path is related to the position and length of shadows.
Outcome	● Can describe the shape of the path of the Sun across the sky.

OBJECTIVES

● To know that the path of the Sun across the sky is due to the movement of the Earth, not the movement of the Sun.
● To understand that the Sun is at the centre of the Solar System and the Earth orbits it.

RESOURCES

Main teaching activity: OHP or torch, globe, name cards for the nine planets and the Sun, paper, pens, pencils.
Group activities: 1. Photocopiable page 192. **2.** Secondary sources of information about the Solar System – books, CD-ROMs, videos, access to the Internet (see Preparation).

PREPARATION

You will need to find, in advance, web addresses with content suitable for the age and ability of your class if you wish the children to research further on 'space' topics on the Internet. There is a vast amount of 'space' information on the Internet, and much is far beyond the access of 7–8 year olds. The Nasa website www.nasa.gov contains much useful information.

Vocabulary
rotation, orbit, solar system, universe

BACKGROUND

The Earth has a diameter of 12 756km at the Equator and is the third planet from the Sun in our solar system. The Sun is at the centre of our solar system and in all there are nine planets that orbit the Sun.

The Earth rotates around the Sun, a journey that takes

Planet	Distance from the Sun (million km)	Diameter at Equator (km)	Time to orbit the Sun (Earth time)	Time to turn 360 degrees (Earth time)
Mercury	57.9	4879	87.97 days	58.65 days
Venus	108.2	12 104	224.7 days	243.01 days
Earth	149.6	12 756	365.25 days	24 hrs
Mars	227.9	6786	686.98 days	24hrs 37min
Jupiter	778.3	142 984	11.86 years	9hrs 55min
Saturn	1427	120 536	29.46 years	10hrs 39min
Uranus	2870	51 118	84.01 years	17hrs 14min
Neptune	4497	49 528	164.8 years	16hrs 7min
Pluto	5913	2284	248.5 years	6 days 9hrs

365.25 days. At the same time as it is orbiting the Sun, the Earth is rotating on its own axis in an anti-clockwise direction. For the Earth to rotate once on its own axis takes 24 hours – an Earth day. At any one time only half of the Earth is lit by the Sun and is in daylight; the other half is in darkness – night-time. Because of the rotation of the Earth these halves are continually changing. Throughout this, the Sun remains static so that any apparent movement of the Sun across the sky is in fact due to the rotation of the Earth.

A similar effect is experienced when you are sat on one of two trains standing side by side in a railway station. If you watch the other train as yours departs you experience an illusion that the other train may be moving when in fact it is still in the station. Because you have no fixed points of reference you assume that the other train is moving. Similarly with the Earth and Sun, it is the Earth's rotational movement that causes us to experience the illusion that the Sun is travelling across the sky.

It is important also to realise that this effect is due to the Earth's rotation on its own axis and not its orbiting around the Sun. A simple orbit with axial rotation would not produce the same effect.

INTRODUCTION

Begin the lesson by recapping on the work from previous lessons looking at the path the Sun takes across the sky. Ask the children to once again explain this to you. Ask the children if they know which is moving, the Earth or the Sun.

MAIN TEACHING ACTIVITY

Talk to the children about the Solar System, how the Sun is at its centre and that the planets orbit the Sun. Demonstrate this by using the children, in groups, to model the Solar System. You will need one child to be at the centre and represent the Sun. Other children, carrying name cards for the planets, should orbit the Sun. As they are orbiting the Sun, ask the children to rotate on their own axis and to look straight ahead at all times. This will mean that they see the Sun for only part of the time (each planet's daylight hours).

Working with one large group at a time, and using a light source such as an OHP or torch and a globe, model the relationship between the Sun and the Earth to recreate the effect of the Earth rotating on its axis as it orbits around the Sun. The children should record their observations in words and diagrams.

GROUP ACTIVITIES

1. Distribute copies of photocopiable page 192 for the children to complete. There are six mixed-up sentences to re-write correctly. These sentences reinforce the key concepts being taught in the lesson and when correctly written should read:

The Sun is the centre of our universe.
All the planets orbit the Sun.
As the Earth spins, it turns to face the Sun.
During the day, the Sun appears to move across the sky.
The Sun does not really move from east to west in the sky.
Really, the Earth moves around the Sun.

   The children are then asked to draw a diagram to show the Earth and Sun and to explain why the Sun appears to move across the sky during the day to reinforce their prior learning.

2. The children could use secondary sources to find out more about the Solar System and the orbits of the nine planets to create a series of 'factfiles' with key information about each planet. (Lessons focusing on the Solar System are provided in Unit 8 of *100 Science Lessons: Year 6/ Primary 7*.)

DIFFERENTIATION

Lower-attaining children may need support in carrying out the activity on the photocopiable page. The phrases could be enlarged for the children to cut out and paste together. Higher-attaining children work unaided and give a clear explanation of the Sun/Earth relationship.

ASSESSMENT

Mark the children's work for evidence of understanding of why the Sun appears to move across the sky even though it stays in the same position in space relative to the Earth. All of the children should be able to match up the sentences correctly and most should be able to give some explanation of how the Earth orbits the Sun. Check that this is clearly stated and that the children do not still hold the misconception of the Sun moving across the sky.

PLENARY

Ask some of the children to demonstrate the modelling of the Earth rotating around the Sun and the Sun remaining stationary. Reinforce this concept.

   Ask some other children to share their research into the Solar System with the class. Play a game of 'Guess the planet' by asking some of the children to give some simple 'planet facts' for the others to guess the identity of the planet.

OUTCOMES

● Can explain why the Sun appears to move across the sky even though it stays in the same position in space relative to the Earth.
● Can understand that the Sun is at the centre of the Solar System and that the Earth orbits it.

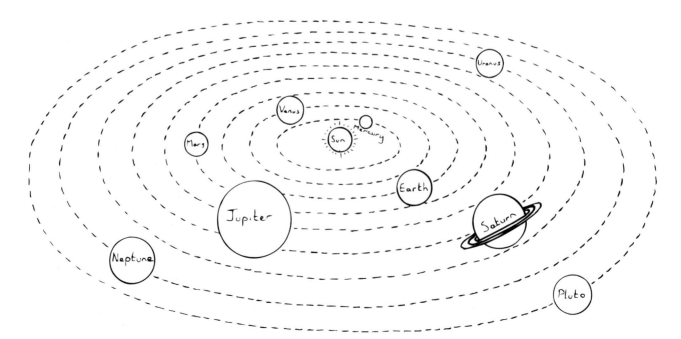

LESSON 8

OBJECTIVE

● To know that shadows can be used to tell the approximate time of day.

RESOURCES

Main teaching activity: A sundial (or a picture of one).
Group activities: 1. Flat wooden boards with a central hole drilled to fit pieces of dowel (one per group, but you can share if necessary), paper templates (one per group), art materials, glue to fasten the dowel in place, reference materials, such as guidebooks for stately homes, showing old sundials (optional). **2.** Copies of photocopiable page 193.

PREPARATION

Prepare materials for making sundials.

Vocabulary

approximate, calibrate, cast, estimate, measure, shadows, sundial

BACKGROUND

Shadows are formed because light travels in straight lines and is unable to bend to go around objects that will not allow light through. On a bright sunny day, the Sun casts shadows that are very sharp at the edges. On overcast days the shadows are more indistinct and fuzzy.

Shadows have been used for many centuries to help man mark time. We know that the Earth rotates around the Sun giving the illusion that the Sun is travelling across our sky. This has been used to mark out the passage of time during the day. The first sundials were used, it is thought, over 4000 years ago by the Chinese. Today they are generally only used for decorative purposes due to the unreliability of certain climates. A sundial works by casting a shadow from a simple pole onto the dial below. After calibration, they can be used alongside our time-keeping and measuring system.

INTRODUCTION

Begin the lesson by asking: *What time is it? How do you know?* Most will be able to tell you about clocks and watches and many will have a sound understanding of time. Ask the children if they know how people used to tell the time before watches and clocks were invented. They may be able to give you a number of ways of measuring the passage of time, such as sand timers or tickers, but this is obviously slightly different.

MAIN TEACHING ACTIVITY

Lead the discussion by suggesting that one method of telling the time is connected with something that is always present even though we may not be able to see it. Give clues that will lead the children to think about the Sun as a means of telling the time. Introduce the idea of a sundial and show the children an actual sundial (or a picture of one). Set the sundial up and see if the children can use it to tell the time.

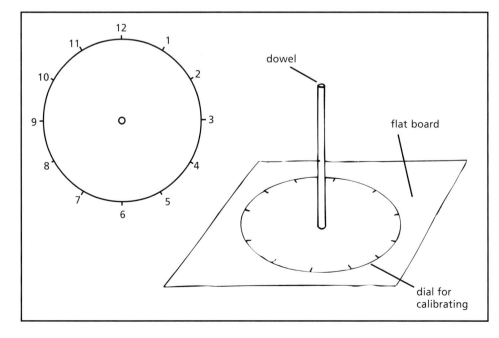

GROUP ACTIVITIES

1. Use flat boards with a vertical piece of dowel to make a simple sundial. A face can be made from a circle of paper with a central hole that can be slotted onto the sundial. (See diagram, left). The children could research historic designs of sundials, reproducing them or using them as inspiration for their own designs. Guidebooks from stately homes and historic houses or gardens often contain pictures. The children may observe that real sundials do not usually cover the full 24-hour period; ask them why this is. (There is no sunlight at night.)

The sundial will need to be set up and calibrated by marking the position of the shadow at specific times, preferably on the hour. This will need to be repeated every hour so that a calibrated dial can be set up. After this the children can use the sundial to estimate the time. Set them a series of challenges to estimate the time using the sundial and then checking the time on a clock. With experience, can they improve the accuracy with which they use the sundial to estimate the time (although there will be an accuracy range of several minutes)? The children can record their estimates in a table:

Estimate of time using sundial	Actual time	Accuracy

2. Distribute copies of photocopiable page 193 for the children to complete. This involves the children looking at sundials and estimating the time shown on them.

DIFFERENTIATION

Lower-attaining children may need some adult support with photocopiable page 193. Higher-attaining children work unaided.

ASSESSMENT

Using photocopiable page 193 and through observation and questioning, assess the children for their ability to tell the approximate time using a sundial. The answer to question 1

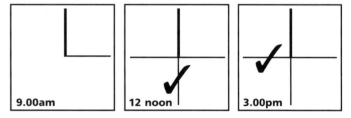

9.00am   12 noon   3.00pm

is shown on the right. For question 2, most of the children should be able to tell the approximate time. (The time would be 12 noon.) Higher-attainers will be able to be more specific and precise in telling the time. For question 3, sundials are not used very often today for several reasons: they are inaccurate, they are unreliable and we have alternative methods of telling the time.

PLENARY

Ask the children to demonstrate their sundials and their skill in telling the (approximate) time using them. Ask the children to think about why sundials are not a very efficient, reliable or accurate way of telling the time.

OUTCOMES

● Can make a sundial.
● Can use a sundial to tell the approximate time of day.

LINKS

Unit 7, Lessons 2–4.

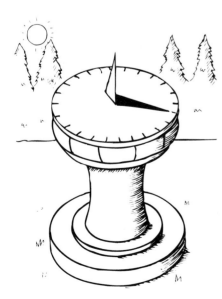

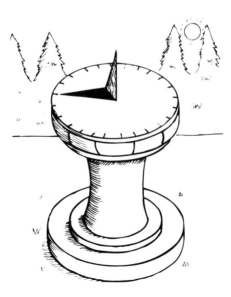

LESSON 9

OBJECTIVES

● To assess the level of understanding of the path the sun takes across the sky and the relationship between the Earth and the Sun.
● To assess the understanding of the use of shadows in telling the time.

RESOURCES

Assessment activities: 1. Copies of photocopiable page 194, pens and pencils. **2.** Copies of photocopiable page 195, pens and pencils.

INTRODUCTION

Begin the Assessment activities by giving the children a vocabulary test – this could be oral or written. Remember the activity is an assessment of scientific knowledge and understanding, not of writing skill. Either give a word and ask for a definition or a definition and ask for a word.

ASSESSMENT ACTIVITY 1

Distribute copies of photocopiable page 194 to the children and allow them time to complete it individually. You may wish to tell the children that you want to find out what they have understood and that it is important to complete the sheet individually. You will need to collect these sheets in order to mark them effectively.

Answers

1. The path drawn by the children should be arc-shaped from east to west.
2. The Sun appears to rise in the east.
   The Sun appears to set in the west.
   At midday the Sun is in the southern sky.
3. The illustration should show the Earth orbiting the Sun and not vice versa.

Looking for levels

Assess the children's work in Assessment activity 1 for evidence of understanding. Most children should be able to answer questions 1 and 2. Many should be able to give an explanation of how the Earth orbits the Sun for question 3.

ASSESSMENT ACTIVITY 2

Distribute copies of photocopiable page 195 to the children and allow them time to complete it individually. You may wish to tell the children that you want to find out what they have understood and that it is important to complete the sheet individually. You will need to collect these sheets in order to mark them effectively.

Answers

1. Children should write 'Sundials need the sun to be useful'; 'Sundials can be used to give approximate times'; and 'Sundials use shadows to show the time' in the 'True' column. The other five statements are false.
2. The illustration and explanation should give some indication of how sundials work and are used.

Looking for levels

Although requiring a good level of literacy skill, most should be able to complete this task. You may like to read the sentences in question 1 for lower-attaining children as this is not a test of reading but scientific understanding.

PLENARY

Discuss the Assessment activities and address any misconceptions still held by the children.

Sunlight

Look at the diagram. Shade one side of the Earth to show the side that is dark. Write 'day' and 'night' on the correct sides of the Earth picture.

Sun   **Earth**

Explain how day and night are caused.

Day _____

Night _____

Complete these sentences. Choose from these words:

earlier	later	shorter	longer

In summer the days are _____ because the Sun sets _____.

In winter the days are _____ because the Sun sets _____.

Draw a picture of the Sun in the sky in summer and a picture of the Sun in the sky in winter.

Summer	**Winter**

Why is it dangerous to look at the Sun?

_____

Name

Matching shadows

Here are some shadows.
Can you match them to the object that cast them?

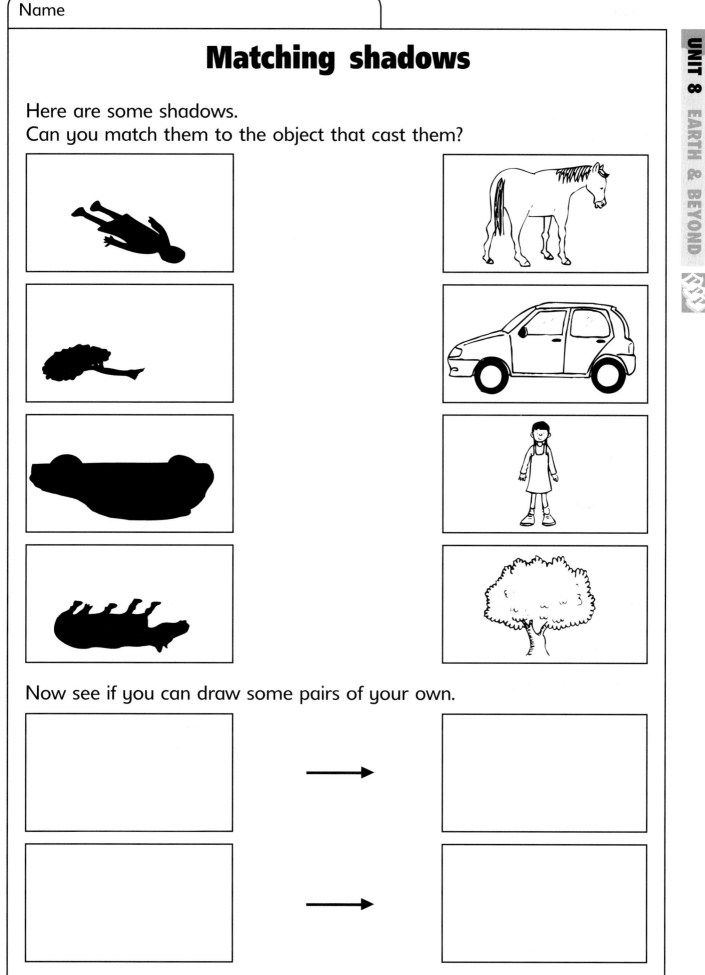

Now see if you can draw some pairs of your own.

Look at the objects and their shadows. Describe what you notice about the shape of each.

The Sun and the Earth

Look carefully at all these phrases. They fit together to make six statements about how we see the Sun in the sky. Can you match up the parts to write the statements correctly?

The Sun is   **orbit the Sun.**

All the planets   **appears to move across the sky.**

As the Earth spins,   **around the Sun.**

During the day, the Sun   **from east to west in the sky.**

The Sun does not really move   **the centre of our Solar System.**

Really, the Earth moves   **it turns to face the Sun.**

Now write the six statements.

1. _____

2. _____

3. _____

4. _____

5. _____

6. _____

Draw a diagram to show the Earth and the Sun. Explain why the Sun appears to move across the sky during the day.

Telling the time with shadows

This is a stick. The first box shows its shadow at 9.00am.
Put a tick against the correct shadows for 12 noon and 3.00pm.

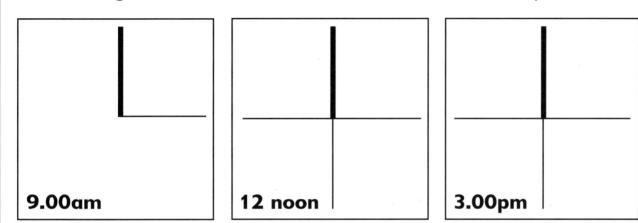

9.00am	**12 noon**	**3.00pm**

A sundial can be used to tell the time. If the Sun is shining from the direction of the arrow draw the shadow on this sundial.

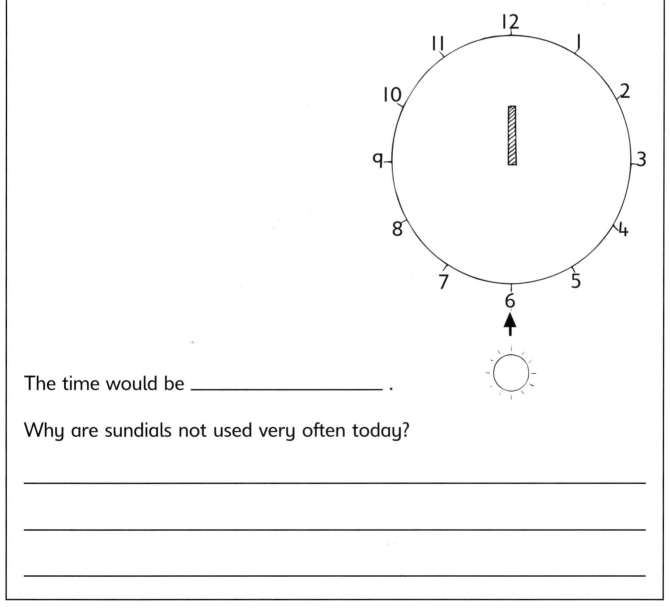

The time would be _____ .

Why are sundials not used very often today?

_____

_____

_____

The Sun and shadows

1. Draw the path of the Sun as it moves across the sky during the day.

east   **west**

2. Complete these sentences.

The Sun appears to rise in the _____.

The Sun appears to set in the _____.

At midday the Sun appears to be in the _____ of the sky.

3. Draw a picture to show how the Earth orbits the Sun.

Use this space to explain more about your drawing.

_____

_____

_____

The Sun and shadows

1. Put these statements about sundials into the correct column:

Sundials are accurate.
Sundials can be used on cloudy, overcast days.
Sundials are easy to carry about.
Sundials can be used inside.
Sundials need the Sun to be useful.
Sundials can be used to give approximate times.
Sundials are a modern invention.
Sundials use shadows to show the time.

True	False

2. Draw a picture of a sundial and explain
   how to use it to tell the approximate time.

National Curriculum in England

LINKS TO QCA SCIENCE SCHEME OF WORK

SC1 SCIENTIFIC ENQUIRY

1 Ideas and evidence in science

a that science is about thinking creatively to try to explain how living and non-living things work, and to establish links between causes and effects

b that it is important to test ideas using evidence from observation and measurement

2 Investigative skills – Planning

a ask questions that can be investigated scientifically and decide how to find answers

b consider what sources of information, including first-hand experience and a range of other sources, they will use to answer questions

c think about what might happen or try things out when deciding what to do, what kind of evidence to collect, and what equipment and materials to use

d make a fair test or comparison by changing one factor and observing or measuring the effect while keeping other factors the same

Investigative skills – Obtaining and presenting evidence

e use simple equipment and materials appropriately and take action to control risks

f make systematic observations and measurements, including the use of ICT for data-logging

g check observations and measurements by repeating them where appropriate

h use a wide range of methods, including diagrams, drawings, tables, bar charts, line graphs and ICT, to communicate data in an appropriate and systematic manner

Investigative skills – Considering evidence and evaluating

i make comparisons and identify simple patterns or associations in their own observations and measurements or other data

j use observations, measurements or other data to draw conclusions

k decide whether these conclusions agree with any prediction made and/or whether they enable further predictions to be made

l use their scientific knowledge and understanding to explain observations, measurements or other data or conclusions

m review their work and the work of others and describe its significance and limitations

SC2 LIFE PROCESSES AND LIVING THINGS

1 Life processes

a that the life processes common to humans and other animals include nutrition, movement, growth and reproduction

b that the life processes common to plants include growth, nutrition and reproduction

c to make links between life processes in familiar animals and plants and the environments in which they are found

2 Humans and other animals – Nutrition

a about the functions and care of teeth

b about the need for food for activity and growth, and about the importance of an adequate and varied diet for health

Humans and other animals – Circulation

c that the heart acts as a pump to circulate the blood through vessels around the body, including through the lungs

d about the effect of exercise and rest on pulse rate

Humans and other animals – Movement

e that humans and some other animals have skeletons and muscles to support and protect their bodies and to help them to move

Humans and other animals – Growth and reproduction

f about the main stages of the human life cycle

Humans and other animals – Health

g about the effects on the human body of tobacco, alcohol and other drugs, and how these relate to their personal health

h about the importance of exercise for good health

3 Green plants – Growth and nutrition

a the effect of light, air, water and temperature on plant growth

b the role of the leaf in producing new material for growth

c that the root anchors the plant, and that water and minerals are taken in through the root and transported through the stem to other parts of the plant

Green plants – Reproduction

d about the parts of the flower and their role in the life cycle of flowering plants, including pollination, seed formation, seed dispersal and germination

4 Variation and classification

a to make and use keys

b how locally occurring animals and plants can be identified and assigned to groups

c that the variety of plants and animals makes it important to identify them and assign them to groups

5 Living things in their environment

a about ways in which living things and the environment need protection

Living things in their environment – Adaptation

b about the different plants and animals found in different habitats

c how animals and plants in two different habitats are suited to their environment

Living things in their environment – Feeding relationships

d to use food chains to show feeding relationships in a habitat

e about how nearly all food chains start with a green plant

Living things in their environment – Micro-organisms

f that micro-organisms are living organisms that are often too small to be seen, and that they may be beneficial or harmful

SC3 MATERIALS & THEIR PROPERTIES

1 Grouping and classifying

a to compare everyday materials and objects on the basis of their material properties, including hardness, strength, flexibility and magnetic behaviour, and to relate these properties to everyday uses of the materials

b that some materials are better thermal insulators than others

c that some materials are better electrical conductors than others

d to describe and group rocks and soils on the basis of their characteristics, including appearance, texture and permeability

e to recognise differences between solids, liquids and gases, in terms of ease of flow and maintenance of shape and volume

2 Changing materials

a to describe changes that occur when materials are mixed

b to describe changes that occur when materials are heated or cooled

c that temperature is a measure of how hot or cold things are

d about reversible changes, including dissolving, melting, boiling, condensing, freezing and evaporating

e the part played by evaporation and condensation in the water cycle

f that non-reversible changes result in the formation of new materials that may be useful

g that burning materials results in the formation of new materials and that this change is not usually reversible

3 Separating mixtures of materials

a how to separate solid particles of different sizes

b that some solids dissolve in water to give solutions but some do not

c how to separate insoluble solids from liquids by filtering

d how to recover dissolved solids by evaporating the liquid from the solution

e to use knowledge of solids, liquids and gases to decide how mixtures might be separated

Lessons where curriculum content is the main objective are listed below. Lessons where content is included but is not the main focus are shown below in brackets.

Unit 1: Ourselves Teeth and food	Unit 2: Animals & Plants The needs of plants and animals	Unit 3: The environment How the environment affects living things	Unit 4: Materials Natural & manufactured materials	Unit 5: Electricity Electricity and communication	Unit 6: Forces & motion Magnets and springs	Unit 7: Light & sound Sources and effects	Unit 8: Earth & beyond The Sun and shadows
UNIT 3A	UNIT 3B	–	UNIT 3C, 3D, (3E)	–	UNIT 3E	UNIT 3F	UNIT 3F
					3	10, 12	3
	8				(8)	10, 12	
	4, 12, 14	4	13, 14		5, 8, 9, 10, 11	10, 12	
	13, 15, 16, 17	8	5, 10, 11, 14		5		
	13		10	3, 5, 6, 7, (8)	5, 8	10, 12	5, 8
2, 3, 5, 6, 9	4, 5	4	9, 11		5		4, 5
5	18						4
1, 2, 8	1, 3, 10, 11	(1), 3, 4, 7, 9	(1)	(1), 4	1, (4), 5, 7	1, 3, 8, 9, 11, 13	1, 4, 5, 7
	2, 7, 9	5, 6, 8	2, 8, 12		2, 6, 9	2, (4), 10, 11	2
	8		3		3, 7	5, 6, 7	3, 6
			13, 14		3		
(1), 4, 7, 9, 10	12		4, 7	(2)	5, 9, (12)	(10)	5, 6, 8
	6	2	6		9, 10	6, 7	6, 8
(2), (3), (4), (5)	(1), 2, (4), 5, 6, 7, 8, 19						
	(1), 2, (19)						
(1), 6, 7, 8, 11							
2, 3, 4, 11	(9)						
(1)							
(1)	3, (4)						
(1), 5							
	10, 11, 12, 13, 15, 17, 18, 19						
	16, 18, 19						
		7, 9, 10					
	14	1, (2), (3), (4), 5, 6, 10					
		(3), 5					
		8					
			1, 2, 3, 4, 5, 6, (7), (8), 15				
			9, 10, 11, 12, 13, 14, 15				
			1				
			(1)				

SC4 Physical processes overleaf

National Curriculum in England (cont)

LINKS TO QCA SCIENCE SCHEME OF WORK

SC4 PHYSICAL PROCESSES	**1 Electricity – Simple circuits**	
	a	to construct circuits, incorporating a battery or power supply and a range of switches, to make electrical devices work
	b	how changing the number or type of components in a series circuit can make bulbs brighter or dimmer
	c	how to represent series circuits by drawings and conventional symbols; how to construct series circuits on the basis of drawings and diagrams using conventional symbols
	2 Forces and motion – Types of force	
	a	about the forces of attraction and repulsion between magnets, and about the forces of attraction between magnets and magnetic materials
	b	that objects are pulled downwards because of the gravitational attraction between them and the Earth
	c	about friction, including air resistance, as a force that slows moving objects and may prevent objects from starting to move are pushed or pulled
	d	that when objects are pushed or pulled an opposing pull or push can be felt
	e	how to measure forces and identify the direction in which they act
	3 Light and sound – Everyday effects of light	
	a	that light travels from a source
	b	that light cannot pass through some materials, and how this leads to the formation of shadows
	c	that light is reflected from surfaces
	Light and sound – Seeing	
	d	that we see things only when light from them enters our eyes
	Light and sound – Vibration and sound	
	e	that sounds are made when objects vibrate but that vibrations are not always directly visible
	f	how to change the pitch and loudness of sounds produced by some vibrating objects
	g	that vibrations from sound sources require a medium through which to travel to the ear
	4 The Earth and beyond – The Sun, Earth and Moon	
	a	that the Sun, Earth and Moon are approximately spherical
	The Earth and beyond – Periodic changes	
	b	how the position of the Sun appears to change during the day, and how shadows change as this happens
	c	how day and night are related to the spin of the Earth on its own axis
	d	that the Earth orbits the Sun once each year, and that the Moon takes approximately 28 days to orbit the Earth

National Curriculum in Wales

SCIENTIFIC ENQUIRY	**1 The nature of science**	
	the link between ideas and information in science	
	1	to apply their ideas and knowledge and understanding of science when thinking about and investigating phenomena in the world around them
	2	to consider information obtained from their own work and also, on some occasions, from other sources
	3	that scientific ideas can be tested by means of information gathered from observation and measurement
	2 Communication in science	
	presenting scientific information	
	1	to report their work clearly in speech and writing using relevant scientific vocabulary
	2	to use a range of methods, including diagrams, drawings, graphs, tables and charts, to record and present information in an appropriate and systematic manner
	3	to use ICT to select and present a range of relevant information, when this is appropriate
	4	to use standard measures and units handling scientific information
	5	to search for and access relevant scientific information, using ICT to do so on some occasions
	6	to recognise that it is useful to present and consider scientific information in an appropriate form, making use of ICT to do so when appropriate
	planning an investigation	
	1	to turn ideas suggested to them, and their own ideas, into a form that can be investigated
	2	that asking questions, and using their knowledge and understanding of the context to anticipate what may happen, can be useful when planning what to do
	3	to decide what information should be collected
	4	that in situations where the factors can be identified and controlled, a fair test may be carried out
	5	to consider what equipment or other resources to use
	6	to recognise the hazards and risks to themselves and others obtaining information
	7	to use equipment or other resources correctly, taking action to control risks
	8	to make careful observations and measurements and record them appropriately
	9	to check observations and measurements by repeating them, when this is appropriate
	10	to use ICT equipment and software to monitor changes
	considering information	
	11	to make comparisons and to identify and describe trends or patterns in data
	12	to use the results of their investigations to draw conclusions
	13	to try to relate the outcomes of their investigation or their conclusions to their scientific knowledge and understanding
	14	to review their work and suggest how their data could be improved
LIFE PROCESSES AND LIVING THINGS	**1 Life processes**	
	1	that there are life processes, including nutrition, movement, growth and reproduction, common to animals, including humans
	2	that there are life processes, including growth, nutrition and reproduction, common to plants
	2 Humans and other animals	
	nutrition	
	1	how the teeth break up food into smaller pieces and the importance of dental care
	2	that the body needs different foods for activity and for growth
	3	that an adequate and varied diet is needed to keep healthy
	circulation	
	4	that the heart acts as a pump
	5	how blood circulates in the body through arteries and veins
	6	that the pulse gives a measure of the heart beat rate
	7	the effect of exercise and rest on pulse rate
	movement	
	8	that humans and some other animals have skeletons and muscles to support and protect their bodies and to help them to move
	growth and reproduction	
	9	the main stages of the human life cycle
	health	
	10	that tobacco, alcohol and other drugs can have harmful effects

Lessons where curriculum content is the main objective are listed below. Lessons where content is included but is not the main focus are shown below in brackets.

Unit 1: Ourselves Teeth and food	Unit 2: Animals & Plants The needs of plants and animals	Unit 3: The environment How the environment affects living things	Unit 4: Materials Natural & manufactured materials	Unit 5: Electricity Electricity and communication	Unit 6: Forces & motion Magnets and springs	Unit 7: Light & sound Sources and effects	Unit 8: Earth & beyond The Sun and shadows
UNIT 3A	UNIT 3B	–	UNIT 3C, 3D, (3E)	–	UNIT 3E	UNIT 3F	UNIT 3F
				1, (2), 3, 4, 5, 6, 7 (8), (9)			
					1, 2, 3, 4, 5, 13		
					(1)		
					(1)		
					6, 7, 8, 10, 11, 13		
					(9)		
						1, (5), 14	
						1, 2, 3, 4	
						(1)	
						(1), (5), (6), (7)	
						8, 9, (13), 14	
						10, 11, 12	
						(13)	
				(12)			(1)
							(1), 2, 3, 4, 5, 6, 8, 9
							(1), 7
							7, 9

Unit 1: Ourselves Teeth and food	Unit 2: Animals & Plants The needs of plants and animals	Unit 3: The environment How the environment affects living things	Unit 4: Materials Natural & manufactured materials	Unit 5: Electricity Electricity and communication	Unit 6: Forces & motion Magnets and springs	Unit 7: Light & sound Sources and effects	Unit 8: Earth & beyond The Sun and shadows
(1)	12						
					2		
(1)	1	1	1	1		1, 7, 8, 12	1, 2
2	2, 3, 6, 10, 11	8, 9	5	1, 2, 4	7, 12		4
2, 3					7, 12	6	4
5			14				
(2)	6	2, 5			4, (12)	6, 13	7
2, 3, 5, 9	14	2, 5		8	1, 7	6	4
	4				5, 11	2, 3, (5), 9, 12	8
	4				5, 11	2, 3, 12	8
	13, 14, 15, 16, 17					9	8
	13, 14, 15, 16, 17	8	5, 10, 11, 14		5		
	18						
		4			8, 9, 10, 11	(5), 9	
8, 10	5		5	3, 5, 6, 7	8, 9, 10, 11		4, 5
6	5	4, 6, 7	7, 12		3	9, 10, 11, 12	4, 5
		2, 3			8	(5)	4, 5
						9, 10, 11, 12	
4, (7)	2, 3, 7, 9	3	2, 3, 4, 8, 9		3, 6, 9, 10, 11	2, 10	2, 3, 6
10	8		5, 13		5	10	4, 8
8				(7)	9, 10		4, 5
		7	6		5	4	
(1), (3), (5), (6)	(1), 2, (4), 5, 6, 7, 8, 19						
	(1), 10, 19						
(1), 6, 7, 8, 11							
2, 3, 11							
4, 11	(9)						
(1)							
(1)	3, (4)						
(1), 5							

Life processes and living things continued overleaf

National Curriculum in Wales (cont)

LIFE PROCESSES AND LIVING THINGS (cont)

3 Green plants as organisms

growth and nutrition

1	to investigate the effect on the growth of plants of changing their conditions
2	that plants need light to produce food for growth, and the importance of the leaf in this process
3	that the root anchors the plant, and that water and nutrients are taken in through the root and transported through the stem to other parts of the plant

reproduction

4	the main stages in the life cycle of flowering plants including pollination, seed production, seed dispersal and germination
5	about the process of pollination in flowering plants
6	how pollen and seeds can be transported

4 Living things in their environment

adaptation

1	to find out about the variety of plants and animals found in different habitats including the local area
2	how animals and plants in two different habitats are suited to their environment

feeding relationships

3	that food chains show feeding relationships in an ecosystem
4	that nearly all food chains start with a green plant variation
5	how locally occurring animals and plants can be identified and assigned to groups, by making and using keys

MATERIALS & THEIR PROPERTIES

1 Grouping and classifying materials

1	to compare everyday materials, on the basis of their properties, including hardness, strength, flexibility and magnetic behaviour, and to relate these properties to everyday uses of the materials
2	that some materials are better thermal insulators/conductors than others
3	that some materials are better electrical conductors/insulators than others
4	to describe and group rocks on the basis of appearance and texture, and soils on the basis of particle size and permeability
5	to recognise differences between solids, liquids and gases, in terms of their properties.

2 Changing materials

1	to explore changes in materials and recognise those that can be reversed and those that cannot
2	that dissolving, melting, condensing, freezing and evaporating are changes that can be reversed
3	that irreversible changes result in a new material being produced, which may be useful
4	that the changes that occur when most materials are burned are not reversible, and result in a new material being produced
5	that mixing materials can cause them to change
6	that heating or cooling materials can cause them to change
7	that temperature is a measure of how hot or cold things are
8	the part played by evaporation and condensation in the water cycle

3 Separating mixtures of materials

1	that solid particles of different sizes can be separated by sieving
2	that some solids are soluble in water and will dissolve to give solutions but some will not, and that this provides a means of separating different solids
3	that insoluble solids can be separated from liquids by filtering
4	that solids that have dissolved can be recovered by evaporating the liquid from the solution

PHYSICAL PROCESSES

1 Electricity

simple circuits

1	that a complete conducting circuit, including a battery or power supply, is needed for a current to flow to make electrical devices work
2	to investigate how switches can be used to control electrical devices in simple series and parallel arrangements
3	that the brightness of bulbs and the rotation of motors can be controlled by altering the current
4	ways of varying the current in a circuit, including changing the power supply, and changing the length of conductor in a circuit
5	how to represent simple circuits by drawings and diagrams, and how to construct such circuits on the basis of drawings and diagrams

2 Forces and motion

behaviour of forces

1	to measure forces between objects and find out how the forces change in size
2	that forces act in particular directions
3	that forces con make things speed up, slow down, or change direction

types of force

4	that there are forces of attraction and repulsion between magnets, and forces of attraction between magnets and some materials
5	that the weight of an object is the force of the Earth on the object and is measured in newtons
6	about friction, including air resistance, as a force between surfaces which slows moving objects and may prevent them from starting to move
7	that objects that are stretched or compressed exert a force on whatever is changing their shape
8	that the change in shape of a spring is used in force meters for measuring forces

3 Light and sound

everyday effects of light

1	that light travels from a source
2	that we see light sources because light from them travels to and enters our eyes
3	we see objects because light falling on them is reflected
4	that most of the light falling on shiny surfaces and mirrors is reflected
5	that light cannot pass through some materials, and that this leads to the formation of shadows

vibration and sound

6	that sounds are made when objects vibrate but that vibrations are not always directly visible
7	that the pitch and loudness of sounds produced by some vibrating objects can be changed
8	that vibrations from sound sources can travel through a variety of materials

4 The Earth and beyond

the Sun, Moon and planets

1	that the Sun, Earth and Moon are approximately spherical
2	the relative positions of the Sun, Earth and other planets in the solar system

periodic changes

3	how the position of the Sun appears to change during the day, and how shadows change as this happens
4	that the Earth spins around its own axis, and how day and night are related to this spin
5	that the Earth orbits the Sun once each year, and that the Moon takes approximately 28 days to orbit the Earth)

Lessons where curriculum content is the main objective are listed below. Lessons where content is included but is not the main focus are shown below in brackets.

Unit 1: Ourselves Teeth and food	Unit 2: Animals & Plants The needs of plants and animals	Unit 3: The environment How the environment affects living things	Unit 4: Materials Natural & manufactured materials	Unit 5: Electricity Electricity and communication	Unit 6: Forces & motion Magnets and springs	Unit 7: Light & sound Sources and effects	Unit 8: Earth & beyond The Sun and shadows
	(10), 13, 17, 18, 19						
	15, 16						
	11, 12						
	14	1, 6, (7), (8), (9)					
		(2), (3), (4), 5, 6, 10					
			1, 2, 3, 4, 5, 6, 7, 8, 15				
			9, 10, 11, 12, 13, 14, 15				
		1					
		1					
				(1), (2), 4, 5, 6, 7, (8), (9)			
				3			
					5		
					2, 3, 6, 7, 8, 9, 10		
					1, 8, 9, 10, 11		
					1, 2, 3, 4, 5		
					(1)		
					(1)		
					(1), 6, 7, 8, 9, 10, (11)		
						1, (5), (6), (7), 14	
					(12)	(1), (5), (6), (7)	
						(1)	
						1, 2, 3, 4, 14	
						(8), 9, 13, 14	
						10, 11, 12	
						(13)	
					(12)		(1)
							(1), 2, 3, 4, 5, 6, 8, 9
							(1), 7
							7

Unit 1: Ourselves Teeth and food	Unit 2: Animals & Plants The needs of plants and animals	Unit 3: The environment How the environment affects living things	Unit 4: Materials Natural & manufactured materials	Unit 5: Electricity Electricity and communication	Unit 6: Forces & motion Magnets and springs	Unit 7: Light & sound Sources and effects	Unit 8: Earth & beyond The Sun and shadows

The Northern Ireland Curriculum

Pupils should be encouraged to adopt safe practices when undertaking science and technology activities.
They should be made aware of potential hazards and the appropriate actions necessary to avoid risks.

INVESTIGATING AND MAKING IN SCIENCE AND TECHNOLOGY

Planning
Pupils should have opportunities to participate in practical activities which involve them in talking to the teacher and each other about ideas predictions and solutions to problems and planning what to make.

a respond to questions
b talk about what they are going to make and the materials they will use
c ask questions, discuss ideas and make predictions
d recognise a fair test
e suggest ideas which can be investigated and make predictions
f choose appropriate materials and components when planning what to make

Carrying out and making
Pupils should have opportunities to participate in practical activities which involve them in exploring familiar objects and materials in their immediate environment and recording what they have done.

a make observations using their senses
b assemble and rearrange materials
c make observations noting similarities and differences
d record observations in a simple form
e explore different ways of joining materials
f reinforce measuring skills using non-standard measures and progress to using standard measures
g develop manipulative skills using a range of materials and tools
h record what they have done or observed using appropriate methods

Interpreting and evaluating
Pupils should participate in practical activities which provide them with opportunities to develop skills in reporting, presenting and interpreting results and evaluating what they have made.

a talk to the teacher and others about what happened or about what they have made
b comment on what happened or what they like or dislike about what they have made
c present their findings using appropriate methods
d relate what happened to what they predicted
e talk about what they have made in terms of materials, colour, size or shape and make suggestions for improvement

KNOWLEDGE AND UNDERSTANDING OF SCIENCE AND TECHNOLOGY

Living things

Ourselves
a recognise and name the main external parts of the human body
b observe seasonal changes and talk about how these affect themselves
c explore similarities and differences between themselves and other children
d develop ideas about how to keep healthy, through exercise, rest, diet, personal hygiene and safety
e be introduced to the main stages of human development
f find out about themselves including how they grow, move and use their senses

Animals and plants
a find out about the variety of animal and plant life both through direct observations and by using secondary sources
b sort living things into the two broad groups of animals and plants
c recognise and name the main parts of a flowering plant including root, stem, leaf and flower
d sort living things into groups using observable features
e find out about animals and their young
f find out about some animals, including how they grow, feed, move and use their senses
g observe similarities and differences among animals and among plants
h discuss the use of colour in the natural environment
i find out ways in which animal and plant behaviour is influenced by seasonal changes

Materials

Properties
a work with a range of everyday materials in a variety of activities
b sort a range of everyday objects into groups according to the materials from which they are made
c explore the properties of materials including shape, colour, texture and behaviour
d find out some everyday uses of materials
e investigate similarities and differences in materials and objects; sort them according to their properties

Change
a find out about the effect of heating and cooling some everyday substances, such as water, chocolate or butter
b investigate which everyday substances dissolve in water

Environment
a identify the range of litter in and around their own locality
b find out how human activities create a variety of waste products
c find out that some materials decay naturally while others do not

Physical Processes

Forces and energy
a explore forces which push, pull or make things move
b explore devices, including toys, which move
c explore how pushes and pulls make things speed up or stop
d find out about the range of energy sources used in school and at home

Electricity
a find out about some uses of electricity in the home and classroom
b know that electricity can be dangerous
c know about the safe use of mains electricity and its associated dangers

Sound
a listen to and identify sources of sounds in their immediate environment
b explore ways of making sounds using familiar objects
c investigate how sounds are produced when objects vibrate

Light
a find out that light comes from a variety of sources
b explore the use of light including colour in relation to road safety
c explore how light passes through some materials and not others

EMU and Cultural Heritage Pupils should have opportunities to develop an understanding of themselves and others by exploring similarities and differences between themselves and other children, and developing a sense of their own individuality. They should appreciate the environment around them, the need to take care of it

Lessons where curriculum content is the main objective are listed below. Lessons where content is included but is not the main focus are shown below in brackets.

PROGRAMME OF STUDY SCIENCE KS1

Unit 1: Ourselves Teeth and food	Unit 2: Animals & Plants The needs of plants and animals	Unit 3: The environment How the environment affects living things	Unit 4: Materials Natural & manufactured materials	Unit 5: Electricity Electricity and communication	Unit 6: Forces & motion Magnets and springs	Unit 7: Light & sound Sources and effects	Unit 8: Earth & beyond The Sun and shadows
2	1	1	1, 2	1	1, 4, 6, 12	1, 8	1
				3	8, 10, 11	4, 10, 12	
	4	8	5, 6			2, 10, 12	5, 8
		8	5, 10, 11, 14		5		
	13, 14, 15, 16, 17, 18	2	5, 10, 11, 14		5		
				(3), 5, 6	8, 10, 11	4	5, 8
6, 8, 10	2, 12		2, 3, 4, 8, 9, 12		2	2, 3, 5, (6), 7, 9	7
					8, 10, 11	4	5, 8
	7, 8, 9	(5), 6	2, 3, 4, 7, 11, 13		3	12	3
	3, 11		10		3, 7	9	5
5	5	4	5, 10, 11, 14		5, 9		4
	13, 14, 15, 16, 17, 18			3, 5, 6, 7, (8)	8, 10, 11	4	
2, 3, 5, 10	4	4	5, 10, 11, 14	(2)	9	9, 11	4, 5, 7
(1), 7		3, 7, 9	1	3, 5	8, 10, 11	2, 3, 4	2, 6
					8, 10, 11	4	6
2, 3, 4, 5, 9, 10	4, 5, 6		5	(4)	3, 4, 7	9, 10, 11, 13	4
		8	5		5, 9		8
	10		6	5	8, 10	4	
1							
2, 3, 4, 6, 7, 8, 11	(9)						
(1)							
5, 9, 10							
	(1), 2, (10), 11, 12, 13, 14, 15, 16, 17, 18, 19	1, 10					
	(1)						
	(1)						
	6						
	2, 3, 4, 5, 7, 8, 19						
		(2), (3), (4), (5), (6)					
			1, 2, 3, 5				
			2, 3, 5				
			2, 3, 5, 9, 10, 11, 12, 13, 14, 15				
			4, (6), 15				
			2, 3, 5, 7, 8, 9, 10, 11, 12, 13, 14				
			1				
			1				
		7, 10					
		9, 10					
		8					
					1, 2, 3, 4, 5, 6, 7, 8, 9, 10, 11, 13		
					1, (3), (4), 8, 9, 10, 11		
					1, (4)		
				(1)	11, 12		
				1, 2, 3, 4, 5, 6, 7, 8, 9			
				2			
				2			
						8, 9, 11, 13, 14	
						8, 10, 12	
						(8), 10, 12	
						1, 14	(1), (2), (3), (4), (5), (7), (9)
						1, 5, 6, 7	
						1, 2, 3, 4, 14	(2), (3), (4), (5), (6), (8), (9)

and how human activities can upset the natural environment. They should consider how some toys and devices work and know that the technology which drives them has been developed over a period of time.

ENVIRONMENTAL STUDIES 5–14 SCIENCE

SKILLS IN SCIENCE: INVESTIGATING

LEVEL	
	Preparing for tasks
	Understanding the task and planning a practical activity.
	Predicting.
	Undertaking fair testing
B	● plan simple approaches by asking questions and making suggestions
	● make suggestions about what might happen
	● recognise when a test or comparison is unfair
C	● suggest a question for exploration and decide how they might find an answer
	● make reasoned predictions about a possible outcome
	● suggest some ways of making a test fair
	Carrying out tasks
	Observing and measuring.
	Recording findings in a variety of ways.
B	● use simple equipment and techniques to make measurements
	● record findings in a range of ways
C	● select and use appropriate measurement devices or make appropriate observations
	● record findings in a greater range of ways
	Reviewing and reporting on tasks
	Reporting and presenting.
	Interpreting and evaluating results and processes.
B	● make a short report of an investigation
	● answer questions on the meaning of the findings
	● recognise simple relationships and draw conclusions
C	● make a short report of an investigation, communicating key points clearly
	● explain what happened, drawing on their scientific knowledge
	● make links to original predictions

EARTH AND SPACE

	Earth and space
	Developing an understanding of the position of the Earth in the Solar System and the Universe, and the effects of movement and that of the Moon.
B	● associate the seasons with differences in observed temperature
	● describe how day and night are related to the spin of the Earth
C	● describe the solar system in terms of the Earth, sun and planets
	● link the temperature of the planets to their relative positions in the atmospheres
	Materials from Earth
	Developing an understanding of the materials available on our planet, and the links between properties and uses.
B	● make observations of differences in the properties of common materials
	● relate uses of everyday materials to properties
	● explain why water conservation is important
C	● describe the differences between solids, liquids and gases
	● give some everyday uses of solids, liquids and gases
	Changing materials
	Developing an understanding of the ways in which materials can be changed.
B	● describe how everyday materials can be changed by heating or cooling
	● give examples of everyday materials that dissolve in water
	● give examples of common causes of water pollution
C	● describe changes when materials are mixed
	● describe how solids of different sizes can be separated
	● distinguish between soluble and insoluble materials
	● describe in simple terms the changes that occur when water is heated or cooled

ENERGY AND FORCES

	Properties and uses of energy
	Developing an understanding of energy through the study of the properties and uses of heat, light, sound and electricity.
B	● identify the sun as the main source of heat and light
	● link light and sound to seeing and hearing
C	● link light to shadow formation
	● give examples of light being reflected from surfaces
	● link sound to sources of vibration
	● construct simple battery-operated circuits, identifying the main components
	● classify materials as electrical conductors or insulators and describe how these are related to the safe use of electricity
	Conversion and transfer of energy
	Developing an understanding of energy conversion in practical everyday contexts.
B	● give examples of being 'energetic'
	● link the intake of food to the movement of their body
C	● give examples of energy being converted from one form to another
	● describe the energy conversions in the components of an electrical circuit
	Forces and their effects
	Developing an understanding of forces and how they can explain familiar phenomena and practices.
B	● describe the effect that a push and pull can have on the direction, speed or shape of an object
	● give examples of magnets in everyday use
	● describe the interaction of magnets in terms of the forces of attraction and repulsion
C	● give some examples of friction
	● explain friction in simple terms
	● describe air resistance in terms of friction

LIVING THINGS AND THE PROCESSES OF LIFE

	Variety and characteristic features
	Developing an understanding of the characteristic features of the main groups of plants and animals including humans and micro-organisms.
	The principles of genetics are also considered.
B	● give some of the more obvious distinguishing features of the major invertebrate groups
	● name some common members of the invertebrate groups
C	● give some of the more obvious distinguishing features of the five vertebrate groups
	● name some of the common members of vertebrate groups
	● name some of the common animals and plants using simple keys

Lessons where curriculum content is the main objective are listed below. Lessons where content is included but is not the main focus are shown below in brackets.

Unit 1: Ourselves Teeth and food	Unit 2: Animals & Plants The needs of plants and animals	Unit 3: The environment How the environment affects living things	Unit 4: Materials Natural & manufactured materials	Unit 5: Electricity Electricity and communication	Unit 6: Forces & motion Magnets and springs	Unit 7: Light & sound Sources and effects	Unit 8: Earth & beyond The Sun and shadows
5	3	2			2, 8	2	3
5	4	6	6	3	3	2, 3, 10, 12	3
			5, 10, 11, 14		5		
	12	7	13		8		
			5, 10, 11, 14		3, 5		5, 8
	13, 14, 15, 16, 17, 18	8	5, 10, 11, 14		5		
5	13, 14, 15, 16, 17, 18			3, 5, 6, 7, (8)	5		4
2, 3	3, 10	2, 7	2, 3	(1)	3	9, 11	3
5	4, 5, 11	4, 8	7, 8, 9, 12		9, (10)		4, 8
3	4	2, 3, 5, 9	5	(4)	9, (10)	9, 11	4, 5, 7
(1), 6, (7), 8, 10	(1), (2), 6, 9	(1)	(1)		(1), 4, 7, 11, 12	(1), 5, 6, 7, (8)	(1), 2
4, 8					5	2	
			2, 3, 4		6		4, 5, 6, 8
9	6, 7, 8	8				5, (13)	
	13, 14, 15, 16, 17, 18	8	5	(2)	9, 10, 11	3, 4, 10, 12	5, 6, 8
		6	5, 10, 11, 14		3, 5		5, 8
		(2), (3), (4), (5)					
							1, (9)
							7
							(7)
			1, 2, 3, 7, 8, 9, 10, 11, 12, 13, 14, 15				
			4, 5, 6				
			1				
						1	1, 2, 3, 4, 5, 6, 7, 8, 9
						1, 5, 6, 7, 8, 9, 10, 11, 12, 13, 14	
						1, 2, 3, 4, 14	
							2, 3, 4, 5, 6, 8, 9
						(8), (9)	
				(1), 2, 3, (4), 5, 6, 7, (8), 9			
					(11)		
					12		
						1, (5), 6, 7, 8, 9, 10, 13	
		(5)				1, 4	
						1, 2, 3, 13	
						1	
					(1)		

Living things and the processes of life continued overleaf

ENVIRONMENTAL STUDIES 5–14 SCIENCE

LIVING THINGS AND THE PROCESSES OF LIFE (cont)

LEVEL	
	The processes of life
	Developing an understanding of growth and development and life cycles, including cells and cell processes. The main organs of the human body and their functions are also considered.
B	● give examples of how the senses are used to detect information
	● recognise the stages of the human life cycle
	● recognise stages in the life cycles of familiar plants and animals
	● identify the main parts of flowering plants
C	● name the life processes common to humans and other animals
	● identify the main organs of the human body
	● describe the broad functions of the organs of the human body
	● describe the broad functions of the main parts of flowering plants
	Interaction of living things with their environment
	Developing an understanding of the interdependence of living things with the environment. The conservation and care of living things are also considered.
B	● give examples of feeding relationships found in the local environment
	● construct simple food chains
C	● give examples of living things that are very rare or extinct
	● explain how living things and the environment can be protected and give examples

Developing informed attitudes

Pupils should be encouraged to develop an awareness of, and positive attitudes, to:

A commitment to learning

● the need to develop informed and reasoned opinions on the impact of science in relation to social, environmental moral and ethical issues

● working independently and with others to find solutions to scientific problems

Respect and care for self and others

● taking responsibility for their own health and safety

● participating in the safe and responsible care of living things and the environment

● the development of responsible attitudes that take account of different beliefs and values

Social and environmental responsibility

● thinking through the various consequences for living things and the environment of different choices, decisions and courses of action

● the importance of the interrelationships between living things and their environment

● participating in the conservation of natural resources and the sustainable use of the Earth's resources

● the need for conservation of scarce energy resources and endangered species at local and global level

Lessons where curriculum content is the main objective are listed below. Lessons where content is included but is not the main focus are shown below in brackets.

Unit 1: Ourselves Teeth and food	Unit 2: Animals & Plants The needs of plants and animals	Unit 3: The environment How the environment affects living things	Unit 4: Materials Natural & manufactured materials	Unit 5: Electricity Electricity and communication	Unit 6: Forces & motion Magnets and springs	Unit 7: Light & sound Sources and effects	Unit 8: Earth & beyond The Sun and shadows
9, 10	4						
(5)							
	(1)						
	(1)						
(1)	2, 3, 5, 6, 7, 8, 9, 19						
(1)							
(1)							
	10, 11, 12, 13, 14, 15, 16, 17, 18, 19						
		(1), (6), (10)					
2, 3, 4, 6, 7, 8, 11		8					
		7, (8), 9, 10					
						(12)	
						(12)	